URBAN PLOTS, ORGANIZING CITIES

Urban Plots, Organizing Cities

Edited by

GIOVANNA SONDA
Istituto Regionale di Studi e Ricerca Sociale (IRSRS), Italy

CLAUDIO COLETTA
University of Trento, Italy

FRANCESCO GABBI
IUAV, Italy

Routledge
Taylor & Francis Group

LONDON AND NEW YORK

First published 2010 by Ashgate Publishing

2 Park Square, Milton Park, Abingdon, Oxon OX14 4RN
711 Third Avenue, New York, NY 10017, USA

Routledge is an imprint of the Taylor & Francis Group, an informa business

First issued in paperback 2016

British Library Cataloguing in Publication Data
Urban plots, organizing cities.
   1. City and town life. 2. Public spaces. 3. City planning.
   I. Sonda, Giovanna. II. Coletta, Claudio. III. Gabbi,
   Francesco.
   307.7'6-dc22

Library of Congress Cataloging-in-Publication Data
Sonda, Giovanna.
  Urban plots, organizing cities / by Giovanna Sonda, Claudio Coletta, Francesco Gabbi.
      p. cm.
  Includes bibliographical references and index.
   ISBN 978-1-4094-0927-4 (hardback)
1. Cities and towns. 2. City and town life. 3. Public spaces--Social aspects. 4.
Spatial behavior. 5. Social structure. I. Coletta, Claudio. II. Gabbi, Francesco. III. Title.
   HT119.S652 2010
   307.76--dc22

                                                                    2010024833

ISBN 978-1-4094-0927-4 (hbk)
ISBN 978-1-138-26090-0 (pbk)

Contents

About the Editors

Claudio Coletta, PhD in Sociology and Social Research – Information Systems & Organizations. In recent years Claudio has carried out research projects on urban and regional issues, with a focus on classifications, narratives and urban space. His field of research involves the interplay between technology, organization and territory. Currently, he is working on a popular approach to innovation.

Francesco Gabbi, PhD in Urban Planning and Public Policies. Francesco is a member of the research unit on the 'Strategies and Actors of the Internationalization of Cities' at the IUAV University of Venice and coordinator of the research line 'Cities between everyday and internationalization processes'. He is also a teaching assistant on Urban Sociology at the University of Trento. His research interests vary from urban regeneration to social policies.

Giovanna Sonda, PhD in Sociology and Social Research. Giovanna's research fields are: urban policies, welfare and third sector, organization studies and Science and Technology Studies (STS). Other research interests deal with memory and conservation, and with forms of representation and sense-making. She has been a researcher at IRSRS for five years.

Notes on Contributors

Beatriz Acevedo (PhD in Management; MA in Sociology, MBA and Gender) is Lecturer on Sustainable Management at Anglia Ruskin University, Cambridge, United Kingdom. As a social researcher and artist, she is interested in exploring the links between arts, aesthetics and management studies. In addition, she has considerable experience in the evaluation of social policies in Latin America: in particular, she has worked on topics such as sustainable development, urban development and alternative development in relation to drugs policy. Her most recent publications in international academic journals such as *Aesthetics*, *Leadership* and *Culture and Organization* address the links between art, imagery, aesthetics and relevant questions in management studies such as leadership, creativity, innovation and sustainability.

Daniela Allocca is a PhD candidate at the University of Salerno (Italy), with a research project about space in female migration literature in Berlin. Daniela is a member of the organizational committee of 'Biennale Est – Europe as a Space of Translation' Culture Programma EU, 2007–2013, Università degli Studi di Napoli L'Orientale. She is curator of some performing art projects for the cultural association 'Il Torchio'. Currently her research focuses on the creative power of migrant writers to develop 'nomadic cartographies' and on the relationship between translation and topologies.

Lavinia Bifulco is Associate Professor of Sociology in the Faculty of Sociology at the University of Milano-Bicocca. Her research and publications focus on the theory and analysis of public action, local policies, public organizations, governance, social and institutional innovations. Among her recent publications are: *Gabbie di vetr* (ed., Milano 2008); *Politiche sociali. Temi e prospettive emergenti* (Roma 2005).

Vando Borghi is Associate Professor at the Department of Sociology, University of Bologna. His current research interests are about the 'regimes of justification' in welfare capitalism and the 'informational basis' of policies, mainly explored in the fields of the transformation of work, the changing relationship between public and private spheres and the active policies and changes affecting the relationship between labour and welfare state. In recent years he published the books *Le grammatiche sociali della mobilità* [Grammars of Social Mobility] (with M. La Rosa and F. Chicchi, Milano 2008), and *L'organizzazione sociale del lavoro* [The Social Organization of Labour] (with R. Rizza, Milano 2006).

Massimo Bricocoli is Assistant Professor in Urban and Regional Planning at Politecnico di Milano. His research focuses on the interplay between spatial and social organization processes, on planning practices and on urban and social policies. Among his most recent publications are *Città in periferia. Politiche urbane e progetti locali in Francia, Gran Bretagna e Italia*, with P. Briata and C. Tedesco (Carocci, Roma 2009), and *Villes en observation. Politiques locales de Sécurité urbaine en Italie*, with P. Savoldi (Editions du Puca, Paris 2008).

Andrea 'Mubi' Brighenti is a post-doctoral research fellow at the Department of Sociology, University of Trento, Italy. He researches both empirically and theoretically into space, power and society, with a focus on the transformations of urban environments through the technologies of control and the practices of resistance and play. Among his recent publications are: *Territori migranti* [Migrant Territories. Space and Control of Global Mobility] (ombre corte 2009), and *The Wall and the City* (edited, professionaldreamers 2009). He is also the editor of the independent online web journal *lo Squaderno* (www.losquaderno. professionaldreamers.net).

Ana Maria Carreira (PhD in History; MSc in Regional and Urban Development; Architect) is Lecturer on History of Art at Universidad Jorge Tadeo Lozano, Bogota, Colombia. Her research interests include the analysis of urban development projects, public spaces and the study of power configurations in the urban context. She has extensive experience in analyzing urban development projects in cities such as Buenos Aires (Argentina), Bogota, Medellín (Colombia) and Mexico D.F. (Mexico), as well as the analysis and evaluation of social policies in Latin America. Her current research concerns the analysis of power in relation to images and aesthetic movements, in particular, the development of a Latin American baroque imagery.

Jérôme Denis is a sociologist at Telecom ParisTech, Paris, France. His research concerns mainly writing practices at work: he studies the production of different kinds of graphical devices, the way prescription is enacted within organizations and the uses of information and communication technologies. He is the coauthor of *Petite sociologie de la signalétique: les coulisses des panneaux du métro* (Presses des Mines 2010). He has a daily blog about ordinary writing artefacts: http://www. scriptopolis.fr.

Barbara Grüning is post-doctoral research fellow at the Department of Science of Communication of Bologna, Italy. Her main scientific interests are public sphere theories, empiric research in the field of memory studies and the field of third places studies. She recently published *Diritto, norma e memoria. La Germania dell'est nel processo di transizione* [Right, Rule and Memory. The Process of Transition in East Germany] (Macerata, Eum 2010).

Claudia Meschiari is a PhD candidate in planning, in the Department of Urban Studies, Roma Tre University. She has studied cultural and urban geography, and is particularly interested in the relations between cultural practices and policies in contemporary cities, and in the changing uses of public space.

David Pontille is a sociologist at the CNRS/EHESS, Paris, France. His research focuses on the relationship between writing, action and cognition in different workplaces: scientific laboratories, bailiffs' offices, biomedical databases and subway systems. He is author of various articles on scientific authorship, a book entitled *La Signature scientifique: une sociologie pragmatique de l'"attribution* (CNRS Editions 2004), and coauthor of *Petite sociologie de la signalétique: les coulisses des panneaux du métro* (Presses des Mines 2010). He is currently working on the politics of graffiti removal in Paris. He has a daily blog about ordinary writing artefacts: http://www.scriptopolis.fr.

Stavros Stavrides is Assistant Professor in the School of Architecture, National Technical University of Athens, Greece, where he teaches a graduate course on social housing, as well as a postgraduate course on the meaning of metropolitan experience. He has published five books, as well as numerous articles (in Greek, English and Spanish) on architecture and spatial theory. His research is also focused on forms of emancipating spatial practices (characteristically developed in his contribution to *Loose Space: Possibility and Diversity in Public Life*, K. Franck and Q. Stevens (eds) Routledge 2006).

Foreword: The City Narrated, the City Organized?

Barbara Czarniawska[1]

The present collection is grounded in word play: it revolves around the double meaning of the term 'plot', as used in geography and cartography, and as used in narratology. This ingenious device is to serve as a link joining urban studies with organization studies; both subdisciplines in recent times strongly under the influence of narratology (see Harding 2003; Boje 2001).

Indeed, one may wonder that this connection was not built earlier, considering how much organizing is involved in constructing, maintaining and running cities. The reasons are probably historical: organization theory is grounded in engineering (Shenhav 2002), and has a long history in common with the history of industry. Urban studies were historically close to architecture, city planning and political sciences. Narratology provides a good meeting place.

But the word 'plot' has more than two meanings. Actually, narratology borrowed it (like the word 'text') from textile vocabulary: since time immemorial, people have been spinning stories and weaving them into plots. But, is this meaning not rather far from the fragmentation and mobility typical of contemporary cities, one may ask? The editors and the contributors claim that it is not – that there is something like a 'fabric' of the city, the 'texture' of which can be described. They even evoke the Penelope myth to corroborate their point (after all, she stayed in the city of Ithaca while Odysseus wandered around). And although women often stood for symbols of cities (Czarniawska 2010), this one is new.

As the use of devices, literary or otherwise, is a matter of technology, the editors stabilize the link they are constructing with little help from STS – science and technology studies. A large part of STS, namely actor-network theory, is also of narrative origins (it was inspired by Greimasian narratology, see, for example, Greimas 1976 [1989]).

Will the link hold? It may if, as the editors suggest, it is to be seen not as a static bridge between two subdisciplines of social studies, but as a small, reusable linking pin that allows the construction of action nets – this time in urban research – among like-minded scholars.

Will the link work? The answer to this question is in the hands (and in the eyes) of the readers. The editors have on offer a reading perspective as well –

---

1   Gothenburg Research Institute, University of Gothenburg, Sweden.

serendipity: a peregrination across the text that may be bountiful in gains, the existence of which the traveller did not even know in advance (Merton and Barber 2006). Walter Benjamin could have called this volume a 'phantasmagoria' of city pictures, big and small, from different cities, countries and continents, seen from different angles. The general impression concurs with my observation that cities are organized but disorganized, managed but unmanageable, orderly but disorderly (Czarniawska 2002). Only hybrid vocabularies and polysemic terms – like those skilfully applied in his volume – can be of use in grasping this complex phenomenon: the contemporary city.

Introduction: Urban Plots, Organizing Cities

Giovanna Sonda, Claudio Coletta and Francesco Gabbi

This book brings together contributions that focus on the interpoint between urban studies and organization studies in an endeavour to draw a new space of discussion which will hopefully prove profitable to both fields. The aim is to account for the processual nature of urban phenomena, considering the organizational aspects of urban space and the material features of organizations as having a common, heterogeneous ground. From this perspective, we propose an analytical repertoire based on the twofold concept of plot and organizing to investigate and understand urban complexity.

The concept of plot is as old as the idea of storytelling. Aristotle first introduced it in his *Poetics* as the element that should provide a story with a beginning, a middle and an end, thus making it a connected and self-contained series of events in a structure designed for closure. In this way, a plot 'can weave into the story the historical and social context, information about physical laws, and thoughts and feelings reported by people' (Czarniawska 2004a: 125).

Todorov (1977) proposed a minimal definition of 'plot' which consisted in the passage from one equilibrium to another. A plot is thus the structure that enables sense to be made of a list of events, so that, on this view, a plot becomes a means to organize space, time and causality (Zimm 2005). On the other hand, in everyday language 'plot' has a wide spectrum of meanings evoking a deeper connection among the social, fictional and material dimensions of spatial matters: according to the Oxford English Dictionary, 'plot' also denotes 'An area or piece (of small or moderate size) of ground, or of what grows or lies upon it', 'The place on which a building, town, city, etc. is situated; site, situation', 'A ground-plan of a building, city, field, farm, or any area or part of the earth's surface; a map, a chart', 'A scheme or plan indicating the disposition and function of lighting and stage property in a particular production'.

Thus, 'plot' indicates both the space and the cartography shaping it; it is a way to associate objects and the representations of objects. Accordingly, emplotment indicates the involvement of the characters in this interaction. Such emphasis on continuous reorganization rejects the idea of the plot as a control instrument and insists, on the contrary, on its openness as an added value.

The notion of plot leads us to a discourse on method. This book, in fact, originates from a research project entitled 'Penelope: the emerging patterns of urban texture',[1]

---

1   Penelope consists of a qualitative research project on the fabric of the city of Trento (Italy), funded by Fondazione Caritro, Comune di Trento and IRSRS. It investigated

the aim of which was to investigate the social and material fabric of urban organization by means of qualitative research on the city of Trento (Italy). It focused in particular on how media imagery, urban practices, urban artefacts and urban management visions interact and shape the city. Our fieldwork started from some basic questions: how does the so-called 'historic city centre' differ from the 'suburbs'? What are the mechanisms that connote them as different and contrasting?

We first examined local newspapers in order to become acquainted with controversies related to the use of public spaces and to find clues to guide the fieldwork. From this perspective, studying cities is like an endless search for clues, changes, layers – as suggested by the project title evoking the myth of Penelope.

Since it is in the news that different positions become visible and dramatized, our work consisted in a sort of 'reverse engineering' of mass media discourse in order to re-territorialize urban space through urban practices and narratives. Consider, for example, the use of the term 'Bronx' as it emerged from our review of the local press. The metaphor was used both by newspapers to define a specific area of the city and by its inhabitants themselves to describe the place where they lived in order to press for public policies. Use of the 'language of emergency and decay' was a tactic to draw attention to their problems, and they tried to intercept institutional discourse by using the same mass media rhetoric in description of the area. News reports evoked an imagery that was appropriated by the inhabitants to represent the place where they lived and to demand concern for their problems.

We maintain that the double thread that linked the languages of the media and the inhabitants (Bifulco and De Leonardis 2005) – together with Park's (1940) contention that news orients rather than represents the public discourse – highlights the performative nature of news: local news is 'local' to the extent that it *localizes* and *connotes* spaces. The localization of public discourse that we adopt goes together with the idea of the contested nature of urban space: the former is rooted in Foucault's notions of governmentality and disciplinary power; the latter draws on Latour's (2005a) concept of 'matter of concern' as opposed to a 'matter of fact'.

A matter of concern is the machinery around which entities are assembled and challenged. Cities are intrinsically indeterminate entities, and they are constantly constructed through controversies where action is distributed among actors and actants that assemble, re-present and translate each other. This perspective makes it possible to read 'urban space' as a controversial setting and provides privileged access to understanding of the entanglement of cities: urban space is defined through processes of localization and delocalization where policies, practices, imagery and artefacts[2] are intertwined to 'perform' places.

---

press-related, administrative and grounded narratives as clues to grasping less-noticed yet relevant phenomena that can orient the public discourse and suggest different and innovative modalities of living and managing urban issues.

2   The performative and social role of artefacts and non-human actors has been introduced and studied by Actor-Network Theory scholars (Callon and Latour 1981; Akrich

The issue of public noise in the historic city centre as reported in the local newspapers provided useful insights into this mechanism. To prevent the public performances of street musicians from invading the peace of private homes, the local authority had arranged specific areas with coloured and visible signs where busking was allowed. The criterion on which such areas were distributed around the city was the LTZ (Limited Traffic Zone): street musician areas were all located around the old city centre, so that a sort of border was drawn between the pedestrian zone and traffic flows. Hence, a traffic management device (organizational artefact) was employed to discipline busking, and it performed a sort of acoustic gentrification which divided a city's silent, pedestrian, shopping-oriented old centre from its busy, working part. In addition, this organization of spaces established a standard of actions allowed in the city centre, thus strengthening a specific imagery. But every framing action entails an overflowing effect (Callon 1999) and requires account to be taken of the relation among public policies, urban planning and everyday practices. This research perspective enabled us to establish a connection between actor-network theory (ANT) and interactionist approaches to territory. For the latter, territory is the product and the process of practices of use (Crosta 2009), and they consider that the action itself of public policies lies in their by-products (Donolo 1997). It is impossible to define actorship and policy *a priori*: they are defined through the traces they leave and by following them. Crosta (2003), drawing on Dewey, identifies two kinds of interaction: weak and strong. The former conceives the elements of interaction as already constituted (that is, policy makers vs. policy takers), taken for granted, and part of a linear and ordinary plot, while the latter envisages a completely different process, where the actors are enlisted in the ongoing interaction. Considering the two kinds of interaction as different ways to make sense of phenomena, we tried to account for the 'strong' version by considering a territory as the plot emerging from fieldwork. It is at this point that spatial processes merge with organizing ones. This concerns the relation between the researcher's situated view of phenomena and the way in which phenomena happen and orient the investigation. The concept of action net introduced by Barbara Czarniawska (2004b) can be used to account for the relation between the methodological and empirical levels:

> The concept of action net has no analytical ambitions, its introduction is an attempt to minimize that which is taken for granted prior to the analysis. A standard analysis begins with "actors" or "organizations"; an action net approach permits us to notice that these are the products rather than the sources of the organizing-taking place within, enabled by and constitutive of an action net. Identities are produced by and in an action net, not vice versa. (Czarniawska 2004b)

---

and Latour 1992; Law and Hassard 1999; Latour 2005b), and Organization Studies scholars, particularly by Gagliardi (1990), who considered them as remains of corporate identity and pathways for action.

What are the action nets that shape urban space and organize city discourse?

We may answer this question by reconstructing a controversy and the action net that developed between an artefact and its stakeholders. In an industrial area of Trento, the construction of a warehouse had been a matter of concern discussed in the local press for several months. The controversy concerned the wall of the warehouse, which was much higher than shown by the designer's graphic rendering, and consequently produced a strong visual impact in the neighbourhood. The difference between the actual height of the wall and that of the graphic design provoked the reaction of the inhabitants, who set up a local committee to campaign against the visual pollution. The company's counter-action consisted in attributing the entire responsibility to the urban development plan, which classified the area as industrial and thus legitimized the construction. For its part, the local administration justified its decisions as coherent with standards and planning rules, while the local newspapers utilized a synecdoche that reduced the whole warehouse to one of its parts.

On the one hand, this episode helps understand the political and acting capacity of artefacts; on the other, the contradictory and complex ensemble transformed the wall into an infrastructure built on manifold levels and not confined to its materiality alone. The episode highlights how a wall was embedded in and enacted an action net which associated narratives, objects, practices to orient the way in which relations developed and eventually produced urban space. Besides the separation between media news language and the language of lay people dissolving into a common narrative, the separation between institutional action and lived experience collapsed in favour of an ecological vision of organizational processes.

Based on our research, we propose three analytical categories to follow the composition of action nets: practices, narratives, artefacts, as illustrated below:

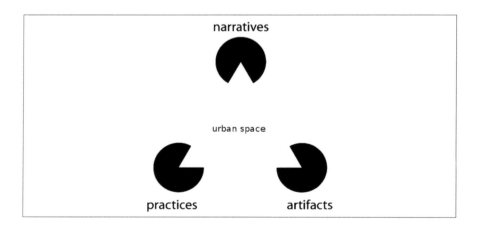

Figure I.1 The Urban Gestalt

This visual device explicitly recalls Gaetano Kanisza's optical illusion whereby a figure is visible but is not effectively drawn: we cannot frame the triangle unless we constantly switch between the background and the foreground. Our difficulty in focalizing the triangle is the same difficulty that we encounter when we try to account urban phenomena without connecting artefacts, narratives and practices together. In other words, we emphasize that the single categories come into being and work only through their interplay. We have chosen to visualize this process by means of this optical illusion because it conveys the ephemeral nature of every analytical category. The controversy on the height of the warehouse wall suggests that a wall is not merely an artefact; rather, it consists of narratives enacting other practices. Another purpose of the triangle is thus to depict the mobile nature of categories.

So far we have dwelt upon why the focus of this book is on urban plots and on the categories used by the contributors to interpret urban phenomena. But it is now time to reveal that the book, although it is a collection of research studies, has its own plot.

The book's rationale may not be immediately apparent on looking through the list of contents. In fact, it presents case studies on cities in every part of the world, ranging from medium-sized Italian towns to European capitals, to Medellín in Latin America. What do these have in common? What value derives from dealing with such diverse urban settings? We addressed these questions when analyzing the chapters and discussing them with the authors, and we came to the idea that the book's purpose was to provide a research-based account of contemporary urban issues, and that its focus would be both on the relevance of the events, controversies and episodes discussed in the chapters and on how they have been described, analyzed and interpreted by the researchers. The heterogeneity of the material presented in what follows thus yields an added value which fulfils our intentions: first, to demonstrate that addressing urban issues from an organizational perspective enables researchers, managers, planners and city users to grasp the ephemeral, multiple nature of cities; second, to underline that there may be a method, a 'gaze', with which to look at urban phenomena. The triangle in Figure I.1 acts as the device that holds the different contributions together; it is the map that situates them and is the key to their interpretation.

What holds the chapters together is thus the research perspective adopted. The epistemological and methodological observations made by the authors in their chapters are based on empirical data and result from a situated gaze. Saying that the linkage between the chapters consists in the research perspective is not to imply a homogeneity of theoretical background or a shared view on the mechanisms that organize cities. On the contrary, the book provides a multidisciplinary and transdisciplinary understanding which may be helpful in addressing urban complexity. Given the domain in which the contributors move – the triangle of narratives, artefacts and practices – the reader will find connections and references among chapters that are all the more interesting because they are unexpected. Such connections are reciprocally stimulating because they increase the overall understanding, although the chapters tackle different issues and are based on different urban settings.

The authors, in fact, engage jointly in the overall editorial project by providing their distinct gazes on the processes of 'continuous experimentation inherent in urban forms of sociality' (Stavrides). On this shared basis, each author then develops their own remarks based on their field work. Accordingly, the book gathers the sensibilities, experiences and professional backgrounds of the authors.

The following presentation of chapters and their relations outlines the plot of the book. It should provide the reader with directions with which to move within the book, discovering cross-references and different approaches to urban issues. We suggest tackling the chapters in a serendipic manner, thereby discovering new connections and the different levels of reading that they offer. The idea is that of following their tracks as in the tales of adventurous travellers who made decisive discoveries, by accident and sagacity, of things that they were not seeking (Merton and Barber 2006). This evidential perspective (Ginzburg 1979) challenges our categories and allows us to reconsider the way in which we approach urban space.

We shall thus discover the narrative and practice-based nature of artefacts (in the chapters by Brighenti; Denis and Pontille; Bifulco and Bricocoli) and public policies (Bifulco and Bricocoli; Borghi and Meschiari); interpret how places change through scripts and narrative paths of memory, language and popular culture (Denis and Pontille; Grüning; Allocca; Borghi and Meschiari; Acevedo and Carreira); and experience the unstable nature of cities through conflict and practices of appropriation (Stavrides; Acevedo and Carreira; Grüning; Brighenti).

In the first chapter, Jérôme Denis and David Pontille accompany the reader on an immersive journey through the Paris subway. The ANT perspective they adopt enables observation of the non-human action of signage and how it enacts different pathways for action. The way in which these *scripts* work induces the authors to rethink urban flows by dismantling a cognitive-centred vision in favour of an account that connects policies, signs, artefacts and bodies. In the Parisian subway 'the rider is never performed only as a reader who would catch some meaning from various texts', above all because signs are not complete texts, but rather systems of elements. Denis and Pontille's ethnographic research shows that, contrary to a tradition of study that considers cities as texts and promotes a *literate accountability*, designers 'strive to fit out a *graphical accountability*' which preludes a wide range of actions.

This remark recalls the metaphor of 'translation' in the chapter by Allocca, who writes that 'the translating eye undoes reality, tripping up significance and opening up the possibility of the creation of new conceptions of space. We are confronted with a process that acts on the topological structure of spatial perception, and as Barthes points out, this is what always occurs in the encounter with a foreign language'. Here the foreign language may be the signal system that enacts a personal use of that item of information in order to find a way through the subway.

Things and their organizing processes are also the main topic of the following chapter by Andrea Mubi Brighenti, who refers to what he calls two 'uncanny' objects: the wall and the mobile phone.

Brighenti focuses on walls and mobile phones in order to verify their substance and function, which are traditionally perceived as divergent: walls divide, while phones connect. By contrast, Brighenti's study draws on Foucault's notion of governmentality to show how both walls and mobile phones organize space 'through their specific, often criss-crossing and overlapping combinations'.

After tracing how walls have been conceptualized and have changed their function over time, Brighenti relates the present function of these artefacts to 'the capillarisation and infiltration of power devices at every scale' and traces their analytic qualities: materiality, territoriality, visibility, rhythm, uses. The way in which these qualities are combined affects the mobility range of *dispositifs*. Both walls and mobile phones call into play the interweaving of space and social relations and the vision of the city as an ecological infrastructure. Accordingly, Brighenti suggests that these artefacts should be viewed not merely as objects, but rather as convergence zones between the material and the immaterial, since both walls and network infrastructures concern the relationship between bodies and their environment. In this respect, such artefacts can be addressed as spaces of public life in which social and political conflict has a simultaneously technological, cultural and legal nature.

Whereas Brighenti explores the socio-technical character of conflict, Stavrides addresses urban conflict, focusing on contestation concerning the meaning and the use of public space. Looking at urban struggles involving the neighbourhood of Prosfygica (Athens), he centres his discussion on the concept of temporal and spatial *porosity*. A city is a space where collective memories, uses and political visions constantly interact and clash with each other. In this respect, the notion of porosity is both a category with which to account for urban organizing and a feature of urban settings. In fact, Stavrides traces the contested nature of urban spaces back to spatial-temporal porosity and in this plot locates the potentiality of multiple uses summarized in the effective notion of 'city as a right'.

The concept of porosity connects with that of *hybridization* proposed in the chapter by Acevedo and Carreira. Used by Science and Technology scholars (Latour 1993) to emphasize the radical indeterminacy of actors, here hybridization refers to the anthropological tradition and is more focused on cultural practices. The authors present and discuss two episodes of redevelopment in the city of Medellín (Colombia) regarded as emblematic in understanding narratives of urban development. The first describes how local people appropriated the administrative rhetoric of modernization and incorporated it into their practices within the city. The second deals with an attempt at mediation between development and tradition: the municipality used popular culture within a project of public transportation to normalize people's behaviour. This illustrates a twofold process: on the one hand, people reconfigure the standard of development established by the local administration, on the other, it is the urban management that incorporates local culture into urban renewal projects. The authors point to popular culture as a key factor in understanding the hybrid dynamics driving the development of Latin American cities.

This discourse on forms of mediation between the practices/narratives of urban management and practices/narratives related to uses of the city takes us to the chapter by Bifulco and Bricocoli. They examine two cases: one relating to social housing policies in Turin, the second to health services in Trieste. They follow the impact and by-products of these policies on social organization, that is, the interweaving between making the city and making society. The chapter is based on intensive fieldwork and comprises excerpts from interviews conducted with inhabitants of the neighbourhoods investigated. The chapter describes how mediation comes about in practice: the authors draw on their case studies to identify the elements that foster a good balance between institutional intervention and respect for social organization, for instance, the involvement of those often considered to be mere beneficiaries of initiatives. In these dynamics, conflict plays a distinctive role in institutional learning by supporting processes of connection and institution-building.

Borghi and Meschiari consider institutional processes within cultural management. After discussing the role of culture in the construction of the public sphere and the arguments in favour of public intervention in culture, they analyse the controversy relating to renewal of a disused foundry in Modena (Italy). The foundry was a place replete with memories and meanings mostly relating to the struggles for employment in the 1960s and, more recently, to the de-industrialization of the urban landscape. The public debate on the potential of that space inevitably drew attention to the building's historical, emotional and political value resulting from a stratification of meanings and uses over time. Consequently, the decision-making process was informed by different positions which claimed different destinations, thus opening up multiple and conflicting possibilities for the foundry. In this sense, culture acts as the organizing principle which drives urban restoration and governance practices.

The book comprises various contributions in which memory has become a major issue within discussion on urban reorganization. Grüning's analysis is emblematic in this regard, because it deals with the urban transformation of East German cities, and particularly with the 'tangle of symbolic and material traces of the city of Leipzig'.

Grüning analyzes how different urban and memory practices, such as media narratives, construct and stabilize specific representations of East German society. She addresses both the symbolic dimension (memory, imagery, rhetoric) and a material dimension of such transformation in order to show how they shape new cities and how these multiple visions stratify and condense.

The reconstruction of East German cities exhibits the opposition between post-modern architecture and traditional culture, as if the past were perceived in the same way by everyone. For this reason, Grüning questions which collectivity we refer to when talking about 'collective imagery' and 'familiar reality', given that those cities are characterized by strong and controversial memories that open up different scenarios.

The chapter by Allocca makes an original attempt to address the process of transformation of spaces from the perspective of linguistic translation. According to the author, translation creates a metaphorical space: that is, a space for the negotiation and recreation of (linguistic) codes so that one can understand and be understood. Is this not exactly what happens in the everyday routine of our cities? The need to reframe (materially and conceptually) the space in which we dwell in order to reach agreement with our neighbours evokes Sennett's work 'The Uses of Disorder' (1970), which addressed the problem of urban complexity and stressed the role of individual responsibility in making urban life. Sennett argued that city life is an experience of encounter, an exploration of alterity, which implies a constant testing of our schemes and biases concerning how the city should be and should function. Similarly, Allocca's remarks on the translation process are based on the inescapable need for negotiation that creates a space of dialogue and the possibility of multiple uses. In other words, both Allocca and Sennett suggest that a space is not given once and for all, because it is narratively constructed and depends on the dwellers' capacity to explore and recreate its potentiality. Narratives indeed create new spaces and new vocabularies that are used to construct a specific version of the city.

It should by now be clear that places are not prominent in this book: it is not a book that aims to give a picture of the condition of contemporary cities. Rather, the purpose of the contributions is to show the potential of addressing urban complexity by considering the action net embracing artefacts, practices and narratives, that is, the 'plot' that in our version constitutes urban life.

The terms 'plots' and 'organizing' used in the title thus act as a chiasmus highlighting both the shape and the process. They suggest that account should be taken of both the organization that results from action nets and the organizing process embedded in those nets. Whereas 'plot' enables us to express our interest in both the urban fabric and the discourse about it, 'organizing' highlights the research perspective concerned with the processes of urban reorganization.

The research dimension of this book is crucial, and it forms the basis on which different tracks develop and interweave to shape the book's complex plot. Having said this, however, the book is more than a collection of urban stories: it is an invitation to those who study or manage cities to go in depth and let themselves be carried away by the flow of action, so that they may understand how fruitful a serendipic exploration into urbanity can be. Moreover, the value of this perspective is that it gives awareness that the meanings and uses of places continually change, and that we may direct the change process. This remark emphasises our responsibility for urban development no matter what role we play in it, for urban life produces the action nets to which we inevitably belong.

Acknowledgements

The authors wish to thank Istituto Regionale di Studi e Ricerca Sociale (IRSRS) for supporting the project 'Penelope' (co-funded by Fondazione Caritro and Comune di Trento) and the further steps that finally give birth to this book.

Chapter 1

The Graphical Performation of a Public Space: The Subway Signs and their Scripts[1]

Jérôme Denis and David Pontille

Introduction

Amid the deep transformations that cities have known in the last decades, the increase of mobility practices has played a central role (Amin and Thrift 2002). As a main feature of contemporary capitalism, it notably contributes to the emergence of new forms of exchange (Kellerman 2006; Urry 2007), which strongly articulate spatial configurations and informational devices (Lash and Urry 1994). In modern urban spaces there is no distinction between, on the one hand, the 'virtual' world of information and the circulation of a so-called immaterial knowledge, and on the other hand, the 'real' world in which bodies move and material constraints are plenty. New information and communication technologies play a great part in the day-to-day organization of cities.

Actually, the articulation between places and information is not new. As Latour and Hermant (1998) showed about Paris, urban spaces are both material and informational. The city is 'intellectual' (Simmel 1989), it holds plenty of signs and inscriptions among which some were in place long before the emergence of the new technologies of information and communication (Petrucci 1993). The public display of signs is inherent to the organizing process of urban settings: cities are made of semiotic landscapes.

Numerous urban signs are notably a matter of way-finding. They provide a whole graphical layer for the accountability of places and the everyday organization of public settings. Street nameplates, traffic lights or signboards inform the passer-by of their own location in the city ('this' neighbourhood, 'this' street) and give indications about the suitable behaviour to adopt ('stop here', 'turn left'). By

1 This research is part of a collective project entitled 'Ecologies and Politics of Writing' (Département Sciences Économiques et Sociales, LTCI (UMR 5141) CNRS, Telecom ParisTech and Équipe Anthropologie de l'écriture, IIAC (UMR 8177) CNRS-EHESS) and supported by the Agence Nationale de la Recherche, Grant n°ANR-05-BLAN-0272-02. We gratefully acknowledge the people from the Régie Autonome des Transports Parisiens (RATP) for their active cooperation and the time they devoted to this study. We also thank Claudio Coletta, Francesco Gabbi and Giovanna Sonda for their willingness to make this book possible and their useful remarks on a previous version of this chapter.

marking sites, giving places a name, designating directions, these signs are what
H. Garfinkel (1996) terms 'territorial organizational things'. They produce an
ordering of the city within which:

> practitioners are required to read descriptive accounts alternately as instructions.
> They do so occupationally, and as skilled matter of course, as vulgarly competent,
> specifically ordinary, and unremarkable worksite-specific practices. These are
> chained bodily and chiasmically to places, spaces, architectures, equipment,
> instruments, and timing. (Garfinkel 1996: 19)

In this chapter, we will study such an ordering process from an actor-network
theory (ANT) perspective. The strength of ANT is to enlarge ethnomethodology's
programme, and its definition of social order as situated accomplishments, to
non-humans (Latour 2005b). Agency is always distributed between people,
artefacts and other entities such as principles or rules (Cooren 2004). According
to this model, collectives as nations or organizations arise from heterogeneous
assemblages (Latour and Weibel 2005), and cities are not organized 'upstream',
nor ordered by invisible forces. Urban spaces are the result of a continuous process
carried out by day-to-day practices and mundane objects (Farias and Bender
2009). Performation, as Latour (2005b) puts it, is a useful notion to describe such
a process. It insists on the dynamic of organizing and the necessity for collective
entities to be maintained day after day. Furthermore, the notion offers a multilateral
view: performation processes concern sites as well as their inhabitants whose
practices and attitudes are constantly shaped by their environment. The signboards
or the street nameplates can thus be seen as utter components of the performation
of modern public spaces. Urban signs both order physical spaces and configure the
action of their dwellers.

The role of signs in the ordering process of places has already been stressed
in two kinds of settings: airports and supermarkets. For the former, Fuller showed
that the standardization of displayed arrows and names produces a hybrid setting
within which 'the distinction between the building and its signs, between the
text and the territory, becomes indistinct' (Fuller 2002: 236). With the airport's
signage, travellers are no more explorers: invited to follow the directions of a
'familiar authority', they are transformed into navigators. Within supermarkets,
Cochoy and Grandclément (2005) showed how things such as logos, price labels
and nutrition facts tables are key features of consumers' choice. Both the spatial
configuration of shelves and these various signs displayed on products' packagings
have transformed the modern customers into *homo œconomicus*.

Airports and supermarkets are 'non-places' (Augé 1995): they are mainly auto-
referential and their organization is focused on very specific concerns. On the
contrary, urban spaces are highly heterogeneous. Their graphical ordering deals
with issues that largely overflow flux management or choice improvement. In this
chapter, we tackle such a complexity and try to understand the way in which urban
signs confer specific positions to the dwellers in public spaces.

Subway Signs in Paris

We will focus on the case of subway signs, using the results of an ethnographical fieldwork within the *Régie Autonome des Transports Parisiens* (RATP). In Paris, subway signs became a central issue at the beginning of the 1990s. At that time, a team of specialists (designers, cartographers and architects) was gathered to reconsider the whole organization of subway signs. Surveys, field studies and experiments were conducted that resulted in the creation of a complete way-finding system (a 'signage', *signalétique* in French) and the redaction of a particularly ambitious policy. For the first time, the content, shape, size, colours and emplacement of subway signs have been standardized and detailed in extremely precise guidelines.

In doing so, the RATP established a real 'writing policy' (Foucault 1977) that deeply transformed subway spaces. Its main idea was to provide riders with as many on-the-spot instructions as they need to successfully 'use' the transportation network:

> An electric iron, if there's nothing written on it, if there are no instructions on it, well … one does not know how it works. Here, it is the same: there are people who are moving, there are all these different spaces, one does not see what is happening behind, so our choice was to include instructions within each station.
> (L.T., Responsible for Signage Normalization, RATP)

There is of course an important issue here about what riders 'need', and more generally about who they are. Our aim is to discover which figures of users such a project conveys, that is, to identify the kind of riders this new graphical organization of subway space supposes. To understand how signage performs in a specific public space, we will study it as a technology in which users' representations are inscribed. Thus, we follow Woolgar (1991) when he writes that innovation processes are 'configuring the user' as much as the technology. Moreover, we adopt the position of Akrich (1992) who showed that the innovation process could be compared to the writing of a 'script' that attributes tasks and positions to people and things, and organizes relations between them. As Akrich puts it, 'technical objects define actors, the space in which they move, and the ways in which they interact' (p. 216). This approach is extremely useful to analyze mundane graphical devices such as way-finding systems because, for once, it allows to go backstage and surface the work carried out behind signboards. By studying the riders' representations inscribed within signage, we can identify the behaviours supposed to take place in subway spaces, and shed the light on the 'framework of action' (Akrich 1992: 208) that the Parisian policy of subway signs supports.

We developed a twofold methodological approach. First, we focused on internal narratives that accompany the signage policy. We conducted thorough interviews with RATP employees from the signage design and normalization department, and we systematically gathered documents that present the signage policy: the guidelines themselves, but also information leaflets, the slides of a presentation performed within the organization to announce the new signage, and articles of internal journals. If this set of data gives us access to the vocabulary used both to describe the great principles of the policy and to detail the subway signs' new organization, it also contains numerous assertions about the riders, their 'needs' and the ways they are supposed to use the new way-finding system.

Second, we tried to understand what it takes to follow the signage scripts in practical terms, that is, to adopt specific positions within subway spaces. In order to fully experience the scripts as frameworks of action, we had to reduce way-finding to the sole use of subway signs, whereas ordinary riders always mobilize heterogeneous resources to find their way (Lacoste 1997; Ingold 2000). Therefore, we elaborated a phenomenological experimentation that consisted in the accomplishment of real rides within the Parisian subway system, during which we systematically gathered a picture and our comments for each board, sticker and poster we relied on to reach our destination. Since the use and the signification of the signage components were sometimes at the centre of on-the-spot debates, we regularly confronted our own interpretations to take decisions and pursue our trip. This experiment offers two advantages. First, photographs are particularly useful to study visible materials (Wagner 2006). In the case of signage, the strict 'shooting script' we followed (Suchar 2007) offered a means to put all the signs mobilized during a ride on the same level and to force us, as researchers, to question each of them. Second, noting our comments and debates was a rich way to surface interpretation processes, which might have remained tacit if we conducted such experiences alone.

Thus, following the trail of their scripts, we studied the Parisian subway signs as organizational artefacts: we both gathered the narratives about the riders' needs and attitudes that are inscribed in them, and discovered the practical tasks their situated uses require. We identified four distinct scripts that we will detail in the next sections: *information, planification, problem solving* and *reaction*. For each one of them, we will precis the riders' definition it relies on, the type of signs that are supposed to carry it and what it really takes in the situation to follow it; that is, what one has to do to effectively become an informed rider, a planner, a problem solver or a reactive entity.

Information

In the first script we identified, the signage is conceived of as a set of tools that inform the riders. The informed rider is a familiar figure within the RATP, which has been striving for long to provide a convenient amount of information to its users. Yet, for years, the issue of information and the figure of the informed rider used to refer almost exclusively to perturbed situations. It was a crucial dimension for the service's quality that riders had to be informed each time the normal conditions of network were disturbed. In other terms, people were supposed to become informed riders only when things went wrong in the transportation network.

With the new signage policy, the informational script has been noticeably enlarged. The figure of the rider who seeks help during perturbations has been gradually replaced with another one who needs to be continuously informed. Within the internal documents and during the interviews such an ordinary informed rider is omnipresent and the need for information appears as an essential dimension in the designers' definitions of subway users. But information is not mobilized as an abstract notion to describe all kinds of situations and everything subway signs have to provide. It is tightly attached to the notion of control. The informed rider is a person who tries to gain more control on the mundane circumstances of her rides.

> We also have to provide riders a control of time in the course of their rides, by informing them [...] about waiting time according to real traffic conditions. (RATP 1993: 14)

Such a script clearly takes part in the larger historical trend of the formation of technological societies. Signage here goes with the numerous devices that transform the modes of government from surveillance to communication, where government itself 'relies on the existence of the informed citizen' (Barry 2001: 48). Providing information within subway spaces is a way to perform an informed rider who can fully control her displacements.

Signboards that provide information are specific ones. They are discursive, that is, they are designed to provide 'messages' to the riders. For example, in certain halls posters can be found that list the names of stations currently undergoing renovation works and inaccessible during a particular period. Recently, electronic real-time devices have also been put up on platforms in order to display the time remaining until the next two trains arrive. Here, signs are mainly texts. They perform a discursive ordering of riders' environment by letting them know that 'this station is unavailable', 'the next train will be here in eight minutes'.

Within subway spaces, the rider has to read in order to be informed. This sounds obvious, but is not so: the circulation of information is never a straightforward and transparent operation. To read a poster's text is one thing; to make up a piece of information (and thus a resource for action) from what it is written is another. To become an informed user, not only has the rider to decipher the linguistic content of a signboard or a poster, but she also has to match this content with the actual situation (dates, places, and so on). For example, if a board displays the schedule of first and last trains according to weekdays, weekends and holidays, one has to align two things to really be informed: what the board reads and the current day and time.

Furthermore, because all information does not appear in a single board, to become informed, the rider generally has to forge a chain of multiple readings in the course of her ride, from one discursive sign to another. In other terms, the rider does not have to simply grasp information, as it would be 'naturally' displayed in the surroundings. As we did several times during our rides, she has to articulate different texts and messages with her own situation, in order to produce a comprehensive informational resource.

Planification

The second script draws the figure of a pretty different rider. Here, she is staged as a person who needs to prepare her ride: she's a planner. The figure points to two distinctive dimensions. The first one is anticipation. As a planner, the rider is considered a strategic human being who makes rational projections for her future actions. The second dimension is calculation. In the documents or interviews which mention such a rider, she is conceived of as someone who collects different kind of facts (station names, lines number, connections, and so on) and computes all these data to produce an operative scenario. The planner translates her displacement ('to go to this particular place') into a point-by-point itinerary, using several calculative operations.

At home or at work, riders have a lot of tools at their disposal to plan their trips before they enter a subway station. But the RATP signage policy aims to provide specific devices that can be consulted *in situ*. These devices, such as maps or timetables, display abstract representations. They offer a simplified panoramic view of the network that makes its spatial characteristics (stations' geographical positions, trains' routes) and its temporal ones (timetables and frequency of trains) commensurable. These signage components perform a calculable setting. For example, timetables support the organization of a trip by anticipating the time of departure and the potential connections to reach the final destination.

Although one could think so, such devices are not identifiable to 'cognitive artefacts' (Norman 1991): they do not produce calculation themselves, contrary to the altitude alert system that Hutchins (1995b) described, for example. The planification work largely remains on the rider's side.

> A map is still an information system that forces the person to work. […] The map tells you everything and nothing at the same time, that is: you have to find the map's instructions, you have to find your departure point, you have to find your arrival point and then manage to understand everything that we put in the map … to see the connections, and this and that … (Q.W., Responsible for Cartography Department, RATP)

During our phenomenological experimentation, we decided to do unusual rides compared with our regular experience of the Parisian subway network. These cases always began in front of a map by struggling with the multitude of signs in order to anticipate the lines and connections that would be relevant to reach the final destination we chose.

Such a script puts the rider in the same position as the person that Suchman imagined for her well-known example of rapids' run, who 'sits for a while above the falls and plans [her] descent' (Suchman 2007: 72). The location of the specific signage components, supposed to equip the rider planner, plays an important role to perform such an anticipatory operation. Timetables and maps are essentially displayed within halls and not corridors or staircases.

However, subway stations are not rapids. First, planning cannot be done from a geographical position that overhangs the entire landscape. In subway systems, the rider is never 'above the falls', she can never watch the whole settings of her future displacements. For planning, she faces graphical representations from which she gathers specific kinds of instructions. In contrast with the canoeist, she has no means to plan 'I'll get as far over to the left as possible, try to make it between those two large rocks' (Suchman 2007: 72). The rider only knows that she has to 'take *line* 2 towards *Nation*, change at *Saint-Lazare* for *line 3* towards *Pont de Levallois*, and stop at *Wagram*'.

Second, because of the semiotic nature of planning devices, the rider cannot completely 'abandon the plan and fall back on whatever embodied skills' (Suchman 2007: 72). When in corridors, she will no longer have access to the rich representation of maps and timetables. In a way, the signage radicalizes the frontier between places (and times) where riders can plan and places where they have to move. The success of their rides depends then both on the memorization of the instructions that compose their plans and on their ability to locally understand the indexicality of each sign.

Problem solving

The third script involves a rider who has problems to solve. Here, the figure is drawn from a micro-level perspective and refers to the description of each ride as a series of choices to be made. But these choices are more like dilemmas than options. The rides are not peaceful and the problem solver figure is mainly a worried person. Subway spaces are presented as real labyrinths that put the riders in a state of maximal uncertainty. The problem solver, as she moves, is assailed with questions:

> Where can I make a phone call? Where can I buy a ticket? Which bus should I Take? On her path, at each moment, the rider wonders. (RATP 1997: 2)

The aim of signage here is to give to the rider every possible means to get out of what is presented as her 'natural' state of indecision. Thus, if the figure of problem solver is imported from the cognitive sciences where it is central (Simon and Kaplan 1989), it is actually far from their mentalist perspective. For the signage designers, the graphical objects put in the environment are conceived of as external resources that should help the rider in search for a solution. Here, the problem-solving operations are then inscribed within a large cognitive system. Cognitive tasks are distributed between humans and artefacts (Hutchins 1995a) and do not depend on a sole individual engaged in a self-reflexive deliberation. As the responsible for signage normalization told us, within subway stations, the signage and the riders are supposed to 'work hand in hand'. If we focus on the figure of the rider, that means that she is performed as an equipped person: confronted with a multitude of choices, she is supposed to gain a significant advantage by delegating some solutions to signboards, instead of thinking for herself.

The signs that support this figure are mainly the directional ones. They display both places' identifications (lines' numbers, destinations, streets' names) and arrows. They play a crucial role in the ordering of spaces by marking the links between sites. Their presence performs a hybrid environment (Fuller 2002) that is as much architectural as cognitive: a setting that supports decision-making. In a way, associated with the figure of the problem solver, what the signage does to the subway spaces can be compared to what Cochoy (2004) showed about the packaging in grocery stores: not only does it provide the resources to decide, but it performs the conditions for the choice itself:

> [With signage], at any time one is confronted to a choice that divides the universe in two parts: what can be reached by turning left and what can be reached by turning right. Then, one direction of our system applies to half of the space and the other direction applies to the other half. (L.C., Information Systems and Telecommunications Department, RATP)

But the felicity of such an 'equipped choice' setting cannot be understood with the sole vocabulary of the distributed cognition model. If signboards are clearly designed to become cognitive resources, they are, at the same time, constituted as constraints. In the performation process we try to describe here, both the environment and the riders are shaped. Not only is the rider invited to rely on various signs during her displacement; she is also invited to mobilize them in a certain manner. This is extremely clear for the problem solver figure for which some signs are designed in order to bypass any deciphering operation at a certain distance. Words that appear on them are made to be spotted, not read:

> The important thing is that a destination is a shape that I spot. That is: it is clear that "Neuilly" and "Chateau de Vincennes" cannot have the same shape. And to do this, we need to write in capital letters and lower-case letters on the one hand, and to reduce the letters height on the other hand, in order to obtain what's absolutely necessary to be seen, to be read when one stands from a certain distance and beyond the shape of words becomes imperative. (L.C., Information Systems and Telecommunications Department, RATP)

This last point stresses an important feature of the problem solving script. During some parts of our rides, our choices have to be made not in deciphering messages but in spotting specific signs and recognizing 'outlines of drawn words' (RATP 2002: 15 [slides]). In order to become an equipped rider, one then has to leave some habits behind, which is a real competency. Here, one has to accept not to read.

Reaction

The last script defines the rider as a reactive entity. Neither in a position of control, nor in a situation of uncertainty, she is staged as a person who goes smoothly through corridors, halls and platforms, almost without thinking. She does not have any imperative for organizing her trip in advance and does not engage in self-reflexive deliberations. Intensely aware of the surroundings, she is mostly reactive. The rider is here driven by basic automatic reflexes:

> No sooner seen than glimpsed ... [...] All the signs that compose the new signage are taken at first glance. The repertoire is mostly constituted of signs that have existed for a long time within the RATP signage policy and that, modernized, provoke immediate user reflexes. (RATP 1997: 2)

Specific features of subway signs, such as materials and colours, are designed to support this reactive attitude. Some of them are generally inherited from a longer history than subway systems themselves. It is the case of certain colours, or shapes, that are used to operate a real 'semiotization' of the signboards. Fraenkel (2006) constituted this kind of conventional work as a key issue of her theory of writing acts: some actions can be fully inscribed in the material support. Here, colours and shapes support the differentiation between the boards and the identification of the distinct functions that are attributed to them. Such a semiotic investment relies on a standardization process. In order to accompany reactive movements, colours and shapes have to remain strictly the same all over the subway network. Because they perform a strongly ordered setting, they are key components of the stabilization of the space itself.

 To become a reactive entity, the rider has to adopt an almost animalistic attitude within this stabilized surrounding. She has to restrict her way-finding operations to sheer 'perceptive procedures' (Hutchins 1995b). By walking on corridors or platforms, she has to identify signs at first glance and at a great distance. For example, she can easily follow the 'exit' boards thanks to their glossy dark blue in Paris. In a way, she has to stop thinking and to use only her eyes, in order to delegate the control of her ride to the artefacts installed in the surroundings. In the course of our rides, we regularly adopted this reactive position, notably when we followed the colour of the relevant line for the next connection. We only had to glimpse the colour while moving and mainly focusing our attention on one of our stimulating theoretical debates.

 In such a framework of action, each sign has to be grasped as a clue to go on and movement is performed in a series of perception/action sequences:

> During the whole trip, signage should be followed as the best of guides. Signs take over one from another; one has simply to follow them in order to get to the city and to reach closer to her destination. (RATP 1997: 2)

Thus, the rider must be able to engage in a step-by-step process, following one lower-level instruction after another, what the designers called an 'Ariadne's thread' (Wiart, Le Roux and Lomazzi 1998).

This form of engagement between the rider and her environment is close to Bessy and Chateauraynaud (1995) termed the '*régime d'emprise*', where people and things are tightly bounded, which cancels any human pretention to objectivization. To become a reactive entity, the rider has to accept this dependency on the surroundings. She then reaches a particular state that 'is characterized by the absence of rupture between entities [... and] leads to the impossibility of any kind of detachment' (Bessy and Chateauraynaud 1995: 263).

What is performed here is the seamless circulation of bodies through the network. The riders are configured as entities moved by the fluidity of traffic. From this point of view, the script is pretty different from the previous one where people are supposed to stop at each junction, even briefly, and make choices between options clearly exposed by the signage components. Even if both scripts involve a similar process of delegation to the environment, they perform two distinct rhythms of movement.

Conclusion

What have we learned from the details of Parisian signage scripts and from the analysis of the embodied practices they require? Above all, we showed that the accountability performed by subway signs is plural. We identified four different figures of riders: the informed one, who wants to control her trip and has to read messages; the planner, who anticipates the conditions of her ride and has to use calculation devices; the problem solver, who calms down her anxiety by finding clear options exposed on recognizable signboards; and the reactive entity, who circulates smoothly by responding automatically to specific graphical features of the surroundings.

In the Parisian subway spaces, the rider is never performed only as a reader who would catch some meaning from various texts. Sometimes she is more 'active' (when she has to compute data to plan her trip), and sometimes more 'passive' (when she has to react automatically after perceiving the shape or the colour of a signboard). Signage displays neither a text, nor a discourse. It is made of the 'a-signifying elements of time, space, rhythm, movement, bodies and so on' (Fuller 2002: 241).

Such a plurality strongly contrasts with the metaphor of reading that still has great resonance in the analysis of urban settings and where streets, squares, buildings, and cities themselves are supposed to be legible (Stierle 2001). This metaphor invites one to study cities as texts and implicitly promotes a *literate accountability*. In contrast, we saw that designers strive to fit out a *graphical accountability* that relies on a wide range of actions.

Interestingly, in designers' discourses, the riders' figures are never reduced to 'types' of riders or marketing targets. They neither mobilize ontological definitions of individual users, nor pretend to describe any kind of diversity within the population. The pluralistic accountability that the signage provides concerns each single rider. The same person may go throughout various frameworks in the course of a single trip. Generally, she actually has to do so.

Thanks to signage, plurality is a feature of the surroundings. However, it does not mean that every figure is supported any time and everywhere. Precisely, the graphical ordering aimed to support the 'success' of rides is performed by the spatial and temporal distribution of the signs, and the riders' states they are intended to generate. Subway spaces are designed as pathways where the available resources for orientation change according to the section one goes through. Successful rides should be performed by the successive encounters between the riders' adequate states and the standardized signboards, that is, the progressive actualization of different scripts.

That is how the signage performs a public space: it ascribes states and positions to people according to the sites they cross. Such a performation process accomplishes a con-figuration, that is, an articulation between particular figurations of spaces and certain figures of riders. But while the first ones are in the hand of the designers and the placement workers (Denis and Pontille, forthcoming), the second ones remain virtual. To be actualized, they have to be enacted on the spot by disciplined riders who, as the pedestrian in Paris described by Latour and Hermant (1998), go through one device to another, through one user's figure to another:

> I'm not simply passing through Paris: the "I" also passes through forms of action, regimes of intelligence that are virtually unrelated to one another. [...] From one second to the next different regimes of action relayed one another, leading me from one competence to the next. I'm neither in control nor without control: I'm formatted. I'm afforded possibilities for my existence, based on teeming devices scattered throughout the city. I go from one offer to the next. To progress a little further I grasp the small bit of program that others have stuck onto each device for me. (Latour and Hermant 1998: 68)

But, unlike to the various devices present in the streets that address different senses (hearing, sight, touch ...), the signage confronts the riders with a single kind of artefact. Its plurality remains within the world of signs, and the regimes of action that it supposes are always a matter of gazes and visibility. In other terms, the graphical accountability provided by signage inscribes a *politics of attention* in public settings.

Goffman (1959) insisted on the human side of public spaces. He showed the importance of 'civil inattention' that occurs within cities, that is, the ability of people to be aware of others without conspicuously focusing on their movements and attitudes. The case of signage shows that non-humans can also become a crucial matter of concern in the organizing of public settings (Latour 2005a). To properly use the Parisian subway system, the riders have to be aware of numerous graphical artefacts. Dwelling in subway spaces requires, besides a civil attention, a *graphic attention*, which, as we showed, demands several specific cognitive skills. And not only have the riders to dispose of these skills: they also need to juggle with them, from one site to another, from one moment to another.

This politics of attention rests on the designers' desire to build an omnipresent graphical apparatus, meant to encompass all kinds of uses. Largely inspired by social theories that took part in Design Research and Human Computer Interaction Studies (such as 'situated action' and 'distributed cognition'), it performs a user-centric world. It is then highly individualistic. Even if signage is a form of public lettering, devoted to several people in the same time (Petrucci 1993), it actually provides an interface that each isolated person can use to navigate the world. The four scripts of the Parisian subway signs, which inscribe various ways to distribute some features of the human cognition within the surroundings, all require a 'face-to-face' relationship between a rider and the signage components. They clearly rely on an individual cognitive availability. In other terms, the Parisian signage is meant to equip a rider who could be all alone. By following the sole signboards directions she could still manage to find her way within the transportation network.

The Parisian signage thus performs a very specific public setting. In order to more precisely understand it, one can ask one of the favourite questions of actor-network theory: what is delegated in this artefact? We saw that signage is not representational. It then has nothing to do with the public display of matters of concern, that is, things we collectively consider (Latour 2005a). Actually, the signage operates a twofold delegation. Signs are meant to replace and, above all, expand the presence of employees of the carrier who could verbally help the riders. But they also replace the collective of co-present riders. From the designers' view, the fact that a rider asks the way of another rider is considered as a failure. What is at stake with the omnipresence and the standardization of signboards is not public consciousness, but strictly personal guidance. It seems that this kind of individual gear is currently growing, with the success of numerous Global Positioning System (GPS) devices on the one hand, and real-time information urban displays on the other. This twofold equipment, of people and places, perform public settings that are augmented with an informational layer, a whole interface, and that are evaluated in the sole terms of operability and efficiency. It sets the basis for public spaces where dwelling together counts less than successfully navigating side by side.

Chapter 2

The Wall and the Mobile Phone:
Organizing, Governing, Resisting

Andrea Mubi Brighenti[1]

Facing Walls, Calling Out

In this chapter I would like to explore the *continuum* that stretches between two 'uncanny' objects: the wall and the mobile phone. The wall is an apparently trivial object, and one long neglected by social theory. The practicalities of the social life of walls are largely under-researched compared to their symbolic value(s). Walls stand for the universal symbols of separation and division, but from this perspective they are rather univocal and do not have much to say: they are, as Simmel (1997) first put it, 'mute'. Additionally, in hi-tech contemporary Western society walls appear to be rather low-tech devices when compared to smarter social control devices, such as the 'surveillant assemblage' (Haggerty and Ericson 2000), increasingly based upon immaterial, digital flow tracking (Lyon 2001).

While old brick walls are neglected, there is a lot of hype (and business) about mobile phones and the other new mobile media. Quite a good deal of sociological research on mobile communication, and more broadly the new media, leans towards the techno-enthusiast side.[2] There is a discourse of empowerment that goes with the celebration of such empowerment. Representatives of techno-enthusiasm tend to stress a number of features of mobile phones, first of all flexibility, and ubiquity. Mobility plays an extremely important role in such an empowerment. The fact that you can now make plans for meetings on the go allegedly allows for a new kind of sociality, essentially an urban sociality that is highly flexible (Kwan 2007). In short, to their advocates mobile communication means total accessibility and provides the ultimate form of the network society (Castells et al. 2004).

So, the apparent antithesis could be put as follows: walls do not communicate, while mobile communication does not know walls since it has little or no material constraints at all. As Mitchell (2003: 7) put it synthetically, 'walls, fences, and

---

1   I wish to thank the reviewers of an earlier version of this chapter and all the participants at the *Organizing Cities* workshop for the useful comments and the ensuing lively debate.

2   For instance, research on the education (Islam and Doyle 2008), health care (Maglaveras et al. 2002), safety (Pain et al. 2005) and new urban cultures (Beiguelman et al. 2008).

skins divide; paths, pipes, and wires connect'. My aim here is to challenge this view. Consequently, in this chapter I propose to look comparatively at how both walls and mobile phones organize space in the city through their specific, often criss-crossing and overlapping combinations of 'mobilities and moorings' (Urry 2009).

City Walls, Cities of Walls

In both imagination and practice, walls are boundaries. Kevin Lynch (1960) famously described boundaries as one of those essential elements people use to make sense of urban space in navigating it. Together with paths, districts, nodes and landmarks, boundaries or edges define the image of the city in the imagination of its users. Architects usually say that boundaries create places and container spaces in which social situations occur.

Historically, walls emerged as boundaries *of* the city and subsequently turned into boundaries *in* the city. The walls that surrounded medieval towns were walls of protection. In his classic history of urban culture, Lewis Mumford (1996 [1938]) observed that the capitalist economy overcame medieval restrictions pushing towards an unforeseen spatial expansion of cities (which today we call sprawl). As cities spread in every direction in the mainland as well as overseas, the walls that surrounded the medieval town centres were demolished both practically and symbolically.[3]

Once removed as boundaries of the city, walls became boundaries inside the city. For instance, segregation processes can be described as walling different communities instead of the whole city. Such an enclosing function is present, for instance, in the late-medieval Jewish ghetto (see Calimani 2001 on the Venice ghetto) and prolongs into modern ghettoes and their self-reproducing dynamics. As Louis Wirth (1964: 92) remarked, 'though the physical walls of the ghetto have been torn down, an invisible wall of isolation still maintains the distance between the Jew and his neighbours'. The Chicago school of human ecology, interested in studying how the selective, distributive and accommodative forces of the environment produce and affect social life, argued that spatial differentiation and spatial segregation in the city emerge from below, in a spontaneously patterned way. Park, Burgess and McKenzie (1925: 56) considered that:

> This differentiation into natural, economic and cultural groupings gives form and character to the city. For segregation offers the group, and thereby the individuals who compose the group, a place and a role in the total organization of city life. Segregations limits development in certain directions, but releases

---

3   More recently, Peter Sloterdijk (2005) has traced how this tearing down of walls was the pivot of what he describes as the second wave of globalization, or nautical globalization, which occurred since the fifteenth century.

it in others. These areas tend to accentuate certain traits, to attract and develop their kind of individuals, and so to become further differentiated.

A different perspective on separation and segregation has been elaborated by Michel Foucault, who regarded walls as architectural arrangements for exclusion and isolation. On his account, segregation and separation do not emerge from mere social interaction, rather are planned as parts of certain *dispositifs* for the government of the population.[4] The shift from the medieval fortification wall to the governmental wall leaves an ominous presence in the cities, the wall of the prison and of the other enclosed institutions:

> The high wall, no longer the wall that surrounds and protects, no longer the wall that stands for power and wealth, but the meticulously sealed wall, uncrossable in either direction, closed in upon the now mysterious work of punishment, will become, near at hand, sometimes even at the very centre of the cities of the nineteenth century, the monotonous figure, at once material and symbolic, of the power to punish. (Foucault 1977 [1975]: 116)

The modern city transforms walls into elements of a *spatial political economy of government*. The outer boundary and its capacity to protect the city from external invasion is no longer what really matters, instead it is the capacity to manage enclaves and islands within the city. Walls are turned into tools for the government of the population. Consequently, it is the power to control settlements and fluxes of people in the urban space that becomes essential. Housing and logistics (stocking, transport, distribution and delivery) become prominent goals for planners from both economic and political perspectives. The Fordist industrial economic model corresponds to such spatial organization, in which walls separate classes, *qua* large occupations groups, that have clearly differentiated lived experiences of the city.

With the crisis of the disciplinary model as an encompassing model for society, the history of the governmental wall enters a third stage. After the medieval walled urbs and the urban wall of the enclosed institution, a further trend towards pluralization and dispersal takes place. It is a process which can be understood through the Foucaultian notion of 'capillarisation' of power. New forms of segregation emerge, based on new 'smart' technologies that increase selectivity in individual access. Walls become virtual: they are pluralized and potentially everywhere. Once the technological infrastructure is implemented, it takes no more than an instant to actualise an *ad hoc* wall. We seem to be faced with a new 'partitioned city' (Marcuse 1995; Caldeira 2001), or dual city. As observed by Stavros Stavrides (2006), 'in today's partitioned cities thresholds are

---

4   In a sense, walls are literally in between disciplinary power (exercised in enclosed institutions) and the *dispositifs* of security (exercised in open spaces of circulation), which form two different aspects of governmentality. Elsewhere, I have attempted to distinguish four analytical diagrams of power in Foucault (Brighenti 2010).

rapidly being replaced by check-points, control areas that regulate encounters and discriminate between users'. Lianos (2001) sums up the features of new 'post-industrial' social control as consisting of three major aspects: *privatization* (fear of 'exposed' public space), *cindynisation* or 'dangersation' (the city interpreted as a field of threatening 'possible events'), and *periopticity* (social control enacted no longer through panoptic surveillance, rather through autonomous and differential individual motivation grounded in competition for access and inclusion).

The impact of governmental diffusion, together with the capillarization and infiltration of power devices at every scale, entail a concurrent multiplication of walls and wall-like artefacts (Brighenti 2010). Therefore the dissemination and the scattering of walls in urban space does not mean their disappearance, least that the materiality ceases to matter. In this sense, Alsayyad and Roy (2006) have spoken of the contemporary urban condition as a 'medieval modernity': contemporary urban geographies appear to be constituted through a constellation of fragmented spaces, as embodied in the exemplary cases of the gated enclave, the squatter settlement and the camp. Similarly, Weizman (2007) has described the complexities of walling strategies in the Israeli 'architecture of occupation' in the Palestinian occupied territories. In all these cases, walls are still among the most widespread and effective devices for the government of populations around the world, especially in urban environments. Arguably, it is so because walls impact so forcefully on the material and sensorial environment. Walls are among the primary boundary-creating objects, but their contemporary use is not as monolithic as it used to be. The general category 'wall' includes, in fact, a wide and increasingly diversified set of separating artefacts, such as barriers, fences, gates, parapets, wire and so on, each of which is endowed with its own specific boundary-making features.

In order to carry on the analysis the pluralization, dispersal and ubiquity of walls in contemporary urban space, it can be helpful to develop an analytic scheme to address the materialities, functionalities and affectivities of walls.

For an Analytic of Wall

From a sociological point of view we can, on the basis of what is said above, identify a series of analytic qualities of walls, which also represent a series of aspects upon which an enquiry can be based.

Materiality

'Wall' is in fact an umbrella term and a shorthand for a series of wall-like artefacts, that is, objects that are primarily aimed at creating and sustaining some sort of boundary. This type of object includes a group of separating artefacts, such as barriers, fences, gates, parapets, barricades, barbed wire (on the latter, see in particular Netz 2004), and so on. Overall, these objects certainly rank as low-tech devices compared to smarter population management devices – used for both human and animal populations. The undeniable effectiveness of walls, however, is due to the fact that they impact directly on bodies, on the materiality of the social. Originally, boundaries act upon bodily movements, hampering some trajectories and facilitating others. This explains the effectiveness of walls as governmental tools, as we have remarked above. Wall-like artefacts should firstly be classified and studied comparatively, on the basis of differential degrees of penetrability, but also permeability, transparency and so on. Materials technologies and building technologies – more precisely, the relationship between these technologies and bodily movements and the mobilities they enable – are the point of departure of our study. Materials range from stone, through glass (a crucial mid-nineteenth-century innovation in architecture), to smart electronic movement-sensitive devices, which are increasingly employed to enforce security in airports (Adey 2008). In any case, it is clear that fixity cannot be taken as a defining feature of walls, given that tactical uses can exploit movable surfaces such as trains, lorries and so on, as visible walls (see the points on visibility and uses below).

Territoriality

Taking the material dimension seriously does not mean discarding the immaterial, but instead studying precisely the points of convergence between the two layers. Walls' territoriality is a case in point because every territory is in fact a mixed entity, material and immaterial at the same time. The specific territorial dynamic consists of the inscriptions of social relationships into a material support (Kärrholm 2007). Territories are better imagined as processes than objects. In fact, making territories equates to drawing boundaries and sustaining the relationships that are defined by and depend upon those boundaries (Brighenti 2006). In this respect, walls are fundamentally vertical, and the first meaning we can give to verticality is *impediment*. As vertical boundaries, walls constrain people flows, transforming a smooth space into a striated one. As we have seen above, the well-known historical example is urban residential segregation, which begins in the form of the walled Jewish ghetto. Incidentally, walls are not the only tools of segregation. Shantytowns and favelas are segregated without being walled, as not many people from the outside wish to go there. More generally, however, urban space would hardly be conceivable without wall-like artefacts and to all appearances, the history of the city is a history of boundaries no less than a history of flows. Most importantly, boundaries are not all-or-nothing barriers, but always a matter of degree and relative speeds. On the basis of a process-based and relational view on territory, walls should be studied not so much in terms of their physical extension and location, as much as in terms of the affects that they create. Here, we can also appreciate that the difference between a wall and a door is in fact quite relative. People who are not admitted will experience the wall-like quality of doors and, for some, taking walls as doors can even become a personal, political or economic challenge. Walls demarcate a within and a beyond and, by doing so, they define flows of circulation, set paths and trajectories for people and, consequently, determine the possibilities and impossibilities of encounters.

Visibility

As soon as we analyse the territoriality of walls, we realise that not only are walls boundaries between territories, but are themselves territories. To people, they are meaningful not only for what they separate or hide, but also in themselves. Consequently, we encounter a second meaning of verticality, namely 'surfaceality'. *Logically* speaking walls are in-between people, vehicles, and so on – yet *phenomenologically* speaking they constitute a horizon, however relative, which is meaningful in itself. In a significant sense, architecture is the science and the art of this relative and close horizon. If for Simmel walls were mute, the events of 1968 – Guattari (1992) reminds us – taught us to read desire on the walls. Although not in a politically explicit way, a whole generation of graffiti writers and street artists understood quite clearly the lesson of walls' visibility – as did advertisers, at least since Simmel's times. Urban walls are surfaces of projection. As Iveson (2007) remarks, they deliver a sort of constant 'public address'. Outdoor advertisement and graffiti are both part of such process of attention-claiming that represents an essential part of the new type of urban capitalism and entrepreneurialism (Chmielewska 2005; Cronin 2008). From this point of view, walls are to be studied in terms of the differential visibilities they possess and consequently confer, as well as in terms of the social effects of such visibility. Walls create *a public* in Gabriel Tarde's (1969 [1901]) sense: as visible surfaces, they define a public focus of attention for a number of viewers and actors who are spatially dispersed. Each wall also collects a *temporally* dispersed audience that, at some point, has transited nearby. Hence, the wall becomes part of the struggle for public attention and key element in the configuration of an urban regime visibility (Brighenti 2007). A politics of visibility – which, with Tripodi (2008), we may also call a *politics of verticality* – is crucial to appreciate the stakes of the social life of walls: corresponding to every definition of a field of visibility are demands and tensions which endeavour to establish a connection between the possible and the proper, between what can be seen and what should or should not be seen, between who can and who cannot see others. Thus, the symbolism of the wall as an exclusionary and containment device can be better understood as a single specific arrangement in a wider field of the politics of visibilities.

Rhythm

A sociological study of walls cannot abstract itself from the fact that walls possess rhythms. As any other boundary artefacts, walls have life cycles, which correspond to successions of points and moments of concentration and dispersal of people, objects and events. Rhythms occur at different time scales, ranging from temporary, occasional and emergency-related (for example, *cordon sanitaire*, police no-crossing line and so on), through regular (to retrieve Simmel once again, a door can in fact be observed and described as a rhythmic wall) and cyclic (circadian, hebdomadal, monthly, seasonal and yearly cycles – like the medieval city gates but also the Jewish *eruv*), to generational (with the Berlin Wall providing a clear example of generational wall), historic, and 'immemorial' walls. All these different rhythms are not simply successive or alternative to one other, rather coexistent, stratified, modulating each other. Urban renewal megaprojects, for instance, can be observed from the point of view of the heavy impact they have on the rhythms of walls in the affected zones. The social life of walls also includes conflicts over the rhythms of these artefacts. Thus, in our study of walls we need to include an analysis of rhythms, based on the factors and determinants of each rhythm, its scale, variance, predictability, and so on.

Uses

By far the most complex dimension is related to the different uses of walls. In the political economy of urban spatiality, walls appear as governmental objects. Foucault (1991 [1978]) describes governmentality as comprising three interlocked elements: a set of institutions and procedures for the exercise of power over a population, the emergent historical configuration of such governmental *savoirs*, and the application of these tools to political institutions, in particular the administrative state. Within this broad framework, one can appreciate the fact that walls are planned and built as part of a strategy aimed at controlling people by means of controlling spatial displacement. A vision, or plan, is at the core of wall-building sciences. From the strategic point of view, walls appear as useful separators and flux managers. Further, not only must walls be built, they must also be maintained, repaired, reconfigured. However, walls do not lend themselves only to strategy. While they are introduced as strategic, they are also always subject to tactical uses. Both strategies and tactics (as classically described by de Certeau 1984) can be regarded as territorial endeavours (Kärrholm 2007). Notably, the classical distinction between strategy and tactics does not mean that established power is only strategic and the powerless are only tactical. On the contrary, social movements, oppositional and subcultural groups often develop strategic lines and, conversely, we often see situations in which the establishment acts tactically. In any case, situational interaction constantly modifies and reshapes the significance, impact and meaning of walls. For instance, graffiti are tactical interventions upon walls, in the sense that walls are built by day and painted by night. Whereas strategy aims at naturalizing walls, pushing them to the background, tactics re-focus them in various guises, pulling them towards new foregrounds. From the tactical perspective, the most remarkable feature of walls is that they offer a visible surface, which becomes a surface of inscription for stratified, criss-crossing and overlapping traces. Such traces are highly visible interventions that define a type of social interaction at a distance. Besides immediate direct interaction between people, urban environments are full of, and sometimes saturated with, such types of mediated interaction. The sociological study of walls must then account for the strategic and tactical uses of walls. It is necessary to tackle how they define, not simply closures, but also fixtures, interstices and all sort of mediated interaction.

Walls and Mobile Phones as Horizons in the Life-World

From both strategic and tactical perspectives, the wall is an urban object that constitutively calls into play the interweaving of space and social relations. Walls, like other territories, are material and immaterial at the same time: they manage space, command attention, and define mobility fluxes that impose conduct, but they are also constantly challenged because of the meaning they assume: they can be reassuring as well as oppressive, they can be irritating as well as inspiring. Marcuse and Van Kempen (2000: 250) claim that 'walls, literal or symbolic, prevent people from seeing, meeting and hearing each other; at the extreme they insulate and they exclude'. In parallel to the modern history of governmentality, which has diffused, capillarized and infiltrated power devices at each social scale, it is possible to diagnose a concurrent multiplication of walls and other wall-like artefacts. In the modern city, walls correspond to planned zoning, according to a politics of connection and separation which has been described by Caldeira (2001) through her metaphor of the 'city of walls'.

At the same time that walls set up such perceptual limitations, however, they also tend to become part of the unquestioned, naturalized background of the here-and-now of a given urban environment. Urbanites do not stare at walls, but that does not mean that walls are unimportant: people look at walls only *a contrario*, so to speak, as dead ends to avoid, literally as *impasses*. Walls are perceived as stable boundaries (Lynch 1960). Consequently, the feature of in-betweenness that characterizes the wall constantly shifts towards the horizon of the life-world. Alfred Schütz (1970) described the social *Lebenswelt* as something that constitutes an unquestioned, taken-for-granted horizon of experience. Experiences take place *within* such frame. Visible, actual problems and issues are placed within an unproblematic background. The phenomenological perspective allows us to make sense of the intrinsic vagueness and 'unmappability' of spatial experience (Miller 2006). It should be added that, if this is the case, it is at least in part because in the majority of occasions one accepts to confine one's spatial experience within a horizon which is never fully or exhaustively interrogated. In a sense, in many situations, walls belong to such unquestioned, invisible horizon.

Mobile phones and, more generally, new media confront us with a similar situation. Phenomenologically speaking, they cannot be adequately understood as mere tools but must be appreciated as whole *environments*. Mobile media are not objects, rather environmental infrastructures. Just like a sociological analytic of walls, the conceptual repertoire for the sociological study of mobile communication should include at least a media ecology, an urban ecology and an ecology of attentions. An ecological perspective does not prevent a focus on power relations in that concepts like 'control' and 'freedom of movement' can themselves be interpreted as ecological concepts. The ecological perspective is useful to explain why it is so easy to concede that mobile phones have changed our sociality but it is so hard to tell whether it was for better or worse. As recalled at the beginning, most new media literature is techno-enthusiast, as a sort of 'iCan-YouCan' discourse, which is the new media advertisement ideology pivoted around the so-called 'user empowerment', seems to pervade the scholarly literature.

Because of this, two crucial elements are largely underestimated in the existing studies referred to above: first, the extent to which new media can become means of control rather than emancipation; second, the degree to which new media can directly and indirectly foster existing social inequalities. While ubiquitous computing and the diffusion of locative media in the city are often emphasised as empowering effects, what is often overlooked is the fact that urban spatial motility is predictably going to become a crucial factor of social stratification in the next future. A number of reasons contribute to this trend, including factors such as the cost of fossil fuel, restrictions to international migration and the increasing partitioning of the city with its associated residential segregation ('hyperghettoes') and self-segregation ('gating') processes. All these factors seem to prefigure a scenery in which mobility – and specifically the twentieth-century dominant model of mobility based on the car (Urry 2004) – turns into a luxury item. Side by side with the right to citizenship and the right to the city, within this decade the right to mobility is predictably going to become a contentious issue.

Paradoxically, even studies explicitly concerned with the political significance of the new media, like Fenton's (2008), are markedly more focused on the ways in which new media allow for a new imagination of hope rather than the ways in which they may turn out to be an additional factor of social differentiation and inequality. Awareness of this 'dark side' of new media – which basically consists in its wall-like qualities – is essential to examine the place and the scope of governmental and resistance practices in the contemporary city. The phenomenological experience of media-saturated spaces is perfectly capture by Adey (2008: 443) in his Deleuzian-inspired description of modern airport travellers as 'ticks':

> Passengers follow the usual procedures of checking-in, going through security control, waiting in departure lounge, going to gate, waiting in gate, boarding plane. Between these processing sites, corridors and walls are constructed to limit possibilities. Such designs are premised upon the imagination of the passenger-as-tick; rendered with a limited set of actions and reactions by the building.

Circulations, Segregations

The phenomenological invisibility of walls makes it possible to reach the high levels of segregation a growing number of observers are increasingly concerned about. Social closure is a process through which communities wall themselves in while walling out the 'others' and, by doing so, destroy solidarity, fostering intolerance towards the outside. It is no coincidence that the world rise of mobile communication is contemporary to this process of fragmentation and social closure. The network age does not at all mean the end of walls, just like it did not entail the dissolution of space proclaimed by the Internet prophets in the early 1990s. Rather, it entails a transformation of walling technologies. How could we describe the relationship between the connections and separations enacted through walls and the connections and separations made possible by network infrastructures? (Graham and Marvin 2001). For many, the simple opposition outlined at the beginning (walls do not communicate, while mobile communication does not know walls) holds. 'If your teeth carried an RFID tag' – writes Mitchell (2003: 77) in one of his smart examples – 'you might make purchases or open hotel room doors by flashing a smile'.

However, depending on who you are, the same RFID could also ensure that it is a jail room that is being opened for you, or that will ensure that you ragged scum do not dare approach retail and consumptions zones. Then, you will certainly stop smiling. The scenery that has emerged since Foucault's and Deleuze's analyses on governmentality and control is marked by the rise of digital locative technology, like radio frequency identification tags, personal digital assistants and other ubiquitous transponders, but the conceptual apparatus they elaborated is still extremely relevant today. Cities continue to operate as organized geographies that sort their populations and regulate flows and boundaries and, from this point of view, the phenomenological experience of urban environments is highly contingent upon this pre-phenomenological, 'machinic' setup (Amin and Thrift 2002).

Contrary to what commonly held, mobile media do not tear down walls. Walls are still present in new technologies, not only in the form of firewalls and checkpoints, but also in a variety of software-sorted spaces (Thrift 2005). Mobile media are no less territorial than brick walls, although their territorializing devices work differently. Research on the mediacity and the interplay between the new media and the city (see, for example, Eckardt et al. [eds] 2008; McQuire 2008) is increasingly revealing this. As observed by Kaufmann and Montulet (2009: 49), 'to travel fast and far does not necessarily mean that one is "freer" in one's movements in space and time'. In a sense, I contend, mobile phones are 'immobile mobiles', if one considers that every mobility they enable is predicated upon the assumption of a series of corresponding moorings and immobilities. Perhaps what we are seeing is an emerging situation in which networks are only for the rich and walls for the poor. The ubiquity of the mobile phone, while experienced as a private and enabling technology, is in fact inserted into a wider architecture of visibility, whereby virtual ubiquitous flows and boundaries function as wall-like *dispositifs* within the modern city.

Ultimately, both walls and the media retain a potentiality for being places not only of government, sorting and resistance, but of *public life* properly speaking (Iveson 2009). In particular, a comparative perspective on different designs and uses of walls and the media should be able to assess walls' situational capacity to *create the public*, that is, to stir movements and affects that resist enclosure, privatization, exclusion, and eviction (see, for example, Blomley 2004; Delaney 2004). Struggles take the form of in/visibilization strategies and tactics. They concern precisely the threshold between sorting objects and environments. Social and political conflict is thus technological, cultural and legal *at the same time*, as it is fundamentally articulated around the techniques or ways of making walls and wall inscriptions either visible or invisible according to different plans, as well as around the meaning that is attributed to such in/visibility and the effects that follow from these attributions. Understood as convergence zones between the material and the immaterial, both walls and network infrastructures concern the relationship between bodies and their environment. The wall is the epitome of *gravitas*, the mobile phone the epitome of *celeritas*. But the speed made possible by the new media is not the totalitarian, absolute speed depicted by Paul Virilio in his many essays on the subject. It is true that contemporary capitalism has appropriated smoothness, opposing it to the striated spaces of industrial and Fordist capitalism. Yet it has also produced an unprecedented number of new spatial striatures and enclosures and a corresponding numbers of exclusions and segregations; it has stratified access to mobility and is increasingly doing so; it has created one-way corridors and militarized access-points. A territoriological analysis could help us to understand the fine-grained compositions of different affects at the intersection of different environments via different artefacts, not least to rehearse our imagination of resistance.

Chapter 3
Redefining the Right to the City: Representations of Public Space as Part of the Urban Struggles

Stavros Stavrides

New forms of public space can be defined and produced in urban struggles, as representations of space acquire a performative character. If people understand public space in terms of quantity only, they tend to focus their demands on quantifiable entities: more open space, more areas for public use, more trees, more public facilities, and so on.. One should not consider such demands as minor or negligible. However, there can be demands and struggles articulated by a different understanding of public space. A qualitative approach can replace the quantitative one: if people tend to appreciate and imagine urban space in terms of specific forms of spatiality, then they tend to demand specific qualities for public spaces.

There is a huge discussion on the essential qualities of public space, and it is indeed difficult to imagine a general agreement on the characteristics that differentiate contemporary urban public space from equivalent spaces in different societies. However, a crucial distinction can structure any relevant discussion: is public space an entity (definable in terms of objective spatial limits) or a process (definable in terms or spatio-temporal relations)? In what will follow, public space will be understood as a spatio-temporal process. The motivating force of this process is a contestation, the contestation over the meaning and use of public space as both the product and the basis of this process. Public space, thus, will be described not only by the social processes which create it but as a condition always in the making. Putting an emphasis on the inherently contestable character of public space can therefore be formulated in this way: '… Public space is always a contestation over the legitimacy of what can be brought and what can be excluded from the life one chooses and is required to have in common with others' (Hénaff and Strong 2001: 4).

Harvey adds to this formulation by elaborating on the meaning of contestation: 'Contestation over the construction, meaning and organization of public space only takes effect, therefore, when it succeeds in exercising a transformative influence over private and commercial spaces. Action on only one of these dimensions will have little meaning in and of itself' (Harvey 2006: 32). Contestation transforms public space because it is constitutive of public space as such.

Contest is always part of the history of a specific society which 'secretes' its own public spaces. We can thus discover in modern cities specific forms of struggle over the production and definition of public space. In these cities, whereas authorities tend to control and enclose public space as an area which expresses and reproduces existing asymmetries of power, urban struggles tend to question the dominant public space production. Public spaces can thus be created through the narratives and practices of people in struggle. Due to the social dynamics characterizing urban conflicts, such contested spaces attain a hybrid status. Images projected through collective demands, collective memories articulated in shared narratives and common values expressed in acts and words, intermingle to produce spatial experiences of 'possible urban worlds'.

The way people project their desires in urban struggles moulds the way they envisage space as a defining aspect of the kind of common life they try to protect or establish. Space, thus, literally 'happens' during the struggle, space is always emergent, as it becomes the common locus created during the struggle.

According to Chris Pickvance, urban struggles make 'urban demands which challenge existing policies and practices' (Pickvance 1995: 198). Most of contemporary urban struggles seem to confront an array of dominant policies which converge in the process of gentrification. Gentrification is characterized by differing acts of recuperation of the urban centres by the middle class. Gentrification creates exclusive and enclosed urban environments which define their users and their users' patterns of public behaviour. Thus, the public space included in gentrification areas takes the form of discriminating enclaves of collective consumption clearly marked by a defining perimeter. Gentrified public space displaces forms of public life which have to do with working class people, immigrants and youth groups by imposing strict rules of use (rules of conduct) as well as terms of use (high prices to be paid for the use of space). Contestation of public space is not tolerated. Normalization of behaviour as well as the establishment of a predictable and peaceful public life is the aim of this policy for which entrepreneurs, city authorities and urbanists combine forces.

This 'model of pacification [of public space] by cappuccino', as Zukin (1195: 28) wittily names it, is necessarily combined with an enormous concern for security. Gentrified public space has to be designed, organized and appreciated as safe space. Gentrification aims to produce 'safe' public space and defines public space as the place of safety. But safety is specifically understood and imposed in this context. Planning safety means declaring a war against all those who are not included in the middle class utopia of peaceful consumption. Planning safety legitimates discrimination, identity control, generalized surveillance and regulated access.

Urban struggles which develop in opposition to gentrification policies have thus to face the dilemmas and opportunities raised in the prospect of combining identity supporting claims with demands for access. On the one hand, defending the ways of life that gentrification displaces has to do with a certain form of identity politics. On the other hand, fighting for the right of the dispossessed to live in city centre areas and improve their life by the public space regeneration plans, has to do with who is allowed to be in and use gentrified public spaces.

A Collective Experience of Urban Porosity

The case of a specific urban struggle in an Athenian neighbourhood can support a possible synthesis of identity and access claims in the form of actualizing a defining characteristic of public space: urban porosity. Taking this as a case study, an effort will be made to trace the ways in which narratives and shared representations create a distinct form of lived and imagined public space.

Those who participated in this struggle had experienced in their common history the power urban porosity has to create inclusive public spaces and neighbourhoods of social integration. Their common experiences implicitly or explicitly formed their struggle for the preservation of the housing complex in which they still live. We may discover in the history of this struggle a developing focus on collective rights that are not limited to the protection of a specific group of vulnerable inhabitants. What is actually at stake is a redefinition of public, communal and private spaces as mutually dependent and connected. As we will see, the idea of urban porosity acquired a central role in the demands, the common reminiscences and the actions of those people. Conversely, this underlying concept is completely absent in the authorities' narratives as development becomes the overarching ideological term to legitimate state actions.

This particular neighbourhood in Athens has a long and troubled history. *Prosfygica* (from the Greek *prosfygas*, meaning 'refugee') is the word indicating a group of housing complexes created in areas that during the 1930s were considered as the periphery of Athens. Those settlements were built by the state in a programme of slum clearance. Who were the people living in these slums in the first place? Were they the ones who would eventually manage to find a decent shelter in the newly built housing blocks?

To begin with, in 1922 there was a sudden increase in the Athenian population of 130,000 newcomers (amounting to 40 per cent of the city's inhabitants). Those people were refugees from Asia Minor who had to leave their homes in a forced population exchange following a war between Greece and Turkey. A lot can be said on the reasons that had produced a disastrous (for both countries) expedition of the Greek army in Asia Minor. Nationalist rhetoric was a propelling force on both sides (Svoronos 1972). What is important in the context of this research, however, is that those people, represented in the Greek dominant ideology as brothers to be liberated, were actually received after the defeat of the invading Greek army as foreign refugees, as outsiders, as others.

State policy kept half the total refugee population of 1,200,000 on the outskirts of the major cities, offering them as a cheap source of labour to the nearby industries and handicraft workshops. This added to the hostility of the local population: refugees were considered responsible for an economic crisis affecting the living standards of the urban poor. As for the middle class, those oriental others were demonized as invaders who would destroy their fantasies of Westernizing Greek public mores and appearances.

However, the people arriving from Asia Minor had a long and rich urban culture, having lived in cities with an impressive cultural and civic life. Even though most of them came to Greece economically ruined, they never abandoned the forms of sociality that were connected with such a public culture. Especially in the flourishing seaside towns of Asia Minor, different ethnic communities had developed a rich network of exchanges and a mutual awareness of cultural similarities and differences. This has produced forms of urban cohabitation which managed to deal inventively with otherness. Nationalism was to destroy this osmotic sociality and population exchanges would create ethnically homogeneous cities deprived of any form of multicultural life. Amorphous shanty towns, produced in a state of emergency, gradually evolved into neighbourhoods with improvised civic facilities and centres of community life. The refugee no-man's-land, was articulated into a network of communicating urban spaces. Shanty towns came to be characterized by the intermingling of public and private spaces, and family shelters, because of the cultural dispositions of the inhabitants, were open to osmotic relationships within the refugee community as well as with the surrounding city (Hirschon 1989).

By the time the state had managed to create mass housing blocks for a considerable portion of the urban refugee population, the prevailing attitude of discrimination towards them took a somewhat new form. Those areas were clearly marked as different from the rest of the city, with the rational 'modernist' building blocks replacing the familiar image of poor Athenian neighbourhoods. Otherness was in a way spatialized not only through a clear demarcation of the refugee neighbourhood but also through the form the houses of those 'others' took. Let us not forget that the buildings belonged to the heroic modernist tradition that was developing throughout Europe during these years and was emblematically formulated in the Charter of Athens.

In the housing complex of Alexandras Avenue, which will be referred to hereafter as *Alexandras Prosfygika*, built during 1934–1935, a typical rational layout prevails, consisting of eight parallel blocks designed for 228 families. Even though people had to live in small identical apartments, the buildings provided adequate cross-ventilation, sunlight and ample outdoor space, ensuring spatial qualities that were to become unthinkable in the crowded developing areas of Athens. In a way, these buildings came to represent a counter-paradigm to the unlimited land speculation as well as the wholesale commoditization of housing that was to prevail in the explosive post-war development of metropolitan Athens.

This social housing project, designed to meet the needs of people unable to produce their own decent family shelter, has created a neighbourhood with controlled population density and a remarkable balance between private, public and communal space. Emerging Athenian neighbourhoods, conversely, due to the important role of land speculation in the Greek economy and to the creation of an expanding apartment market propelled by a 1929 law that has established the status of separate ownership in apartment buildings, have developed by eliminating or privatizing outdoor space and destroying any osmotic relationship between private and public space. A quantitative rather than qualitative approach to living space was to produce and justify neglect towards collectively used spaces, spaces of encounter and common life (Guizeli 1984; Vlachos et al. 1978).

One of the crucially distinctive characteristics of the urban struggle that has emerged in defence of this housing complex, is precisely the collective awareness that such an urban counter-paradigm should be protected and creatively restored. With the help of mobilized architecture academics as well as environmentalists and social activists, the remaining inhabitants have articulated demands that go beyond their right to live decently in the houses for which their refugee fathers and mothers fought. They have actually given specific meaning to a collective right to the city as a whole.

Because of rapidly increasing land prices in Athens, following the uncontrolled urban growth of the post-war years, the Alexandras Prosfygica became a highly attractive and promising target for private land development corporations. With the passing of the years, the area became part of central Athens, and Alexandras Avenue has evolved into a key urban axis whose buildings are primarily offices, banks and large civic buildings and hospitals. The Alexandras Prosfygica were allowed to fall into disrepair, and the outdoor spaces were neglected, eventually becoming makeshift parking lots.

Almost half of the inhabitants were forced to sell their houses to a State Land Development Company, under threat of compulsory expropriation. Governments were supposed to take these measures as a means to improve public space: a park was promised in the place of the derelict housing area. As has happened time and again, this was simply a ploy to ensure the cheap buy-out of land. Michalopoulos, a still-active president of the Panhellenic Refugees Coalition, explicitly showed in an article written as early as 1960, how State Acts (f.e. 111/27-06-1960 Council of Ministers Act) initiated violent slum clearance projects, speaking vaguely about the need to use the occupied areas 'in benefit of the public' (Michalopoulos 1960).

The inhabitants who chose to fight for their houses had thus to confront not only the market but also government rhetoric that once again demonized them, stigmatizing them as marginal others. But this does not imply that their struggle has become a typical anti-gentrification initiative by a group of urban deprived, marginalized and vulnerable residents. As they did throughout their history, these people have responded to the threat by affirming their ability to destroy the sanitary zone of prejudice that was created between them and the city (cf. Marcuse and Van Kempten 2002). Instead of defending an enclave, a collective shelter, they sought to defend a different urban culture which can integrate outdoor public space into a residential neighbourhood.

This complex, created out of a pressing social need but inspired by the then emerging modernist architecture dogmas, was conceived as a concrete manifestation of the '*Existenzmininmum*' logic characterizing the corresponding CIAM[1] declarations. This logic combined an ideology of definable universal human needs with an architectural practice focused on quick, efficient and cheap construction of mass housing. We know today that although this logic was expressing a welfare state approach, both in the East and West, the produced corresponding environments were highly problematic: anonymity, different needs reduced to an optimum minimum common denominator which satisfies nobody, lack of inhabitable public space, areas deprived of any mixture of activities, and so on.

In Alexandras Prosfygica however, people have inventively appropriated the area, projecting on the modernist uniformity their own signs of differentiation, their own transformative acts and constructions (in private as well as in public spaces). One connecting thread in the history of this complex is the ongoing effort to inhabit the in-between areas that integrate private shelter into a rich network of public and communal areas. Benjamin's understanding of Neapolitan life can be taken to describe these experiences of urban porosity. 'Each private attitude or act' was indeed 'permeated by streams of communal life ... So the house is far less the refuge into which people retreat than the inexhaustible reservoir from which they flood out' (Benjamin 1985: 174).

Refugees, their sons and daughters and the children of their children, building upon the rich memories of urban life in Asia Minor cities, have always used their distinct culture to perforate any defining perimeter (Stavrides 2002). Those people who were once forced to stay on the threshold between two opposing countries, both regarding them at times as outsiders, have developed the skill to transform these in-between areas into spaces of encounter. They have transformed the outdoor spaces of the complex as well as the staircases and the collectively used building terraces to rich meeting places where small improvised feasts are often organized. (In Greece, the impact of the refugee culture on Greek cuisine, festive habits, music as well as various urban everyday habits is now acknowledged.)

What was to become an everyday performance of urban porosity, became also a characteristic aspect of the struggle of the Inhabitants Coalition. It was not their narrowly defined interests that they were defending. It was a different way of understanding common interests, a different way of combining the struggle for the life quality of specific inhabitants with the quality of life that concerns all those who use the city centre.

---

1   Congres Internationaux d'Architecture Moderne, especially the second CIAM held in Frankfurt in 1929.

Opposing Narratives

It is interesting to compare the two opposing narratives that have inspired, sustained and legitimated the ongoing urban conflict connected with the future of the Alexandras Prosfygica.

The government authorities, along with the right-wing mayor of Athens, have long supported the idea of demolishing this building complex. Their description of the area is and was full of slighting remarks about the people who still live there, who are most of the times presented as being responsible for their fate. It is not only that those people are described as selfish and irresponsible because they are obstructing 'development'. There seems to be an implicit identification of those people (in the authorities' discourse) with all the ills supposedly present in every derelict area: illegal squatting, immigrants, 'self inflicted' poverty, drugs and illegal activities in general.

The hegemonic narrative of urban development has first to describe urban areas of possible intervention. This act of description acquires performative character as it not only names the characteristics of an area and its inhabitants but also further downgrades the area's economic and social value. 'Territorial stigmatization', as Wacquant explicitly shows, justifies policies that 'further marginalize' the occupants of a place (Wacquant 2008: 240). What is more, instead of stating the problem of an urban intervention in terms of social solidarity and welfare politics, stigmatization policies support 'a form of injustice of spatiality' by presenting targeted areas as 'remainders of urbanity' (Dikec 2009). In this way, the area is represented 'in itself as a problem' (ibid.) and the reasons which have caused the area's decay are effectively hidden.

The defining characteristic of such an authoritarian narrative is a promise for 'urban regeneration' understood as a major sanitizing expedition. The 'metaphor of health' (Donald 1999: 44) prevails. Smith observes that in the rhetoric of 'regeneration', an 'anodyne language' is employed. 'A biomedical and ecological term, "regeneration" … insinuates that the strategic gentrification of the city is actually a natural process' (Smith 2002: 445). The displacement of former residents, which effectively applies a specific class politics, appears as a necessary measure in order for an urban area to be able to 'regenerate' itself almost in the way a forest supposedly does.

As in the case of the 1930s' slum clearance programme that produced the Prosfygica complex, once more in the history of the area, the state intervenes to produce a morally and physically 'healthy' environment in place of an urban enclave of misery. However, what is different this time is that neither the state nor the municipality is offering a specific plan for the area. The thematic of development is vaguely connected to a project for a public park. However, neither the successive governments nor the municipal authorities have produced a project plan that might at least describe this prospect. This was not even done when procedures of 'compulsory expropriation' were imposed, although the relevant law explicitly demands specific proofs for the state's intentions (in the name of common good) in order to authorize such procedures. The area bordering Alexandras Avenue is already a major office building centre. Considering the land prices and the neoliberal logic of the government and mayor, the most probable scenario after the demolishing of the housing blocks, would be privatization and real estate development.

On the other side, people trying to oppose those plans, have developed their own proposals which explicitly express a different set of values concerning city-space. Aided by their supporters in the NTUA School of Architecture, the Inhabitants Coalition did not simply develop a narrative of nostalgia and common identity preservation. True, this area has a long history and the people who have spent their lives there have a common background and common experiences. They did not however produce a narrative based on a somehow idealized image of a past that was actually full of discontinuities and ruptures. Their discourse was built on the idea of proving how valuable the preservation of these buildings is as an alternative to the urban development of central Athens (Stavrides 2007: 187–188). Theirs was a discourse firmly attached to the present, even though memories of a rich neighbourhood life were always accompanying the appraisal of the urban environment of the complex. In a way, people were trying to reverse the stigmatizing image of a derelict place. This place was truly invaded by unauthorized parking which totally destroyed a rich public space. This place was left almost to crumble only because the authorities have abandoned it. And this was not simply a case of neglect: it was one of the ways to make inhabitants leave the area so as the 'development process' could freely take over.

Implicitly sometimes and explicitly too, in their struggle discourse, people were raising the issue of spatial justice. For them, everybody's right to decent housing was actually connected to long struggles during the past. The Asia Minor refugees have experienced what it is to become suddenly homeless. So, having become able to own a house again was already a serious achievement for them. To lose their houses once more would be unjust in every aspect. Even more so, since the Greek state still owes these people: after the 1922 population exchange, an agreement was reached with Turkey based on the idea of balancing the difference between properties the exchanged Greeks and Turks had to leave behind (Greek populations in Asia Minor being a lot more prosperous than Turks living in Greece) by adding to the sum the war compensation Greece had to pay as an invading and defeated country. The Greek state thus literally paid for this compensation with money belonging to the Greek refugees.

For the inhabitants, however, justice was not only connected with their private interests. Urban justice was essentially linked with a collective demand for public space. The space between the buildings was and can be again a rich public space, open to all. Compared to the congested neighbouring areas, this neighbourhood's space can indeed become a community centre full of life. For the inhabitants, to destroy this complex would mean to destroy a constructed urban housing area where a paradigmatic osmosis between public and private space has been and can be possible.

No need for a park, they say: there is one between the buildings (9,783 m^2 of outdoor space in a total area of 14,323 m^2). And instead of a segregated green enclave, this is the opportunity to create a public outdoor space integrated with low-rise housing buildings full of life. This alone will ensure safety and access for all. Such a view completely unmasks the government's plans, reversing at the same time the role of gentrification rhetoric. It is the inhabitants of the complex that propose the area to be of public focus and public use, not the developers or the government officials.

The Prosfygica inhabitants' version of spatial justice puts an emphasis on quality rather than quantity. Theirs was not a demand for more public facilities, for more private and public space, for larger houses and more trees. For them urban justice has to do with the quality of space, private or public. And this eventually means that the area should be protected, renovated and designed so as it becomes a contemporary example of a collectively enjoyed network of communal and public spaces.

A just city, in this prospect, is a city that may contain differing cultures allowed to communicate and negotiate in conditions of equality. What is more, through the educative experience of urban porosity, a just city becomes a city that offers people spaces of encounter and negotiation themselves discontinuous and differentiated.

Inhabiting, using and creating spaces of encounter means accepting that those spaces belong to no one and everybody. Porosity does not only define a communicating condition that is established through a spatial arrangement. Porosity has to do with a spatio-temporal structure. Urban pores exist as in-between places only if activated by inhabitants who use them. Urban 'pores' connect while separating and separate while connecting. This seemingly paradoxical status prevents urban porosity from being identified as an arrangement of check-points that punctuate an enclosing perimeter.

Urban Porosity and the Experience of Negotiating Encounters

Urban porosity can be approached as a potential characteristic of spatial arrangements as well as those spatial practices which constitute the inhabiting experience. Urban porosity is a term that has both descriptive and figurative value. Urban porosity is a metaphor that has the power to describe an experience (the experience of osmotic relations between people who use public space). At the same time, this metaphor can figuratively represent, as if in an emblematic way, a form of understanding and evaluating this experience. Pores are not simply openings – they are more like 'intelligent' filters, constantly at work and alert, which regulate processes of exchange and protection by connecting and separating at the same time 'inside' and 'outside'. To describe specific spaces and inhabiting practices as 'porous', attributes to both space and practice, inseparably, the dynamic character of an adaptable cultural communication system.

Benjamin's seminal essay 'Naples' catches this inherent relation between the form of a city and the culture of its inhabitants as performed daily: 'As porous as this stone is the architecture. Building and action interpenetrate in the courtyards, arcades, and stairways' (Benjamin 1985: 169). For Benjamin, porosity essentially refers to a continuous exchange (spatial as well as temporal) between the so-called public and private realms and actions. We can extend this porosity effect to today's metropolitan spatial and temporal divisions, if we intend to discover practices and spatial forms that perforate barriers and create osmotic spatial relations.

Urban porosity then may become a prerequisite of a 'relational politics of place' as proposed by Massey (2005: 181). If we explicitly depart from the image of space as container, we may understand space and action as mutually constitutive and therefore focus on porosity as a process rather than as a physical characteristic of specific places. Urban porosity can thus result from urban struggles and can motivate those struggles through memories of collective past experiences or collective dreams. Urban porosity can become a form of experience that activates relationality rather than separation, considered in terms of space as well as in terms of time. Space, thus, becomes not an entity to be described, appreciated, valued and possessed in terms of quantity, but a structure of potential relations connecting people, to be evaluated by qualitative comparisons. 'Grounded connectedness' (Massey 2005: 188) becomes socially meaningful as it takes form through this relational spatiality. In urban porosity different lived spaces as well as different times become related and thus compared.

Many urban movements seem to face a serious dilemma which has to do with their priorities and strategies. This dilemma can be formulated thus: is it more important to emphatically defend rights connected with the distribution of space-bound goods (including access to public spaces and facilities) or to defend the right to hold on to and develop situated collective identities?

'Distributional issues colour the politics within explicitly identity based movements' (Ballard et al. 2006: 409) as, for example, proves the case of the identity-based gay movement of South Africa that cannot but deal with 'the distributional questions raised by the poverty of significant proportion of their members' (ibid. 411). Urban porosity can be the defining characteristic of a collective experience sought for by people when they explicitly or implicitly demand for space to be 'open'. To 'open' space means to gain access but also to dispute closed situated identities. Identity issues and distributional issues are, in this way, mutually transformed and intermingled.

Thus, urban porosity can extend or enhance access rights, developing possibilities of urban-spatial justice or 'regional democracy', to use one of Edward Soja's terms (Soja 2000). Urban 'pores' connect, establish chances of exchange and communication, therefore eliminating space-bound privileges. At the same time, urban porosity can provide the means of acquiring different collective identity awareness. Situated identities lose their secluding defining perimeters without, however, becoming totally amorphous or dispersed. In this way, porosity becomes the crucial prerequisite of identity formation experience as a spatially and temporally regulated process.

Societies have long known the ambiguous potentialities of 'porous' public spaces. Anthropologists have provided us with many examples of spaces that characterize and house periods of ritualized transition from one social position or condition to another. What Van Gennepp (1960) has described as 'rites of passage' are ritual acts connected with spaces which symbolize those transitions (from childhood to adolescence, from single to married life, from the status of the citizen to that of the warrior or the hunter). Ritual acts aim, above all, to ensure that an intermediary experience of non-identity (Turner 1977), necessary for the passage from one social identity to another, will not threaten social reproduction. Through the mediation of purification rites or guardian gods, societies supervise spaces of transition, because those spaces symbolically mark the possibility of deviation or transgression. Liminality, however, this experience of temporarily occupying an in-between territory as well as an in-between non-identity, can provide us with a glimpse of a peculiar spatiality that may support urban porosity. Creating in-between spaces might mean creating spaces of encounter between identities instead of spaces characteristic of specific identities. When Simmel was elaborating on the character of door and bridge as characteristic human artefacts, he was pointing out that 'the human being is the connecting creature who must always separate and cannot connect without separating' (Simmel 1997: 69).

This act of recognizing a division only to overcome it without, however, aiming to eliminate it, might become emblematic of an attitude that gives to differing identities the ground to negotiate and realize their interdependence. In-between spaces are spaces to be crossed. Their existence is dependent upon their being crossed, actually or virtually. It is not, however, crossings as guarded passages to well-defined areas that establish a rich osmosis between private and public areas. Rather, it is about crossroads, considered as thresholds connecting separated potential destinations. The spatiality of threshold can represent the limit of a spatio-temporal experience created by urban porosity.

A 'city of thresholds' might be the term to describe such a network of lived and communicating spaces which provide opportunities of encounter, exchange and mutual recognition. Those spaces of encounter constitute a performed alternative to a culture of barriers, a culture that defines the city as an agglomeration of identifying enclaves. Thresholds, by replacing check points that control access through interdictions or everyday 'rites of passage', provide the ground for a possible solidarity between different people allowed to regain control over their lives.

Those spaces essentially differ from the non-places Augé describes (Augé 1995). No matter how temporary or general, the identities imposed in non-places are effective in reducing human life to the rules of contemporary society. 'Transit identities' are nonetheless identities. And, most importantly, these identities do not result from negotiations between equals. Intermediary spaces can be the locus of a potentially emancipating culture only when people assume the risk of accepting otherness as a formative element of their identities.

The City as a Right

The idea of urban osmosis has strong roots in the collective memories and experiences of the Prosfygica inhabitants. This idea has formed their collectively or individually created narratives: Eleni Papavasileiou, an inhabitant and descendent of the Asia Minor refugees, describes her house thus:

> If you come one day to visit us ... you will feel how freely we really move ...
> This is not the typical Athens block of flats with the dark corridors and minimal
> outdoor space. The staircases are full of light and plants. You can freely meet
> your neighbours there, as in the common terraces or in the large outdoor areas
> between the buildings. (Papavasileiou 2003: 37)

Dimitris Eftaxiopoulos, a former leader of the Inhabitants Coalition, recalls in his childhood memories a feeling of freedom connected with the experience of playing in the large, unshaped but safe and friendly open spaces of the complex.

The same idea of urban osmosis forms one of the central claims of the Inhabitants Coalition. As stated in one of their leaflets: 'These buildings represent a distinct quality of built urban environment because the large in-between open spaces of the complex constitute important areas for social encounters and collective initiatives'.

People have also produced, through their actions in defence of the area, various performances to support the idea of an enacted urban porosity. First of all, many public events in the area, which aimed to publicize the struggle and the demands, have taken the form of a collectively organized feast. The most characteristic of all, which took place in the central outdoor space of the complex in 2003, was actually an attempt to celebrate a symbolic recuperation of public space. As people managed to obstruct for one day the parking of cars, space became a multifarious stage for various cultural events: music, theatre, speeches as well as an exposition of architecture student proposals for the redesign of the buildings as contemporary housing blocks.

During the 2003 feast, students and inhabitants have opened some of the abandoned flats and temporarily converted them to a playground and a small neighbourhood info spot. The idea was that in every event and action the possibility of a new life for the complex might be illustrated. It was as if the 'pores' of the complex were temporarily and paradigmatically opened again.

Other events and happenings have followed. Probably one of the most inventive was a dance performance organized by a group in the deserted doorways and flats. Some inhabitants have participated by reciting their memories. The event has culminated in a symbolically arranged collective eating and drinking that has evolved to a small feast for those who have participated.

Other, smaller and more mundane gestures have also contributed to the same spirit. Young people have planted trees between the parked cars, securing little by little small 'liberated' outdoor areas, especially in front of the doorways.

On the opposite side, the state attempted to symbolically efface the area during the Athens 2004 Olympics. In a highly indicative gesture, a large placard was raised in front of the first building facing the Alexandras Avenue. The complex was completely hidden from view during the days of the Olympics mega-event, as if the area was an embarrassing image to be expelled from the organized urban spectacle. Ironically, the placard depicted a glorious view of Athens' historic centre emblematically presented as the cradle of Western civilization.

Completely and explicitly opposing the inhabitants' narrative and actions, the state has produced the ultimate symbolic destruction of the Alexandras Prosfygica. The buildings, blocked behind a 'huge postcard', were sealed off from the rest of the city. In place of a potential urban porosity a gesture of absolute enclosure (Stavrides 2005: 108–114).

If we are to understand the right to the city as the right to collectively create the city, then urban porosity is a crucial part of this process. The city as the 'perpetual oeuvre of the inhabitants, themselves mobile and mobilized for and by this oeuvre' (Lefebvre 1996: 173) is the city of passages, as performed and established through accessing the 'right to urban life' (ibid. 138). Giving form to the spatiality of connecting through separation and vice versa, implies the construction of embedded practices of negotiation that allow no closed urban identities, no self contained definitions of inhabitant groups.

Building upon Lefebvre's ideas, Amin and Thrift suggest that 'cities are truly multiple' (Amin and Thrift 2002: 30). By this they mean that what actually produces the power of urban life to exceed institutionalized control is the prospect of a continuous experimentation inherent in urban forms of sociality. 'Temporal and spatial porosity' essentially provide urban life with this potentiality (ibid. 155). Experimentation, however, needs to be propelled by common dreams and interests realized in the process of discovering common practices to demand and to create. Urban movements and urban political actions may actually create in practice forms of urban experience that will redefine what 'quality of life' means. For this, movements and actions need to both fight for and conceptualize urban porosity as a condition that enables different urban experiences to be compared. Situated identities may thus become comparable and mutually aware.

The Prosfygica inhabitants were forced to experience what it means to cross boundaries that separate situated collective identities, without being able to belong to either of them. Through their struggle to create a new life they have learned how to transform urban boundaries into pores. Their struggle to preserve their houses has gained from this collective memory in which inhabiting in-between areas was a means of giving form to social integration. Defending Alexandras Prosfygica as an urban counter-paradigm to housing development thus means defending a different way of articulating private and public spaces. In place of mutually exclusive areas of urban use, this struggle demands areas to be defined through practices that compare and connect them. Differences in use and appropriation become thus mutually dependent.

People have actually created through their narratives, through their actions and through the ephemeral urban artefacts produced during the organized performances, a regenerated environment of urban porosity. People have produced, have made real, those possible spaces they wanted to fight for. If the city does not only comprise physical elements that define space, but also includes those imagined and performed spaces of collective struggle, then the Prosfygica inhabitants have indeed created new spatial forms. Their implicit focus on urban porosity has demonstrated what it means to fight for the preservation of an urban alternative paradigm.

Urban political action may take the form of demands for a redistribution of urban goods and urban services. This kind of action is usually situated within the dominant distribution networks for goods and services. What appears to be crucial in this context is the problem of access to any situated network. We can, however, understand the city in a different way. If we are to demand 'the right to the city', echoing Lefebvre's emblematic phrase, then we have to ask once again, what can constitute the city itself as a right and not as a medium to be regulated through struggles for access rights? The city becomes a right to be defended only if urban struggles seek to defend and create urban forms that correspond to emancipating practices. It is imperative to search for those urban forms that may actualize in space as well as in time, social relationships directed towards social equality and mutual respect. Can we find indications of such a 'possible urban world' in the practices and discourse of certain urban struggles?

The particular struggle of the Prosfygica inhabitants is implicitly inspired by memories of urban porosity. That is why this struggle has taken the form of demands and actions which understand the city neither as a provider of services nor as an agglomerate of enclaves. Urban porosity can redefine the city as a network of thresholds to be crossed, thresholds that potentially mediate between differing urban cultures as mutually recognized. Urban porosity can thus be the spatio-temporal form that a potentially emancipating urban culture may take.

By defending urban porosity, people in Alexandras Prosfygica have possibly given us the opportunity to understand what it means to defend the right to the city as the right to a new urban culture. Their words and actions have created those public spaces that may possibly sustain this prospect. Their words and actions have made those spaces indeed happen.

Chapter 4

Hybrid Cities: Narratives of Urban Development and Popular Culture, the Case of Medellín (Colombia)

Beatriz Acevedo and Ana Maria Carreira

Introduction

We can choose to live in a state of war or in a state of hybridization.

(García Canclini 1995: 30–31)

According to the introduction of the book, the urban landscape can be seen as the interweaving of different narratives, practices and artefacts. A growing field of scholarship and research has addressed the notion of discourse and narratives towards understanding the city. This approach draws upon the literary theories of Roland Barthes and the cultural materialism of John Berger and Raymond Williams, as well as Michel Foucault's interest in the relationship between the discourses and the exercise of power (Hubbard 2006). In particular, the chapter addresses the encounter of two types of narratives regarding the urban landscape: on the one hand are discourses about development guided by policy makers and international agencies aimed at *modernizing* the city; on the other, those narratives from local people when interpreting, appropriating and applying certain urban projects in the city. Understanding development as an historically produced discourse determined by certain dynamics of power and knowledge (Foucault 1982; Escobar 1995), we analyse how policy makers interpret this notion when proposing development plans in the city following the economic and global changes emerging from the past ten years. Further, we consider the ways in which local people interpret and appropriate such a notion of development in their daily lives and practices in the city. We focus on the case of Medellín, Colombia, in order to analyse how these two narratives meet in the urban landscape. As in many other countries around the world, the economic measures proposed by international agencies with a neo-liberal approach during the 1990s have influenced the public investment in urban projects. In fact, many of these urban projects tend to benefit only some groups in the population who are better equipped to compete in global economies; thus, these projects may be contributing to widening the gaps among classes (Székely 2003; Barrientos and Santibañez 2009; McIlwaine and Moser 2003).

Acknowledging this reality, we start by pointing out some of the paradoxes and contradictions created by certain urban development projects. However, we aim to go beyond these paradoxes by presenting some cases in which the narratives of local people and local culture can successfully be incorporated into the process of urban development.

In order to understand the encounter of these different narratives in the urban landscape, we use the notion of *hybridization* by García-Canclini (1995) to refer to processes where discrete structures mix and combine to create new realities. Applying this view in the analysis of the city, we argue that certain Latin American cities can be understood as the result of different encounters between, among others, two types of narratives: on the one hand, the underpinning assumptions guiding the type of 'modern' projects implemented by policy makers and urban planners; and on the other, the cultural aspects linked to the symbols, practices and customs of local people. In this way the narratives of modernization/development meet and combine with the diverse cultural codes by which local people use, interpret and recreate those projects. Further, we argue that in Medellín, and to some extent certain other Latin American cities, these encounters produce a *hybrid city* in which different aesthetics, rationales and aspirations meet.

The chapter is divided into the following sections: the first analyses the different narratives regarding the notion of development, including the interpretations made by policy makers and urban planners when proposing urban projects and interventions. In the second part we present a brief description of the city of Medellín, emphasising the different views on *urban development* adopted by policy makers and urban planners during this past decade. The third section explores some paradoxes and contradictions caused by an emphasis on particular views of urban development that seem to obey the dynamics of globalization that sometimes deliberately ignore local realities and cultural aspects. We propose the notion of hybridity to understand that these paradoxes can be actually bridged by incorporating the narratives of popular culture into the urban projects. We illustrate this point by presenting two cases in the city of Medellín: first, the popular aesthetic appropriating some projects of sustainable development, and second, the case of *vendedores ambulantes* (street sellers) who actually represent an important part of the informal economy in the city and yet are being prosecuted and marginalized by the current urban policies aiming at recovering the *public space* and promoting a very particular view of economic development. Finally, we conclude our chapter by pointing out potential avenues towards reaching an understanding of the hybrid nature of the city.

Narratives on Urban Development

In the process of creating their own identity and political systems after Spanish rule, Latin American countries looked up to emerging powers such as the United States, England and France for models and inspiration in the configuration of their political and economic systems. The increasing expansion of the British and the French empires during the nineteenth century changed the geo-political configuration, dividing the world between *civilized* and *non-civilized* nations. After the second half of the twentieth century the emerging power of the United States consolidated their influence in Latin American countries (Cardoso and Faleto 1979). The inaugural discourse of President Truman paved the way for the notion of development to become a means of extending the division between countries: thus, the world was divided between developed and underdeveloped (or developing) countries (Escobar 1995). Development has, during the last fifty years, been dictated by the norms and ideals of the industrialized countries following the United States' approach and their main programme of *Alianza para el Progreso* (Alliance for Progress) (Escobar 1995). Latin American countries have adopted a particular view on development through loans and guidelines provided by international agencies such as the World Bank (WB) and the Inter-American Development Bank (IDB) (Carreira 2007). However, it is not only through loans and regulations that the goal of development has become such an unquestioned aim. Complex *dispositifs* of power and knowledge have determined what type of *development* must be followed, without any questioning whether or not this is the route to follow for the peculiar characteristics of each country. Escobar (1995: 10) has proposed speaking of 'development as a historically singular experience [involving] the creation of a domain of thought and action'. Drawing upon the work of Michel Foucault he has analysed the different circumstances that created the division between developed and developing countries, and how the notion of development became a powerful strategy to influence decisions at the geo-political level in a post-colonial era.

The notion of development proposed by these agents implies – directly or indirectly – that the Western model is the only way to ensure human happiness. Indeed, Western countries are compelled – politically and morally – to help those (developing) countries to achieve a specific desired economic situation and becoming *modern* or *developed*. As has been suggested: 'the First World is [thus] the model to be emulated by the rest of the World, as being the engine of a more global and homogeneous history' (Breton et al. 1999: 9, our translation). In this ideal, variations in how development must be achieved have been proposed throughout history. For example, during the 1960s it was thought that the best way to achieve the ideal was by protecting national industries, focusing on industrialization and infrastructural projects. The model prevailed in Latin American countries during the 1980s when the new guidelines started mentioning *sustainable development* following the discussions at the international level (for example, Brundtland Comission 1987). The view, originally focused on more complex aspects of development, shifted toward a new ideal in which the purpose of development should be to become global and economically competitive. In addition to these changes in the type of development to be achieved, proposals have been made regarding how development should be implemented. Traditionally, international agencies have adopted a *top-down* approach, assuming that policy makers and bureaucrats in different countries can plan development in a rational way and that people are blank recipients keen to receive the benefits of this proverbial progress. Latin American countries and their societies are considered as *objects* for developmental programmes. In contrast to this view, some theorists have proposed to include the cultural, social and human aspects of development, in what has been called the 'human development' approach (Sen 1982, 1999). Local communities ought accordingly to participate in the planning process and decision-making concerning development projects. Communities and local people should be considered as *subjects* of development, and therefore development plans must follow a 'bottom-up' route by consulting, involving and responding to the necessities of local people. Within this line of thought streams such as *communitarian development, endogenous development* and *self-development* have stressed the necessity of considering the particular conditions of Latin American countries and their populations (Max-Neef 1991; Cardoso and Faleto 1979).

Although the two models differ in their respective approaches to development, they coincide in embracing the ideal of development as the unique avenue to become *better*, as in *modern, global* or *economically viable*. In their search for this type of development, Latin American countries try to emulate borrowed images of development and modernity as experienced in First World countries (García-Canclini 1995: 44). When benchmarking Latin American progress against these norms, it is easy then to evaluate it as *backward* or *poor* without considering other factors, indicators and particular circumstances. The notion of development seems to be the panacea for Latin American problems: politicians, urban planners and communities promise, demand or aspire to attain what they consider *development* to be. Latin American societies are, though, after almost six decades of development programmes, not achieving their economic goals; moreover, development programmes as implemented so far are, rather, increasing the inequalities not only between classes but also the relative poverty of the less advantaged elements of the population (Székely 2003, Barrientos and Santibañez 2009).

In Colombia, major cities such as Medellín have embraced this notion of development and some of its multiple manifestations. Regarding urban planning, development is often focused on the *physical* aspects of the city, rather than on the complex dynamics involved in a comprehensive understanding of the city (Carreira 2007). The analysis of a number of *Planes de Desarrollo* (Development Plans) in this region reveals that the city is often defined as a *complex field* involving social, cultural and economical aspects. In practice, though, the city is treated as an *object*, depopulated and inert, and in need of being filled with *projects*. In this view, the city's development plan aims exclusively at administrating the *physical* dimension of development, whereas the social and cultural aspects are *factors* or *externalities* excluded from the planning process. As the analysis reveals, the main purpose of *development projects* during the last ten years has been to transform or to adequate the city and its territory (such as land, natural resources, and so on) for the international market by means of investment in business centres, technology and specific projects of urban space (Carreira 2007). From time to time some variations in this ideal have been proposed: for example, the idea of achieving sustainable development, following the 1980s concern about environmental issues. However, these types of approach are often short-lived, although these *aims* remain present in discourses and documents; in practice, the main force driving urban development is to transform the Latin American cities into economically competitive places.

Following Foucault's archaeological approach it is possible to trace back in history some of the processes that have determined why and how a city chooses a certain path for its evolution. In the case of Medellín, socio-cultural factors have influenced the evolution of the urban landscape. As will be shown next, the cultural characteristics of local people and the socio-economic structure are crucial elements in understanding the current situation of the urban landscape. Here, we provide a brief description of the city of Medellín and its cultural aspects, while focusing on selected trends in urban development proposed for the city during this last decade.

A Tale of a Latin American City

Medellín, Colombia's second city, nestles in a mountain valley at 1,500 metres in the central Andean *cordillera*; it is the capital of the Department of Antioquia. An important industrial centre, its metropolitan area population exploded from 380,000 in 1951 to an estimated figure of around three million in 2005 (Departamento Administrativo Nacional de Estadística 2005). Because of the constant influx of migrants, around 60 per cent of Medellín has been built outside planning controls in the form of squatter settlements and informal development (Brand 1995). The city has nevertheless embarked on a number of projects aimed at upgrading the city as an international and competitive metropolis.

The city was founded in 1675 by Spanish colonizers many decades after the main colonial cities of Bogota and Cartagena were established (Botero Herrera 1996). The area of Antioquia is characterized by a rugged territory and a wild and sometimes hostile nature, and the colonization took a different path in contrast to other city centres in Colombia (Tobón 1985). Consequently, the type of society and culture developed in this area had a lot to do with both the landscape and their history: families rely on their own effort and social cohesion in order to colonize wild nature; at the same time religion played a crucial role in ensuring this social cohesion and providing *meaning* to the sometimes difficult daily life. These socio-cultural features have prevailed through history, and people in Medellín (kindly regarded as *paisas*) are characterized as hard working, stubborn, entrepreneurial, austere, responsible, religious and conservative people, with strong family ties (Henao 1990).

Thanks to the buoyant coffee trade and the discovery of gold, by the end of the nineteenth century Medellín had become the most important city in Antioquia and the second most important city in the country (Botero Herrera 1996). This dominance continued during the twentieth century when the Medellín's élite promoted a successful industrialization process through textile factories and manufacturing activities. The offspring of the élite usually travelled abroad, especially to Europe, in order to acquire the best education and also to further their families' businesses. The influence of Medellín's élite went beyond the industrialization process by determining, furthermore, the way in which the city of Medellín was developed (Botero Herrera 1996; Roldán 2003; Ocampo and Dover 2006). Aimed at transforming the old colonial village into a *modern* metropolis, the city's élite of entrepreneurs and bourgeoisie imported models from Europe, with a few architects who were invited to re-design the urban landscape (Botero Herrera 1996: 19).

By the 1950s and 1960s the city had begun to acquire a shape according to an ideal of modernity supported by the knowledge gained in Europe, stimulated by the prominence of entrepreneurs and industrialists. In this process, the private values of the industrial groups combined with the *civic* values of the population. However, private interests very often prevailed over public matters, as is expressed in the city, where private buildings replaced the public spaces following a discourse of *development* (Botero Herrera 1996: 133). At the same time, the city of Medellín received a major migration of people from the rural areas. Countryside people brought with them a range of traditional hand-crafting skills and the aesthetic of the traditional house into the new urban neighbourhoods (Fraser 2004: 230). This *paisa aesthetic* of baroque compositions today expresses and mixes among buildings of modern designs. The city began to expand beyond control while settlements and *barrios* were established in the way of the typical houses in the small towns and rural areas. Traditional working-class neighbourhoods were transformed during this period into sites of intense competition for housing, resources, jobs and political primacy (Roldán 2003: 131).

The economic strength of Medellín continued during the 1970s when the city became a trade centre in goods such as coffee, gold and textiles. This situation prompted the further migration of people from rural areas who managed to fulfil their dream of social and economic mobility in the city (Roldán 2003: 129). The urban development favoured, however, only some well-off sectors of the city, and the urban landscape displayed a high level of social, spatial, and economic inequality among its residents. The inequality in the distribution of wealth and access to public services created *two cities*: the geographical situation of the territory and the location of the city nestled as it is in a valley, meant that there was little available flat land on which to expand. Migrants had then to settle on the geologically perilous hillsides around the perimeter of the valley and a number of illegal settlements were also established. As noted by Roldán (2003), Medellín has been the scene of contrasting influences marked by inequality and discrimination:

The gulf separating lower class inhabitants from the city's wealthy has historically been spatially, morally and politically defined. Poor neighbourhoods cling precariously to the slopes that ring the city while the principal administrative, commercial, political and cultural establishments are located in the city's valley. (Roldán 2003: 137)

Changes during the 1980s and 1990s within the context of globalization affected Medellín's industrial strength. The former manufacturing and commercial model was affected by the economic changes, promoting both open markets and less protection to national industries. During the same period, the emergence of drug trafficking affected the whole structure of the city. The narcotic boom vastly inflated prices for urban real estate and redefined the stylistic taste and characteristics of urban neighbourhoods and architecture (Roldán 2003: 130). At the social level, violence and urban gangs recruited from the poor neighbourhoods of the city, normally known as *comunas*[1] terrorized the region (Velázquez 2006; Bergquist et al. 2001).

At the beginning of the new millennium, the city was facing a number or problems. Firstly, there were the challenges produced by the shifting economic measures and globalization process; secondly came the socio-cultural consequences of the drug-trafficking regime of terror; and thirdly, the changing view on development favoured one or other approach for public investment. As mentioned above, development plans became a key tool in planning the urban landscape. These plans reflected simultaneously local interests of certain powerful groups and the latest trends in the conceptualization of development as suggested by international agencies and other institutions. For our study, two distinctive discourses about development and its urban impact in Medellín can be identified.

The first one refers to the beginning of the 1990s, when the international trend, supported by scientific knowledge, advocated for a type of sustainable development. The discourse on environmentalism became linked to certain strategies for conflict resolution; therefore, significant attention was paid to the environmental variable in development plans, especially in terms of social development. Buzzwords such as *inter-generational sustainability* and *recuperation* became common terms in the official discourses on development. In particular, during the administration of Juan Gómez Martínez (1998, 2000) the environment became a key element for social cohesion and conflict resolution. In fact, this view reflected some of the symbolic values of Medellín's people regarding good housekeeping and their relation to nature, as well as the possibility of creating employment using basic skills for these types of projects (Brand and Prada 2003). Among these projects, the revival of the

---

1   *Comunas* is the name given to those informal settlements located in the periphery of the city. These are normally poor neighbourhoods that have been established informally and are lacking basic services such as water supply or energy. Over time, these settlements have acquired those services but their social and economic conditions are still very precarious.

Medellín River became a key programme in the aim of sustainable development as well as in the recuperation of the city's pride and a sense of belonging.

The second one refers to the following years, when the new administration of the Mayor, Luis Pérez (2001–2003), brought the idea of modernization and globalization as the main driving forces for urban planning. His council dismissed the successes and processes linked to environmental goals when proposing economically strategic projects aimed at modernizing the city. As a result, a number of new buildings and projects are re-shaping Medellín's urban landscape. In the city centre, there have been some important transformations, among which are: the substantial development of the Metro and cable car systems for the city; the expansion of the administrative complex of *La Alpujarra*, a hub of different governmental institutions and public services; and the construction of a new International Business Centre, *Alpujarra II*, aimed at enhancing the global profile of Medellín as a key trade centre in Latin America. The main objective of these projects has been to improve the facilities and infrastructure of the city to render it more competitive and *global*.

Within the ideal of globalization, markets and commerce are the main sectors to be developed. As is the case in many other cities in the world, also in Medellín the ubiquitous shopping mall has become part of the city landscape in certain neighbourhoods. The shopping mall, usually copied from other cities in the world, is normally appreciated as a symbol of *development*. Against this, informal commerce prevails in the city centre where new projects are due to be established. In this process, the value of the land changes and the small business or the poor resident in the city centre is unable to pay the higher rents or taxes. In Medellín, the *development* crusade is accompanied with a moral purpose: the association between informal commerce and delinquency is highlighted as a key factor to be addressed by urban development, as is the possibility of *cleansing* these areas taken by *deviants* and poor people (both marginalized economically and also morally) who shall be displaced or *developed* (Brand and Prada 2003: 94).

It seems that two cities co-exist: on the one hand lies the wealthy, global and modern city of beautiful buildings and harmonious architecture, trees and parks; on the other are the populous *barrios*, dynamic and vibrant, where animals and people share the small streets, and in which houses appear spontaneously with no building controls or planning. Such disparity has been widely documented by researchers studying Latin American societies and it has become a useful analytical framework within which to understand the contrasting narratives of the city (Caldeira 2001). While important, the view may neglect some of the processes through which these disparities occur and how differences are transformed. While hegemonic groups define and design the city, subordinate groups may be displaced or marginalized; yet since these subordinate groups represent the majority of people in Medellín, the groups actually re-configure the city by using it and living it. The re-configuration of the city thus takes place neither within the economic sphere of major investments, nor does it occur in the dispute regarding what type of urban development is required; as we illustrate in this chapter, it is within the realm of certain local narratives that the bridge between the narratives of what is planned and how it is used can be found. The narratives imply not only written discourses about what development may be in the city, but also the aesthetics of popular taste linked to local culture.

We argue that Medellín's urban landscape can be understood as the result of different encounters between infrastructural projects guided by the narrative of development (in its different modalities) and the diverse cultural codes by which local people use, interpret and recreate those projects. The purpose of this chapter is therefore to propose a way of understanding the city by weaving two types of threads: on the one hand, the discourses guiding the type of *modern* projects implemented by policy makers and urban planners and, on the other, those narratives produced by the daily use of the city by its people, and the way in which they interpret and appropriate these projects.

Hybrid cultures/hybrid cities

The term *hybrid*, originally used in biology, refers to processes of crossing among species, as well as other dynamics of combination and mixture. From this former use, normally associated with conditions of inferiority and contamination (Raab and Butler 2008: 1), the term has gained popularity while being adopted into several disciplines such as anthropology, sociology and linguistics, to describe processes of *mestizaje*, the intersection of cultures and languages, and other types of combinations. The concept of hybridization often includes divergent notions such as *mestizaje*, which applies mainly to studies regarding race or ethnicity; *synchretism*, alluding to religious combinations or symbolic transactions; and *creolization*, referring to certain zones of contact and exchange. In particular, the term *mestizo* does not translate into the English language; the word in Spanish is used when referring to miscegenation, half-breed, mixed blood and *hybridity* (García-Canclini 1995, 2004). The concept of *hybridization* has been applied in the analysis of a wide variety of phenomena, including globalizing processes, travel and border crossing, and artistic, literary and mass communication fusions (Martin-Barbero 1987). As argued by Raab and Butler, 'the concept of hybridity itself is a hybrid construct, which is based on a number of – at times highly divergent – theoretical and ideological perspectives and assumptions, and which has been a site for continuous academic and political contestation' (Raab and Butler 2008: 2).

Bhabha (1985) first applied the term *hybridity* to defining interethnic contact in the context of decolonization processes. He argued that hybridity is to be understood as the name for the strategic reversal of the process of domination through disavowal – that is, the production of discriminatory identities that secure the pure and original identity of authority. Hence, in the process of building a new post-colonial identity, hybridity becomes 'a *third space* between colonizer and colonized that effects the hybridization of both parties rather than embracing both in however explosive a mixture' (Fludernik 1998: 13). Harald Zapf extends the use of this concept by referring to 'diverse linguistic, discursive and cultural intermixtures' while stressing that 'this mixture should not be understood as homogenizing fusion but rather as a connection of different parts' (Zapf 1999: 302).

Cultural anthropologist Néstor García-Canclini follows a different route by using the term in the analysis of certain social and cultural processes in Latin America. For him, hybridization refers to 'socio-cultural processes in which discrete structures or practices, previously existing in separate form, are combined to generate new structures, objects and practices' (García-Canclini 1995: xxv). He suggests going beyond the traditional use of the concept usually limited to *describing* cross-cultural mixing by giving the concept a hermeneutical capacity, making it useful for interpreting relations of meaning reconstructed through mixing. His object of study is not *hybridity* but the *processes of hybridization*:

> If we speak of hybridization as a process to which one can gain access and which one can abandon, from which one can be excluded, or to which we can be subordinated, it is possible to understand the various subject positions implicated in cross-cultural relations [...] Hybridization, as a process of intersection and transaction, is what makes it possible for multicultural reality to avoid tendencies toward segregation and to become cross-cultural reality. (García-Canclini 1995: 30–31)

This approach contrasts with the use of the term in post-colonial studies. Although Garcia-Canclini acknowledges the importance of the Spanish colonization of Latin America, he suggests understanding hybridization by focusing on wider cultural processes. He argues that Latin American countries should be understood as 'the result of the sedimentation and juxtaposition and interweaving of indigenous tradition (above all in the Mesoamerican and Andean areas), and catholic colonial Hispanism' (García-Canclini 1995: 46). He states that Latin America lives in a state of 'multi-temporal heterogeneity' and of 'intercultural hybridization', because in Latin America traditions continue while modernity has not yet completely arrived (Raab and Butler 2008). The historical subjection of Spain to the Counter-Reformation and other anti-modernist movements determined the path of its colonies and thus 'only with independence could [Latin America] begin to bring [their] countries up-to-date' (García-Canclini 1995: 41). Since then, Latin American countries have became part of the geo-political configuration of powers; consequently, they have adopted certain ideals and paths in their relatively recent history. As mentioned above, one of the main paths adopted by Latin American societies is the notion of development across its multiple representations in, for example, policy-making, urban development and consumption markets.

Hubbard (2006: 30) explores the notion of hybridization while trying to make sense of science and technology as creators of the urban landscape. He alights on the concept of hybridity to propose an approach to the polymorphous materiality of the city. We follow a different route: we use García-Canclini's view of hybridization as a dynamic process encompassing social, cultural, economic and technological transformations. We believe that this wider approach can explain the interrelations between diverse narratives within processes of urban development in the Latin American city. We propose a view of a hybrid city not as the combination between technology and physical urban space, but through understanding the city as the result of the encounter and combination of different cultural narratives that can be framed within García-Canclini's approach to processes of hybridization. Particularly, we have chosen two cases representing how divergent narratives can combine to create a hybrid meaning for urban projects.

An encounter of narratives

In the previous sections, we have argued that the urban landscape in certain Latin American cities can be understood as the result of a complex configuration of power and knowledge expressed in architectural arrangements and urban investment. In this complex context, we have identified two main narratives regarding urban projects: on the one hand, a narrative of development adopted by policy makers following international trends and global precepts; on the other, the narratives of popular culture as they interpret and give new meaning to these urban projects. The processes of hybridization created by the inter-relation of these two narratives can be either spontaneous or planned. The two cases presented here illustrate how policy makers can actually acknowledge the influence of popular culture and, in particular, popular aesthetics, in the implementation of urban projects.

In the first case, we explore the discourse of sustainable development as implemented in the city of Medellín and reveal how local communities interpret this narrative by transforming urban projects using certain aesthetic devices. As mentioned above, the view of *sustainable development* was adopted by the city of Medellín during the 1990s. In a context of violence and poverty, policy makers suggested that the environment may be an appropriate context in which to promote peace processes and civic feelings:

> El medio ambiente se asocio discursivamente con las nociones de equidad, seguridad, coexistencia pacifica, racionalidad y armonía, o sea, todas la cualidades tan notoriamente ausentes en la vida social de la ciudad de ese entonces. (Brand and Prada 2003: 114)[2]

In particular, the revival of the Medellín River for the city was proposed. After years of abandonment and pollution, the programme *Mi Rio* (My River) was created with the purpose of building a new relationship between the River and the inhabitants. A number of projects were proposed, including botanic expeditions

---

2 'The environment became part of the discourse of development, egalitarianism, security, peaceful co-existence, rationality and harmony ... in other words, all those characteristics that were notably absent of the city during that time' (our translation).

and scientific research, as well as creative and cultural events aimed at celebrating
the renaissance of the river. This experience drew upon the *recuperation* of rivers
in big cities in Europe (for example, the Thames in London). Similarly, policy
makers in Medellín adopted the idea of recovering the river. They designed
boulevards and bank-side paths in order to encourage citizens to walk along the
river. It was also determined that without the involvement of communities, the
project could not succeed. Consequently, local people were invited to participate
in the project, which resonated with the cultural values of good housekeeping
and social cohesion. Schools, local neighbourhoods, voluntary associations and
non-governmental organizations (NGOs) played a crucial role in the planning and
implementation of the river's recuperation.

One of the most evident outcomes of this participation was that the River
became a major hub of the traditional Christmas celebrations. Every year,
anticipation of the *Christmas lights* is a major event in urban life; the lights across
the river became a major attraction. Local communities and neighbourhoods are
responsible for the designs and motifs for the lights, expressing their taste and
aesthetic through these figures. As a result, the popular aesthetic *paisa*, baroque
and colourful, infiltrated these new spaces and architectural arrangements.
Gigantic adornments for the River Medellín included naive elements in decoration:
enormous butterflies, childish frogs and fairy-tale characters, as well as the
traditional imagery of the Nativity, the Virgin, the Three Wise Men and shepherds,
were selected as the main figures to represent the Christmas spirit. Bright colours,
realistic images and elaborate ornamentation were used for the decoration of the
river. For those familiar with the *paisa* culture, the images may resemble those
painted by Colombian artist Fernando Botero: his voluptuous women, exotic fruits
and sensuous imagery resonate with the way in which this artist has represented
his own origins in Medellín.[3] Similarly, the images and arrangements used for
the decoration of the river are unsophisticated arrangements of light and colour,
reflecting the traditional aesthetic of local people: the baroque arrangements, the
childish and humorous figures, and the figurative aesthetic inherited from the
Catholic Church.

---

3   As a representative artist of Medellín and Antioquia, Botero's work represents 'the
hallmark of a modern Creole culture in Latin America' (Hanstein 2003: 13). His paintings
reveal his '*paisa*' background: 'the tranquillity and security of small-town life, the pompous
pageantry of upper-crust society, the carnal sensuality of women, the mystery and drama
of the Catholic church, and the meticulousness of the military and government are frequent
subjects of Botero's brush, often rendered with a warm nostalgia, a piquant whimsy, and
a satirical sense of humour' (Rodriguez 2001: 95). At the same time, Botero's art follow
a very classic tradition of the Old Masters in the Italian and Spanish Art. This dialogue
between the *high* art and the *popular* art has informed the development of art in Latin
America, and that in the case of Botero, has become his signature and style (González
2006). This hybridity is one of the main characteristics of the Latin American art, and that
explains its vitality and originality (Lucie-Smith 1993).

The exuberant aesthetic devices may appeal less to the *high cultural taste* of the élite; in fact, many despised the popular aesthetic, saying that it *spoiled* the urban landscape. Yet, despite this clash of *tastes*, the project *Mi Rio* proved to be a successful means of involving local communities by creating a sense of ownership while promoting sustainable practices. In this sense, the local traditions regarding a high importance given to the aesthetic of the *house* is enhanced by expanding this feature onto the public space and the environment. Although certain élite groups have criticized the involvement of the community via the inclusion of certain baroque and childish imagery in the project as a *popularization* of the project, the truth of the matter here is that these images and aesthetic devices contribute to the appropriation and involvement of communities who actually make, use and enjoy these projects.

The second case refers to the conflict between the dynamic *vendedores ambulantes* (street sellers) and the use of the public space. The street sellers offer a wide variety of products including fruit and vegetables, stationary, cigarettes, lottery, live animals, manufactured goods and mobile phone renting, or *minutes*. They are part of a traditional form of commerce in the city and they reflect the aesthetic of *paisa people*. Street sellers not only proffer their merchandise on the pavement, they also have kiosks, carts and pushchairs. Their goods are packaged in a colourful and baroque fashion. Although they are an important part of the city and its culture, from the 1990s the city authorities have targeted street sellers as a threat against a *clean and tidy city*, and also as an obstacle to the expansion of business centres. Street sellers are regarded by urban planners as *problems* that need to be removed from the public space. Some areas of the city, known for the concentration of informal commerce, are also considered as undesirable obstacles in the purpose of *modernizing* the city. Street sellers represent all sort of negative characteristics: the untidy, the disorganized, the chaotic and the illegal. Even though it is true that these street sellers do not pay taxes, it is also clear that they do not enjoy the social protection and security of formal labour. Furthermore, street sellers are constantly harassed by police and urban authorities, who sometimes abuse their power by confiscating their goods, stealing their cigarettes or asking for bribes for letting them off. The conflict between urban authorities and street sellers is a crucial problem in the configuration of the city. From peaceful demonstrations to more violent confrontations between police and street sellers, this conflict is evidence of the clash of two narratives: on the one hand, the desire of urban planners and public servants to recover the public space as communitarian right, and on the other, the exercise of the right to work by these people who are unable to access other types of employment and resort to the street to generate some income. Similar approaches in *controlling the crowd* are explored by De Giorgi (2000) when analysing the political economy of punishment and the criminalization of migrants across Europe and the United States. Although the problem of street sellers in Medellín does not address the racial and colonialist aspects of those in Europe, they represent certain type of *otherness*, one that defies the rationality of an organized city and formal commerce. Policy makers fail to realise that street sellers are in fact resourceful entrepreneurs responding to a growing demand for less expensive items in certain parts of the city. In Medellín, as in many other cities in Latin America, street sellers are a traditional feature of the city life as well as an important part of the informal economy. As demonstrated by a recent study of the World Bank (Cortés 2009) the informal economy in Colombia represents 39 per cent of GDP, comparable to Brazil (40 per cent) and Peru (60 per cent). Although the term 'informal economy' presents some difficulties in its definition, Ramírez (2002) defines it as all those small businesses of less than five employees, as well as independent workers who participate in commerce, such as these street sellers. Data concerning the dynamics of the labour market in Colombia shows that the informal sector represents 50 per cent of the labour force and this proportion tends to increase in periods of recession and high unemployment (López 1996; Garay 2002). For instance, the informal economy grew to 60 per cent of the labour market during the 1990s when the neo-liberal measures affected many of the former protected sectors in the Colombian economy.

The street seller is not only an important economic actor, but also, it is part of the traditional culture of the city, and his presence has been registered in movies (such as *La vendedora de rosas*, dir. Victor Gaviria 1998), postcards and also in paintings such as those by Colombian artist Fernando Botero. In spite of the cultural and economic importance of street sellers, the city government has been trying to reduce the number of them working in the public space. A new rule in the Code of Transit (Art. 76, Proyecto Ley 087/2007 Code of Transit) stated that street sellers were an obstacle to the right of movement of people in the city, thus, they would be prosecuted or fined. In response to that, street sellers decided to *move* with the city, so they adapted some pushchairs, normally used for babies and small children, to *circulate* across the city. Their resourcefulness and adaptability should be regarded as entrepreneurial skills, and thus, programmes related to economic recovery or growth could rely on these abilities by proposing some economic projects and strategies of commerce development. Instead, authorities prefer to relocate people from the city centre to some other places in the city, normally outside the commercial areas. These efforts are short-lived: despite the authoritarian and sometimes violent methods used to *remove* people from the city centre, it is just a matter of days before the street sellers reappear in the urban landscape.

When analysing these two cases it can be seen how different narratives meet in the context of the city. One strand involves the *rhetoric* of development used by policy makers to promote their view on how to organize the city, following the precepts of international agencies, educational systems, training courses and other complex devices of power and knowledge; their aim is to impose a particular path for Latin American countries. The view on what constitutes development is often accompanied by a type of aesthetic borrowed from First World countries, which represent a symbolic yet no less important means of exercising power. As argued by Foucault (1982), apart from the power relations exerted by means of language, there are also systems of signs and symbols exerting influence upon another person or persons. In this case, it is possible to see how the symbolic notion of *urban development* is also expressed through a certain aesthetic, a more refined, civilized or metropolitan aesthetic represented in monuments, transport systems or urban equipment. In contrast, we have established evidence that local communities react to this ideal of development through using their strategies based on popular culture and its narratives. Although the latter groups hold little or no economic power, neither do they have the capacity to influence the production of knowledge concerning the constituents of development, they have instead a powerful arsenal of symbolic and cultural narratives. According to Foucault, 'there are no relations of power without resistances: the latter are all the more real and effective because they are formed right at the point where relations of power are exercised' (1980: 142). In this view, Foucault does not suggest a sort of duality of power and counter-power; rather, he proposed understanding the multiple manifestations of power and its exercise. Thus, in our analysis it can be said that the non-élite groups react to and interpret urban projects, which are derived from certain operations of power and knowledge at the same time, by using their own symbolic and aesthetic means. They introduce their taste, their traditions and their imagery into urban projects implemented following particular ideals about development. García-Canclini's view on hybridization allows an understanding of what happens next, once the dynamic exercise of power and resistance has created a new reality: in our case, it is a hybrid city.

Urban projects are transformed aesthetically, functionally and symbolically through the narratives of local communities, linked to religion and baroque imagery. Although the cultural ideals of hegemonic groups seem to prevail, less evident processes show that popular groups create their own style based on their own *taste* (García-Canclini 2004). This popular *taste* linked to the *paisa* culture is baroque in expression, sometimes with deep, elementary emotions and sensuality. By extending this view to our consideration of popular culture exhibiting a baroque aesthetic, this suggests that it breaks the rules of *good taste* imposed by the hegemonic groups, while in the process creating a hybrid taste both dynamic and vibrant. According to Bourdieu (1987) the category of *taste* is created by the necessities of certain social groups. Thus, it would be possible to say that the aesthetic search of subordinate groups is limited by its own *habitus* and expenditure. In this logic, only the dominant groups are able to develop *taste* as expressed in monuments and urban development in the city. Subordinate groups, although constrained economically and socially, nevertheless actually re-create and re-appropriate those monuments and projects in their own particular way. By re-elaborating the symbolism of places and urban projects, local people develop their own popular culture, one that is not subordinated to or controlled by the dominant model, but a new kind of taste rich in symbols and meaning (García-Canclini 2004). Notwithstanding, urban planners and policy makers should include these views, aesthetics and symbolism throughout the process of decision-making and implementation of these projects. It is necessary, thus, to consider planning as an ongoing process that will not end only with the materiality of the physical city. Instead, it is clear that without the participation of people and local communities, urban development projects only represent the interests of some particular groups and indeed they may be contributing to the exclusion and marginalization of communities.

On the other hand, as some cases may prove, the inclusion of local traditions in process of urban development can produce positive results such as major ownership of the projects, citizenship and social identity. The case of the Metro in Medellín can illustrate this point. For many years, policy makers in Medellín proposed building the first metro in Colombia. Against growing opposition from both several sectors in the city and from the national level, mainly because of the increasing costs of the project, the Medellín Metro was finally inaugurated in 1995. The Metro connects the north and the south of the city, and beyond its functionality it has become a symbol for the people of Medellín. The Metro represents the character of the *paisas*: entrepreneurial and stubborn, a society driven by development and modernity. As part of this important investment, the Municipality decided to include the cultural factor within the construction and planning process. Policy makers and urban planners had, during the planning stages, identified high levels of violence and vandalism by gunmen and drug traffickers as potential threats to the project. It was also found that traditional values such as religiosity, social cohesion and local pride could be used to counteract the influence of these anti-social groups since, paradoxically, gunmen and drug-traffickers were deeply traditional and religious. A foundation called *MetroArte* was created in order to invite artists and communities to participate in the project. The artists invited proposed to include religious imagery in the form of Virgins to be placed in prominent sites at the different stations: *Virgen del Rosario, Virgen del Perpetuo Socorro, Virgen María Auxiliadora* and *Virgen de la Milagrosa*, the last being famously depicted as the Virgin of choice for gunmen in the film *Our Lady of the Assassins* (dir. Barbet Schroeder, 2000).

The result of this symbolic inclusion of religious images resulted in a diminishing of vandalism against the Metro. Indeed, residents from all social backgrounds take pride in the Metro, with social control exerted against any threat to it. The symbolic efficacy of these initiatives improved both security in the Metro and the feeling of ownership among residents. Nowadays, the Medellín Metro is not only a modern and useful artefact; it has become a source of civic pride for local habitants. The design of the Metro stations and the success of the religious imagery may evidence the process of hybridization of two narratives: on the one hand, the narrative of development, that as previously described, tends to increase the social inequality and benefit few groups of the population; and on the other, the religious narrative of images and virgins firmly rooted into the local culture and traditions.

The plethora of cultural manifestations in the city evidence the richness of popular culture and its capacity to attract, adapt and re-create elements initially imposed by the twin logic of globalization and modernity. The role of popular culture in the appropriation of the urban projects and the creation of the hybrid city is a necessary element in the understanding of the urban dynamics in Latin America. The city is the place where exchanges between high art and popular culture, modernization and traditions, functionality and sensuality, take place. In the images given we present examples of how people actually re-create and appropriate these urban interventions by using their own local idiosyncrasies, aesthetics and symbols. In summary, it may be claimed that in response to the differences and contrasts created by certain urban projects, local people react by introducing their own interpretations and uses; the exchange takes place in a cultural realm, rather than in the traditional power bases of public administration, knowledge or architectural arrangement. In the urban landscape, a popular taste expressed in aesthetic narratives and religious practices offers an informative contrast to the relatively more constrained aesthetic of the shopping mall and the international business centres. Such popular culture is made of the re-interpretation and appropriation of certain ideals offered by global brands, TV and other agents. As García-Canclini (1995) states, popular culture in Latin America enables people to enter or leave modernity. The re-creation and re-appropriation of the city by its habitants follows no clear logic; rather, it is the spontaneous action of groups and individuals creating a way for them to live in the city. It is not a contest against the development projects and changes, either. In fact, people in general truly believe in the benefits of development and their claims are for a greater number and range of development projects.

As a Way of Synthesis: Organizing the Hybrid City

Latin American cities exhibit a complex combination of traditions, popular cultures and local customs with global trends, modern ideals and international patterns of consumption. The case of Medellín examined in this chapter shows how these different tendencies mix and combine, as interventions in the urban landscape toward competitiveness and increasing economic infrastructure are challenged and re-created by the practices and uses of the local communities who live with them. Residents welcome the city's transformation, while they also seek to participate in these changes using their own cultural codes and practices. In this process, they create a new city, one neither a copy nor a pure authentic place, but a hybrid city where transformations and exchanges take place in the public space. Through applying García-Canclini's view on hybridization it can be understood that the complex process of transformation of the identities of Latin America actually weaves elements from First World countries (*via* colonization, internationalization or globalization) with the local traditions and indigenous ideals.

It must be acknowledged that Medellín, as many other Latin American cities, can be many types of city simultaneously: linked or disconnected, harmonious and chaotic, global and local, functional and playful, violent or sensual. Residents find creative ways to provide meaning not only to this heterogeneous space represented by the city but also to the cultural mixture that makes Latin America such a unique place to live. As evidenced in the case of Medellín, capitalist logic fails to dominate all spaces of daily life. The dominant groups aspiring to build the global city meet with the constant re-creation of and challenge to their symbols and projects. However, winners or losers cannot be simply identified. Even if a successful hybridization occurs, there are forms that become richer due to the exchange and intersection, while there are also aspects that lose value or their original features. Similarly, accelerated processes of hybridization prompted by globalization will result in the exclusion of certain parts of the population as well as unequal access to the goods and messages of this type of development.

One of the main conclusions of this paper suggests that a possible response to the contradictions and contrasts created by different appreciations of what constitutes development and progress in the urban landscape consists in acknowledging the potential of mixture and hybridization. In this sense, we do not attempt to elevate one narrative over the other, the local over the global, or *vice versa*. Instead, we argue that several narratives co-exist and create a distinctive texture of the urban landscape. Although it is accepted that certain discourses tend to be dominate over others, we also see how these views are contested by local uses and traditions; in this conversation, new narratives emerge. The challenge for policy makers and urban planners actually rests in recognizing the potentialities of this encounter, rather than dismissing or ignoring the multiple dialogues created in the city.

As presented in this chapter, the different narratives co-exist and overlap. It is not a matter of *development* or *stagnation*; rather, it is a process in which traditions and uses modify, re-interpret and re-create those models imposed under the development ideal. When the dynamics between what is *planned* and how this is *used* by real people and local communities are understood as a totality, it would be possible to create more versatile and adequate responses to the challenges of a dynamic society moving toward a global order. Since globalization involves the exchange of markets and communications, they may be integrative, yet they may also segregate, producing new inequalities and stimulating differentialists' reactions (Appadurai 1996). Rather than opposing globalization, Latin American societies are trying to adjust participation in this new context. In the process they borrow and exchange with other countries, cultures and models, creating a hybrid context. The solution is not only possible; it can be also a very creative and colourful process. Of course, we must be aware of the structural inequalities and the difficulties posed by the imposition of few alternatives in the conception of *development*; and the challenge for policy makers and public managers consists precisely in democratizing for all the groups access to the means and systems. The city represents a potential scene for the distribution of these means and benefits and for the re-creation of models in a rich process of hybridization and cross-fertilization.

Chapter 5

Organizing Urban Space:
Tools, Processes and Public Action

Lavinia Bifulco and Massimo Bricocoli

Two important lines of research offer promising interpretative contributions on the intertwining between spatial (place) and social (people) organization in the city. The first concerns the symbolical, normative and cognitive dimensions of physical artefacts and spatial settings that shape the urban experience. Following this line, we find the conceptual and analytical approaches discussing the generative dimension of space, with special reference to studies that thoroughly examine the dynamics in which space comes into play as a sense-making medium taking part in the creation of social action and relational contexts (Gagliardi 1990; Weick 1995). Thus, this requires clarifying the ways in which interventions on space set off action nets that call into question organizational practices and forms that are then consolidated through the urban experience, promoting processes of change that make contexts and actors dynamic or, on the contrary, produce and reproduce closures, separations, isolation, 'cities apart' and 'non-cities' (Czarniawska and Solli 2001. The second line assumes that space-based and situated action may be a lever for renovating policies and city organization by integrating interventions which have a constitutive reference to a given space. This assumption is currently a main reference for the so-called 'territorialized' approaches shared by many policy fields, in particular the field of urban government (Monteleone 2007; Bricocoli et al. 2008).

Both of these research lines will act as the main references in the present chapter, which discusses processes that have been affecting the social and spatial organizational asset of public housing neighbourhoods. Indeed, neighbourhoods may be considered key and relevant objects to be put under observation from the point of view of how the coupling of 'places and people' is being organized and managed in an urban context. In fact, this pairing has been taken up by many authors and was initially proposed by Robert Park as the essence of the city (Park and Burgess 1925). Although following specific patterns regulated by cultural norms, values and rules, the combination of places and people shall generally be assumed as loosely coupled (Weick 1976), that is a mix of lack of coordination and chances for local adaptation. Yet the case of public housing estates (on which our attention is focused) is greatly under the rule of the public actor (Sennett 2003). Moreover, the spatial and social asset of a public housing neighbourhood can in this sense be considered, without a doubt, as being significantly influenced by institutional action and specialized policies. Let us take a closer look at the development of a typical public housing estate. On one side, as many authors have remarked, the history of planning and urban design has a solid tradition in structuring the city as a physical set-up in which the action of citizens is to take place (Czarniawska and Solli 2001). The public housing estate is a typical 'object' which we can easily distinguish in the pattern of city development because of its specific outlook, a set of features, which identify a distinction between this urban object and the 'normal city'. Very often, these features are proudly remarked, as a symbol of socially sound city planning. On the other side, the development of this urban object is very much related to its role and use in the city, to its image and the profile of the people living in it. In this respect, the development of public housing estates, in time, is a good reference for understanding how a portion of urban space, that is to say its places and its practices, is the result of a wide set of different institutional actions and filters (as well as overall processes such as migration flows, population change and economic cycles) which intervene in transforming the place.

The reframing of public housing estates from 'solutions' to 'problems' will allow us to discuss them as laboratories for the redesigning of public action and management, at both a local and an urban level. In the following paragraphs we shall discuss some experiences in which public action has addressed integrated approaches to neighbourhood regeneration in Italy. The aim is to investigate whether, while re-organizing urban space, these policies are also impacting upon the social organization and, if so, how (Bagnasco 2003). Recalling a concept introduced by Jacques Donzelot, the aim is to analyze whether these practices while 'producing the city' are also 'producing society' (Donzelot et al. 2003). A close observation of these practices could be promising for a better understanding of how cities and societies are developing. Later in the text we will introduce an understanding of public housing estates as functional devices in a time of growth and development of a modern city. In a following phase, the crisis of the industrial organization of urban economies and of the corresponding welfare systems will lead to considering public housing estates as dysfunctional, that is to say, as problem areas in which social deprivation tends to concentrate.

Public Housing and the Organization of the Modern City

On the day of my arrival in Turin, I took the tram down through the southern districts of the city. The Via Arquata public housing neighbourhood is only about 8 minutes on the tram from the Porta Nuova railway station, and is right next to Crocetta, one of the most wealthy areas in the city. In a few minutes' walk from the tram stop, you are right in the middle of the neighbourhood. At around 6 pm, I was walking along the newly refurbished and pedestrianized street in Via Arquata, running alongside the train tracks. I noticed a short, olive-skinned man in jeans and a simple shirt, inspecting one of the new flowerbeds. Born into a peasant family in Positano, in southern Italy, he left school at 9 to help his father look after the animals. At 14, he got a job collecting fresh milk from mountain villages and bringing it down to a local cheese factory. He worked from daybreak to 11pm, all week including Sundays. In his early twenties he left to seek work and a better quality of life in the North of Italy (most of his friends went further abroad to Germany, France or even the USA). Arriving in Turin in 1973, he got a job at a factory making refrigerator motors. At that time, he said, Turin was an ugly city – dirty, grey and ill-lit. He told me that the street we were on used to be a real no-go area, full of abandoned cars which were used for shelter by homeless people and drug-users. He says there is now a children's playground where the cars used to be. The area feels completely different now. He lives about a 20-minute walk away, across the train tracks from the Lingotto factory in South Turin, but he now comes up to the Via Arquata neighbourhood for his evening "passeggiata" (stroll). His refrigerator motor factory has now relocated to 30 km outside the city (he takes the bus to work), and the old factory building has been converted into apartments.

This short story[1] may act as a reference to introduce the topic of this chapter, that is to say the development and re-organization processes occurring in many public housing projects in the contemporary, post-Fordist, city. Our area of interest is northern Italy: nonetheless we will provide some interpretative keys that may apply for Italy as well, a country that was characterized by a delayed and scattered process of modernization during the time of industrialization. The city of Turin (in which the Via Arquata housing project is located) stands nearly as an ideal-typical of a city, which developed after a peculiar though Fordist model, as a company town, owing its development to Fiat and the car production industry.

From the short ethnographic account, we can identify three different phases that affected the place of the encounter and which we can assume as emblematic of the major changes affecting the role, position and assets of public housing in Italy, as well as in many other European countries.

Housing for workers:
Public housing estates as devices in the development of the Fordist city

If we look back at the history of the European city, we can identify and select some major references and values, which have led the planning and organization of the modern city.[2] In the process of modern city planning, while a series of needs are

---

1   The reference originally in Italian is here translated by the authors. This account is part of an intensive field work that Astrid Winkler and Massimo Bricocoli developed within the Weak Market Cities Research Program and other research projects (Winkler 2008; Bricocoli and Savoldi 2008). We owe the ethnographic description entirely to Astrid Winkler.

2   While in the history of the European city several great plans mark the evolution of city planning and represent landmarks proposing key elements for the government of the

identified, an intense activity of classification brings about the definition of a plan that provides answers, ordering a sequence of functions, that are distributed and organized in space. Since the industrial revolution, together with the traditional provision by private and speculative initiatives, industries and companies, as well as the State, became the direct providers of housing stock for workers, thus confirming the role of industrial production as a principle of economic, social and spatial organization. Public housing estates were conceived as answers to the relevant housing demand, as well as platforms for social inclusion, for urban integration (and control) of the working classes that migrated toward the city (Power 1993, 1997). Design concepts of new estates were developed with the will to find better typological solutions and with the aim of minimizing production costs. Design certainly had a strong regulatory attitude, in wishing to reproduce, through the design of places, a certain model for the functioning of society. It was inexorably a 'modern' and standardized answer, producing dwellings that were all alike as the least common denominator, built to respond in a rapid and economical way to the needs of a standardized nuclear family. Moreover, public housing projects were comprehensive and included the design and provision of basic services targeted at the population. In this sense, the design of a public housing neighbourhood, in its comprehensiveness, is creating very clear references for the setting of standards in modern living and the organization of urban life in the modern city, complementary to industry and its rhythms. We may recall the definition Le Corbusier introduced in the 1920s, naming housing buildings as 'machines for living' with explicit reference both to the conditions of housing production (dwelling as an industrial, standardized and mass product) and the functioning of the housing project as an industrial and functional device.

---

spatial organization of the modern city, in this short note, two main examples may be selected and worth mentioning. The first is the plan that Cerdà designed in 1857 for the expansion of the city of Barcelona. The plan aimed at regulating urbanization of the city following reformative principles of equal distribution of opportunities and social and environmental qualities. The plan offered a sort of scheme – a grid – to be considered as the reference for a virtually unlimited expansion. While regulating urban development along a pattern of streets and built blocks (of a given size, breadth and height), the grid was scattered with provisions of public infrastructure necessary for the organization of urban life. While the regular grid was used as an organizing principle at the urban (and metropolitan) scale, the single blocks displayed quite a variety of building solutions, functions and uses. Within a few decades, the concept proposed by Tony Garnier (in 1899–1901) for the urban development plan of Lyon displayed significant differences (Vayssière 1988). The project of the 'cité industrielle', opposed order and land use destinations (the residential quarter, the industrial zone, services and public infrastructures) to the intertwining of industry and workers' housing in the nineteenth century city (Roncayolo 1990). These two plans represented the reference for the development of principles and references for the design and organization of the modern industrial city, organizing the city more and more along a functional concept. In 1933, 'Living, working, circulating, taking care of body and mind' were the renowned objectives of the Modern Movement's manifesto (Choay 2006; Roncayolo 1990).

If we look back to the time when the public housing project described in the ethnographic account was conceived, designed, built and organized as a functional city-unit in a time of industrial development, we may locate that date (1930s) in the time span starting in the 1920s and lasting for several decades until the economic crisis of the mid-1970s.

While for certain aspects Italy still had to be considered an underdeveloped country up to the second half of the 1950s (Ginsborg 1998), the prosperous years of the post-war period led to an impressive growth in the country's economy as a whole and in that of northern Italy in particular. These changes forced the Italian economy to undergo a process of modernization and within a short time the northern cities emerged as the locomotives of the economic recovery that brought Italy back to the European and global competition. During this phase, the city of Turin was a main destination for mass migration from the south of the country, offering job opportunities to a vast number of newcomers who were very often leaving the poor countryside in the south and becoming urbanites. The construction of mass housing was provided with national funding (derived from a special tax on wages for the specific purpose of public housing construction), and IACPM – the National Institute for Social Housing – was the main actor in the provision of public housing, while only a minor stock was directly owned by local governments.

Turning dysfunctional: Public housing estates as places of the socially disadvantaged in the post-Fordist city

Following the history of social housing over the last century (Power 1993, 1997; Förster 2006) it is generally recognised that the decay and crisis of many housing estates occurred when industry ceased to be the basis for city organization. Instead of being regarded as 'housing for workers', all over Europe, public housing projects started to be known as places where the socially and economically deprived would tend to concentrate (Allen et al. 2000; Briata et al. 2009). The economic crisis of the mid-1970s set overall in Europe a dramatic turn: together with the increasing retreat of welfare policies, investments in mass public housing stopped as the overall growth model of the city started to be in crisis. It is the phase in which neighbourhoods such as Via Arquata were confronted with the increasing retreat of welfare policies and decay: at a time of industrial crisis and structural economic change, many public housing neighbourhoods became, if not dysfunctional, definitely problematic entities in the economy of the contemporary city. From solutions to a set of development-related questions they were more and more perceived as 'problem areas'. While in Italy, given the limited stock of public housing, the phenomenon has not been as severe as in other European countries (such as England and France), this was a time in which many public neighbourhoods started to be affected by a downward spiral of crisis. It became rapidly evident that many of those very neighbourhoods, which had been attractive for large numbers of new workers, were now becoming 'traps of social exclusion' for those who were to be severely disadvantaged in the new knowledge economy (Robson 1988; Cremaschi 2001; Donzelot 2006; Castel 2007).

Given the significant decrease in the supply of affordable housing, the population turnover in public housing estates started to be vastly in favour of severely disadvantaged tenants. While until then the allocation of flats mainly followed priorities determined by wages, in the new context, given the shortage of dwellings and the increasing social vulnerability the elements, the criteria for awarding a public housing flat started to correspond to far more complex social profiles. Only the most severely disadvantaged succeeded in reaching the top of the allocation list. While this process generally followed a social justice principle, it resulted in producing a concentration of vulnerable people in the most decaying housing estates. Those very estates were at the same time experiencing two further changes. On one side, they were experiencing the retreat of public social services and political and labour organizations. On the other, the management of public housing was increasingly shaped along the models of new public management, and housing companies started to contract out many services to private actors: with the aim of reducing expenses, which very often produced the loss of control over the properties. An emblem of the negative effects of this new management style was the removal of the local concierges who used to live in the estate and who were very relevant local units in the housing organization, ensuring social control as well as small maintenance and repairs on a daily base. Their substitution with external private cleaning companies often produced a decrease in the quality of the service as well as the loss of a whole set of minor services which were relevant for the organization of daily life of many vulnerable tenants (the elderly, for example). In this sense, we may clearly identify, in the devices and orientations of public actor themselves, the grounds on which the concentration of disadvantaged social groups occurred and the corresponding processes of disorganization and crisis of many estates.

Opening Black Boxes and Enabling Change?
Recomposing Public Action in Public Housing Estates?

Along the development and life cycle of public housing estates, we can recognize a more recent phase in which, along with some investments and innovative public action, some of the neighbourhoods have been undergoing interventions and processes aimed at redesigning, restructuring and reorganizing their spatial and social asset. While the Italian context had experienced significant programmes for the regeneration of historic city centres, most of the policies had until then been targeted mainly at physical restructuring. At that time, it was evident that the demand for regeneration in many public housing estates was related to problems which, by their multidimensional nature, brought the inadequacy of more traditional methods of action organized along different pillars to the fore. Across the variety of experiences, it became clearer and clearer that the urge of intervention would recall a re-setting, an effective and generalized re-formulation of the rationales and organizational assets concerning local policies and services (Briata et al. 2009). The need for a multidimensional approach was recognized by many as a condition for effectiveness in tackling problems that were multilayered and intertwined in terms of a concentration of various elements of disadvantage (poverty, poor housing and environment, unemployment and so on). In this respect, a fundamental step was to recognize that the strong need for integration did not just concern the measures themselves but the city administration and its organization as well. In this perspective, the tools of government (the programmes funded at a national or regional level for integrated and local neighbourhood regeneration policies) as well as the practical processes of organizing local actions have been generally recalling innovation at the institutional and policy level.

The philosophy leading interventions for the recovery of public housing neighbourhoods is shaping so called 'area-based' programmes (Lawless 2004), which assume the borders of a public housing estate as the field of action of a multitude of actors converging on an overall aim of tackling multidimensional disadvantages. New urban programmes have been developing widely in our country under the influence and positive constraints (as they become major sources of funding!) of European Policies and new programmes financing urban regeneration have been promoted more and more at a national and regional level following European experiences (Balducci 2001; Cremaschi 2001, 2009). From the late 1990s, the model of an integrated, multi-actor, inter-institutional, and (increasingly) participatory approach as a new form of local intervention in tackling multidimensional forms of disadvantage (physical decay, socio-economic disadvantage) started to develop widely in Italy (Palermo 2002). As Laino and Padovani (2000) and Mingione et al. (2001) remarked, developing processes of institutional innovation and new practices of negotiated cooperation between public bodies did support the propensity of experimenting these innovative practices

The most patent effect of this regards the spread of integrated and negotiated styles of public action (Geddes and Benington 2001). In fact, the various programmes have been directed mainly towards promoting integrated forms of action and government for problems, which by their multidimensional nature have foregrounded the inadequacy of more traditional, sector-based methods of action. Integration has been considered a relevant key in Italy for improving the effectiveness of public policies, becoming a mainstream keyword over the last decade. Integration has been used with reference to the joint action in different fields of public action (that is, physical and social programmes) and in this respect area based programmes have played a leading role. But integration has also been used as a reference on issues concerning the capability of joining different sources of funding. These programmes thus lever upon the plurality of institutions and actors (public and private) as identified by the notion of governance, at the same time tending to highlight the need to involve local communities and citizens in the choices affecting them, in the direction of active welfare (Bifulco et al. 2008).

Since 1992, five different programmes for the regeneration of urban decaying areas have been launched on a national scale. An interesting field of observation is, among others, the *Contratto di Quartiere* (Neighbourhood Contract), a regeneration programme funded by the National Ministry of Infrastructure and then in some following phases by some of the Italian Regions. The programme, in its first (1998) and second generations (2002), is specifically targeted to public housing areas. Three main innovative features can be remarked as being shared by the programmes: the promotion of new forms of partnerships, the integration of funding and fields of intervention and the timing of the project to be shared and subscribed by all of the involved actors.

The *Contratto di Quartiere* programmes are among the most significant programmes supporting neighbourhood policies in Italy (Balducci 2001) and have generally offered the context for involvement of new and local actors in urban policies, where the programme was meant to enable joint interventions and partnerships among public and private, institutional and non-governmental actors. The target areas of the *Contratto di Quartiere* are housing estates displaying a majority of public housing stock, diffused decay in physical structures, lack and/ or low quality of services and infrastructures, higher rates in unemployment and social disadvantage and weak social cohesion. The 'contract' approach assumes that the preliminary project to be submitted to the Ministry is shared by a plurality of subjects who subscribe to the *Contratto di Quartiere* and commit themselves to investing resources (human and/or economic) in the promotion and implementation of interventions. Furthermore, for the first time in Italy, an urban planning programme explicitly requires the active involvement of the inhabitants in the development of proposals and actions. Within the Italian context, the experience of the *Contratto di Quartiere* allows a close view on several implications that a programmatic, contractual and integrated approach to housing issues implies.[3]

New Institutional Structures, New Social Practices

Certain experiences and practices of neighbourhood regeneration have been leading to some sort of institutional learning. In these cases, institutions have been capable of re-setting, re-structuring, managing, negotiating and redesigning forms of treatment of issues which are strictly connected to housing and which reflect a context of deep changes due to economic restructuring, erosion of the welfare state and structural uncertainty in the job market. Some of the regeneration programmes have achieved success in creating chances for undermining – and thus 're-organizing' and reformulating – the deeply rooted rationales of administrative treatment of needs (Tosi 1994). Within the *Contratto di Quartiere*, a series of issues which concern dwellings and housing are emerging as something different from the traditional/consolidated consideration of being individual problems and

---

3   These notes refer to Bricocoli 2002.

are treated in a public dimension, through a process that creates conditions for public visibility along the way. Both the interventions in physical (renewal and renovation of the dwellings) and management (moving the families that live in dwellings where major intervention is occurring, social work to accompany the programme, redefinition of the rents after renovation) imply dealing with issues that were previously hidden in the opacity of sector-based work and/or real taboos. Opening up the black box of housing management recalls the assumption of more direct responsibility on the side of political and technical staffs.[4] It is in this domain that the *Contratto di Quartiere* brought along practices that 'teach how to learn' local government and to the housing agency at first point. It is the very nature of a 'programme', with the requirement of respecting rhythms, time schedules, deadlines imposed by the Ministry (and these are compulsory to avoid the loss of funding), that brings to the development of open discussions and makes housing-related issues at the same time visible and visibly relevant for a collective.

Two closely connected elements in this picture carry particular importance. One is the local dimension of the programme that produces conditions and pressures:

- for the 'qualification' of the demand of housing and services;
- for the production of a knowledge framework which corresponds far more to the local context, and allows learning effects for key issues in the lack of policies and guidelines;
- for the coordination among institutions and non-profit organizations in the management of housing and social services;
- for the enabling of inhabitants, that is to say for a process that – where there are conditions for opening and inclusiveness – may create conditions in which beneficiaries become actors that discuss and negotiate (Bifulco and de Leonardis 2003).

The second aspect involves the role played by participation. Thanks to lessons learnt by experience, the second round of the programme, more clearly than in the first, has chosen to give space to the voices of citizens, already soliciting an involvement in the phase of defining the objectives and projects. A lot of regional tenders have identified this involvement as one of the priority criteria in the assigning of financing.

The manner in which this orientation is realized highlights the problems, as well as the opportunities, of participation. One basic problem requiring consideration is ambiguity. The very idea of participation is vague and has uncertain borders compared to similar themes such as activation and negotiation (themes that, in turn, have their own amount of ambiguity). One specific element of ambiguity

---

4 In a way, this is the effect of another key feature of the programme, as it requires the designation of a responsible person within local government and whereas the visibility on the public – and, more in general, public – scene that these programmes actually have brings to a greater exposition of politicians as far as their decisions are concerned.

is the 'bi-frontal' formulation of the programme. On one hand, it has the aim of social equity and solidarity and establishes the inverting of disadvantageous situations through an additional granting of resources; on the other hand, it tends to reward the contexts of better equipped resources and that 'do more' (Bricocoli 2007). Furthermore, there are also more general problems relating to the way in which the theme of participation enters the politics of urban re-qualification, incorporating and contributing to reinforcing a prospect of territorial citizenship (Donzelot 2006).

Participating experiences are in fact heterogeneous with regards to procedures, the key actors and the mechanisms of relationships. However, there are cases in which new institutional structures and new social practices of participation emerge (Donolo 2005) and they increase the 'political' efficiency of participation, which means the effective possibility of influencing decision-making. Therefore, a plurality of voices comes into play requiring a political ability to mediate and recompose. In several *Contratto di Quartiere*, for example, the institutional actors opened a constant flow of very close interaction with the inhabitants starting from the initial thinking phase of the interventions and learning to deal with a number of voices, often conflicting (Bricocoli 2007).

An element playing in favour is the presence of organizations of inhabitants of that activate in the neighbourhood a diversity of points of view without expecting to represent them. But the whole experience of the first round of the *Contratto* documents the important role played by local administration in supporting, recognizing and mediating these diversities. The possibility of change itself appears as a significant product in contexts where the inhabitants, but also many other local actors and public administration staff, would have considered any change simply impossible. If institutional leadership, direction and responsibility are at work, trust in change is viable as well as the possibility for many to play an active role with the implications in terms of responsibility within the process.

Co-determination between institutions and social practices:
Conflicts and public action

Therefore, the analysis of the empirical reality confirms a need to concentrate on the relationship of co-determination between institutions and social practices. On one hand, significant elements are the social resources of action that are available in contexts and their degree of aggregation and integration. On the other hand, what matters are institutions, which create rules of influence, transmit organizational models, and provide incentives, levers for action and power resources (March and Olsen 1989). Therefore, contextual factors such as political-institutional architectures and social-organizational models are just as important as factors that intervene in the process directly, such as culture, political leadership, the design and rules of participation; as well as the social basis of participation.

In some situations the mobilizing of inhabitants (singular and associated) has a marked conflicting register and develops 'against' decisions taken by the administration. In other cases, the administrations themselves take the responsibility of falling into a network of action able to self-fuel potential action that would otherwise be lost or lose potential.

One general fact is that neither the necessary resources required for participation, nor the interest to participate, should be taken for granted. The effective involvement of the inhabitants and the 'political' weight of the involvement significantly depend on the opportunities offered to develop the agency and the voice of the people. This means having access to resources (material and cognitive resources, rights, legitimacy) that allow for expression and being counted in the public deciding scene.

The case of the *Contratto di Quartiere* in Cinisello Balsamo, which has been a major reference nationwide for this generation of programmes, is very useful to understand both the role played by conflict as well as the position of the public actor. As commonly occurs in the *Contratto di Quartiere*, one of the most critical phases involves the transfer of tenants for the time needed to restructure the housing premises. Planners and consultants had organized a lot of meetings for the 'stairwells' in which to illustrate the plans and ways to change housing to the inhabitants. The following notes illustrate a moment during one of these meetings.

Imagine 20, 30 people listening, often in complete silence. Then, after the plan has been presented, chaos breaks out. In one second the climate has heated up, people are all shouting and talking at once.

Meeting for Stairwell 'A':

> "My son is a schizophrenic and has not left his room for the past ten years. We cannot move from where we live." "Who are you people? We want to speak to the Mayor!! The President of Aler!" "I have completely redone my apartment, come and see it! I am not moving" "I have spent 20 million to redo my kitchen, you must be mad." "You have to give me a garage like the one I am leaving," "You are only thinking about the technical elements and not the human element," "I will take you to court, I will get a lawyer, it is not fair that I have to change my stairwell," "I don't trust you for anything," "I am not leaving here," "When does the work start?" "I want to go back to the house where I have lived for 25 years," "I have six children, where am I going to end up?"

A rundown neighbourhood keeps sending its inhabitants a message saying: 'you are not worthy of recognition', 'you do not exist, you are worthless'. Besides the trauma of moving house, besides the fear of losing their house, the thing that the inhabitants were asking for – shouting for – was respect (Sennett 2003).

At the end of the meeting, the conflict regarding the contents of the plan was at its height. The inhabitants were anything but ready to move. A solid wall of refusal and objection had been put up that resulted in the constitution of a Tenant Association and with a public assembly that was greatly fuelled by politicians.

The raising of the conflict was endangering the whole process: not following the contents and the deadlines of the programme could result in reassignment and loss of the funding. But representatives and consultants invested their energies in re-framing the situation and the relations. They started a door-to-door consultation of each single family, to verify the willingness to move into a different flat, as well as to note the specific needs. Beyond listening to individual needs, taking the voice of the inhabitants more seriously as an input for a more effective project was a main learning point. For example, why should a flat which was completely refurbished by its inhabitants be considered in the number of those to be refurbished just because the project had selected its staircase as a main focus? Alongside this intensive process, the necessary technical and administrative procedures were carried out so that the project could include the variations discussed with the inhabitants. Procedures for introducing changes in the project were carried out at the local as well as at the central government in discussing with the heads of the National Ministry who were in charge of the funding.

Therefore, the final project incorporated all of the very complex negotiations through which the Council and the inhabitants (and consultants) learned to cooperate. While the original project was following a technical rationale in the design and organization of interventions, the rationale of the final project is more consistent with a feasibility based on technical, economic and social requisites and ended up to be a major best practice nation-wide. Opening up the black box of problems and output that was made possible by three factors: the 'face-to-face' relationships that played a crucial role in order to learn how to build up relationships; the position of 'listening' and mediation taken on by the administration that was essential so that the voice of the inhabitants could reach and effectively influence decisions that had already been made, and the ability to bring local issues and requests up along a vertical line leading to the technical and bureaucratic decisional arena (The City Council, the National Ministry). So, conflict turned into a learning process thanks to which the neighbourhood project was reformulated and both the context and the people could be assisted.

Connection building

Over recent years, the concept of neighbourhoods has undergone a multitude of classifications – even far ranging – and an abundance of rhetoric emphasizing the 'soothing virtues of places. (…) A new romanticism has sprung up, and with it an expectation that new neighbourhoods and plazas reconcile history and modernity, selfish communities and public spheres' (Cremaschi 2009). The problems of this interest in neighbourhoods are many. In general, one risk regarding territorialized interventions is that they can confirm or reinforce fragmentation or territorial disparity and that the changes end *in loco* (de Leonardis 2008).

As for the integrated approaches to neighbourhood regeneration, concerns may be rising with reference to some key issues:

- how far does the integrated logic of the interventions cross and contaminate the sector-based approach which is deeply rooted in the public and private/ third sector services institutionally in charge for dealing with the issues of urban development?
- to what extent do the interventions succeed in enabling processes of development within the area of intervention?
- how much do the interventions imply a re-thinking, re-setting, an effective and generalized re-formulation of the rationales and assets concerning the organization of the city?

The results of the empirical observations signal that wide and solid changes are normally associated with dynamics that could be defined as 'connections building'. We shall refer to another case in order to highlight them.

The yellow umbrella

Micro-area is an experimental pilot programme, launched in 2005 in Trieste (a middle-sized city in the northeast of Italy, on the border of Slovenia) by the local health authority from a prior experience and later becoming an integral part of regional planning for welfare policies. The programme tests integrated projects on the issues of health, habitat and community development in highly circumscribed territorial areas. These areas have an average population of 1,000 to 2,500 and are normally characterized by the presence of public housing settlements.

As for the organizational structure of the programme, each micro-area has a manager and its own headquarters, normally located inside the public housing complexes. Besides the managers, 'social caretakers', usually workers in social co-operatives, are also involved in the micro-areas. The choice to physically immerse these figures in the different backgrounds of people's lives responds to the need to fill the voids normally created between services and users, and proposes to tear down the institutional, organizational and social obstacles to the involvement of citizens and collectives in the decisions that concern them (de Leonardis and Monteleone 2007).

Some short stories may be usefully quoted to demonstrate the style and orientation of the programme since its beginning, The first steps in the programme saw a crew of operators who decided to start focusing on a housing estate – mainly populated by elderly people – consisting of five-floor buildings with no lift and in a condition of heavy decay. The aim was to increase knowledge of the inhabitants' problems and needs through direct contact. Unexpectedly enough, the easiest way of knocking at each door turned out to not be feasible because of the lack of confidence in these 'newcomers'. Many people did not know the health operators at all but – even more significantly – most people did not really know the Social and Health Services. While for some people seeing a nurse knock at the door, without having been called for, was quite a positive surprise, many others showed resistance and even hostility. During the summer, the group of operators decided to change their approach strategy in how to reach out to the inhabitants. The group realised that stepping out of the district offices was not enough to become visible and accessible and decided to more effectively express their new intentions through a symbolic action. A large, yellow beach umbrella was put in the central square of the estate to draw attention: operators sat under it and waited for the people to notice them. They were apparently both 'wasting' time and 'taking' time. Little by little, inhabitants approached the umbrella: some bringing a chair, some others a drink. They started to question the operators and to tell their own stories: sitting in the square became strategic in order to focus on some lines of action which eventually became crucial in the development of the programme itself. The case highlights how much the interplay between policies and social practices is dense of tactics, detours, oblique narrations and artefacts. Quoting one of the operators: 'We knew that the inhabitants could bring resources, but we did not know what kind of resources they would bring; moreover we had no idea of which public resources could help in supporting the activation and expression of their resources. The only way we found was to approach them, to have a close look, to stay on site'.

Today, four years later, in the same estate the seat of the micro-area is located in a dwelling. When you enter the seat, you do not really understand where you are: it looks like a flat, not an ambulatory. A fully equipped and colourful kitchen, a refrigerator with ice-cream and sparkling wine, a living room with a sofa, and a pressure gauge lying on the table. The responsible operator interacts with inhabitants and does not wear a uniform.

The programme is conceived in a certain way as a device that can provide an understanding of the limits and weaknesses of public action in these areas. Moreover, it is the Public Health Authority that starts a strategic process of re-setting of its organization, after realizing some major defeats in reaching the most disadvantaged users in the city. In this case, a public institution is actively using the neighbourhoods as a ground on which to sample and verify the effectiveness of public action. In a way, the enlightened institution is recognizing that in the given change of economic and social arrangements in the city, public action must be reshaped in order to suit contemporary urban and social changes. Though recognizing the need for local and physical intervention for the improvement of the living environment, the first step to improve living conditions is regarded as a matter of redesigning and reorganizing the relations between public services and the people. This process is definitely not an obvious one and places and people which have been neglected for some years and in which problems and outcomes have been produced and cumulated as through a black box, require innovative approaches.

These approaches imply a number of activities. An important line of intervention entails the elaboration of health-care projects modulated on the specific characteristics of the subject and their background. There are 'door-to-door' home visits for inhabitants in micro-areas thanks to which the referents get the information regarding the use of medicines and can define a series of personalized interventions. Other activities affect daily life in housing blocks and aim at developing exchanges and reciprocal help between neighbours, thus favouring an active role for inhabitants. The organizational ability of the inhabitants gave way to initiatives for the collective that were also visible to the rest of the city such as, for example, neighbourhood festivals and the restoration of public squares and parks. Thanks to this kind of activity, inhabitants learn to participate in their own life contexts and express their own voice (Massiotta 2006).

Connection and Institution Building

As can be noted, the ability to create connections is crucial. It involves developing ties between the subjects and the people living in the places in the city, the construction of an articulated and integrated institutional architecture, and the activation of relationships between scales of action, first of all between the area of intervention and the urban area. This ability is flanked by an operative infrastructure in which 'bridging' organizations play a determining role, creating a bridge between the subjects and heterogeneous groups, and 'linking' them to the different levels of power (Putnam 2000; Woolcock 2001).

These dynamics imply (and in part coincide with) dynamics of institution building. In fact, the coordination between actors is a fundamental element in organizational and institutional architecture of the micro-area case. It entails the construction of a set of norms, cognitive frameworks and rules to sustain and stabilize interactions between a wide variety of subjects. We can find here the key point of a perspective aimed at creating long-term institutions and, simultaneously, guaranteeing the resilience of these institutions.

The micro-area programme lets us throw light on the dynamics involving other cases that we have referred to. Generally speaking, these dynamics are crucial, especially (but not only) if they are aimed at involving disadvantaged individuals and groups, traditionally considered mere beneficiaries of initiatives. This implies drastically reducing or tearing down various institutional, organizational and social obstacles to their involvement, in order to build new action contexts and guarantee the legitimacy and stability of the innovations that have been realized.

Summarizing the analysis so far, the processes of connection and institution building have an effect on:

- *The dynamics of social organizations.* The interventions to public housing neighbourhood are called to deal with the segmentation and tearing of social urban fabric that is sometimes very deep. Society tends to fall apart in these neighbourhoods (Donzelot et al. 2003). Inverting these dynamics means working on the urban space to bring about an effect of integration to weave social connections. An important point is that these effects are produced when the differences, the plurality of vocabularies, the potential reasons for conflict are not annulled but, o the contrary, find a space to be recognized and valued.

- *The relationship between neighbourhood and the city.* Another crucial point involves the relationship between the organizers in the neighbourhood and the overall organization of the city. As far as public housing estates are concerned Italy does not present the degree of urban segregation typical of other European countries but there is an increase in social homogeneous situations in which people chose to live among similar individuals. Furthermore, it appears that the gap between poor and rich areas is growing, with polarized logic that reflects broader social changes (Zajczyk et al. 2007). While they are not segregated, several public building neighbourhoods are, in any case, worlds apart and present a very difficult situation for co-habitation. Interventions in these neighbourhoods are therefore called for due to the need to initiate a double-move: break the trap of exclusion created by the concentration of socially deprived conditions and territorial deprivation (Cremaschi 2001; Briata et al. 2009); re-establish a link between these neighbourhoods and the city, contrasting the separations that can be seen in the social urban fabric. This also means that the changes are more significant the more they invest in the city and its government.

- *The public sphere.* Though it is not as frequent, the revitalizing of public dimensions of urban space is something that can happen. Sometimes it is exactly where the contents of the *Contratto di Quartiere* have implied a highly conflictual process and a close confrontation among inhabitants, institutions and key persons with responsibility over the process that we can recognize the ways of a 'turning into public' of key issues that become first of all visible. This is a necessary step in order to define a way for a public treatment, that is to say a treatment in terms of generality. In other words, it is probably a way to produce public learning, allowing private knowledge to become public, generating institutional learning. Along this path, marked by practices of active listening on the part of public administrations, the renewal of a housing estate can develop new ways of problem-solving and a ground for policies to be more effective.

- *The transcalar dimension.* Besides creating dynamics in the urban decision making arenas, multi-actor and multi-sector interventions such as *Contratto di Quartiere,* can also favour a link between different spatial scales – the neighbourhood, the city, the region, national level and trans-national level. Above all, this seems to occur when the institutional actors manage to contemporaneously fuel and orient the plurality of relationships which design urban governance both horizontally and vertically.

Conclusions

In this chapter, we have discussed a few of the neighbourhood regeneration experiences in Italy. In particular, we have focused on the institutional and social practices that are solicited in public building neighbourhoods by integrated recuperation interventions, with the objective of understanding how and why these interventions reorganize the city-producing society.

The analysis pinpointed public housing estates during the development and crisis of the modern city as the starting point. Conceived as a solution to several problems of industrial development, they were later seen to become problem areas themselves.

Today, the approach for the recovery of public housing neighbourhoods tries to face these problems with integrated and so-called area based programmes. The *Contratto di Quartiere* represent the most significant experiences in Italy relating to methodologies based on the integration and involvement of the inhabitants. Other cases, such as the micro-area programme, are just as significant but tend to remain circumscribed to the territories in which they are developed.

The dynamics of connection and institution building, linked together, are the heart of the experiences that manage, in some measure, to reorganize the urban space producing social organization (Bagnasco 2003). The relevant actors, in this sense, are the institutional subjects – in particular for their ability for active listening and mediation – as well as the social subjects – in particular for expressing their voice. It is a voice that can also be very conflicting, just as much as it can be promoted by rules and formalized procedures. Whether and how a different urban and social order is formed depends on the interaction of these actors and the manner in which institutional rules and self-regulating social forms are combined.

There are still a lot of problems that need to be solved. One decisive problem involves the breadth and solidity of the innovations triggered. Public housing neighbourhoods, that were a tool for building integration in a modern city, are today spaces that offer evidence of dilemmas. The end of the idea of functionality they embodied coincides with the end of one of the pillars of contemporary urban organization. Therefore, we have the problem of how to reformulate the question of living in a city in more comprehensive terms, just starting with public housing neighbourhoods. These neighbourhoods are a space where institutions can solicit, answer and open themselves up to the voices of inhabitants and local communities, in such a way that social integration practices can occur with new and old forms of citizenship taking shape, with the condition that public action is not circumscribed within a limited perimeter.

Chapter 6

Public Sphere in Times of Governance: Public Action, Disputed Building and Local Cultural System in a Northern City of Italy

Vando Borghi and Claudia Meschiari

Through the analysis of a case of a socially and culturally *disputed* urban space in the city of Modena (a medium-sized city in the northern part of Italy), we will explore some more general issues, concerning the *organizing of the public sphere of the local cultural system*. In 2007–2008, Modena has been interested by a large, multidisciplinary research project,[1] developed, among others, on the basis of these questions: how is the cultural field connected to the space of the public action? What is the meaning (the grammars of justification and the terrains of disputes), for a local community, of sustaining and funding public policy of culture? How is the relationship between culture and territorial development conceived in that context?

In the first part, we will introduce some relevant elements of the urban cultural system, as they come from the wide research project, in order to locate the reflections concerning a specific disputed place, in which the relationship between local cultures, public sphere and a concrete urban space are involved. A general mainstream on cultural policy, in which public action is mainly interpreted according to a strict economic perspective and the connection between 'culture', however defined, and 'urban development' is consequently over-simplified, will be then discussed. The case study concerning the local public dispute about the

---

1   The article is part of the results of a broader interdisciplinary comparative research project about 'The field of culture. Situation, places, history and perspectives'. Coordinated by Andrea Borsari (philosopher, University of Firenze), Vando Borghi (sociologist, University of Bologna) and Giovanni Leoni (architect, University of Bologna), the project is promoted by the Fondazione Mario del Monte and financed by the Fondazione Cassa di Risparmio (both located in the city researched). It started around November 2006 and was concluded in January 2009. On the website of the Fondazione MdM – www.mariodelmonte. it – beyond a presentation of the Fondazione itself, many materials coming from the first wave of the project – that have been (and will be) consisting not only of the research activities, but also of seminars, collective interviews, etc – are and will be available. Part of the second year of the project will also be dedicated to activities of dissemination: not only the research reports and publications, but also the realization of an interactive website, public seminars about the results of the different sections of research and workshops.

destiny of a disused foundry, will be finally analysed in this context, showing how the process of 'signification' of a specific place may offer relevant insights to overpass a superficial and privatistic perspective on culture in contemporary cities.[2]

Cultural Instrumentality and the Local System

In large part, the relationship between culture and public policy is constitutively instrumental (Vestheim 2007): culture is mainly interpreted as a means for realizing other (economic, political, social) aims. So it can be useful to make explicit the nature and the internal articulation of that instrumental relationship. According to a clear scheme advanced by Vestheim (2007: 233), it is possible to distinguish three types of arguments in favour of the public intervention in culture:

- the *perfectionist* argument: public support should be directed to what is considered the 'best' art for its 'intrinsic value'; the target of this argument is the 'individual as a private person' and the type of instrumentality deployed is an aesthetical and educational one;
- the *economic* and *social* argument, according to which the promotion of social and economic development is the legitimate argument for public support of the arts and culture; the target, in this case, is the individual as 'a socio-economic being', and the type of instrumentality used in this argument is the socio-economic one;
- the *democratic* argument, in which promoting enlightenment, social consciousness and cultural rights is the motive for public support for the arts and culture, addressing the individual 'as citizen', through a political type of instrumentality.

Of course, in real social life we can only find combinations of these pure analytical categories; but at the same time, that scheme can help us in recognizing the prevalent approach in any given situation. Vestheim himself (2007: 234), introducing that scheme, concludes recording a shift of the relationship between public institutions and culture in the current times: 'Cultural institutions, activities, projects and investments are to a greater extent being considered as business enterprises. To get money from the state, cultural institutions and culture-based initiatives must justify their economic productivity. The state expects something in return, something that

---

2   The case study has been conducted mainly by participant observation and in depth-interviews, applied to local officials (such as the Culture Councillor), activists, local experts and people involved in the process of regeneration. We also examined public reports, local literature, journals' dossiers and documentaries concerning the past of the of the foundry and the current debate about it.

can be measured in quantitative terms'.[3] We are observing, in contemporary cities, a 'syndrome of privatism' (de Leonardis 1997) in dealing with culture, also defined as a part of a general 'commodification' (Gray 2007) in urban public policies.

The situation of the local cultural actors seems to offer some insights to better deepen these general statements.

First, we can affirm that the most important cultural actor is a local private bank foundation (the 'Fondazione Cassa di Risparmio'): its budget – considerably bigger than the one of the city's Councillorship of Culture [*Assessorato alla Cultura*] – financially sustains, directly and indirectly, a great part of the local cultural life and structures.[4] The Fondazione escapes all the criteria identifying a public actor, as we will define afterwards: there are opacities in the processes of building cultural activities, as far as the visibility and the universalistic principles of the public agency are concerned, since the Fondazione is a self-responding and auto-organizing private structure. Its clear economic dominance – certainly a resource, not a problem in itself, characterizing that organization – does not automatically translate itself in a corresponding emptying of the public agency: but under these circumstances, it is clear that *a multiplication and empowering of the public places and spaces of discussion, exchange and knowledge circulation are needed.* Only in this direction it is possible to think about a re-equilibrating effort, otherwise impossible (especially as far as the financial dimension is concerned), with regard to the growing risks of privatism currently characterizing the public policies of culture.

A second element of reflection is related to an almost complete lack of interest about culture on behalf of the main local private actors (economic and industrial organizations): apart from very few exceptions, (the Fondazione is of course the most relevant one), they are not very willing to be involved, even when there are projects clearly linked, directly and indirectly, to local economic matters and history.[5]

Third, a relevant point which is useful to frame the local cultural system is the progressive marginalization of the patrimony of knowledge, competences and experiences the local administration and its personnel accumulated along the way

---

3 It is shift in the cultural dimension of social life that shouldn't be surprising, being coherent with a more general 'post-democratic' turn in which prevails the idea of a mere coincidence between society and market (Mastropaolo 2001, Crouch 2004).

4 Even only considering a very raw indicator, the fact that the local government planned to spend about 11,005,675,98 euros for the whole matters of youth, sport, tourist marketing and cultural policies in 2007, whereas the Fondazione, in 2006, spent about 14,155,816 euros for cultural activities, we can get a significant picture of the concrete processes.

5 An evident example of this can be seen in the case of the current project of 'House-Museum Enzo Ferrari', with evident implications with the local industrial history (the founder of the famous car's brand was born in this city) and sure positive effects on the tourism: also that project didn't receive any particular attention from the local economic and industrial actors.

in projecting and realizing cultural activities. It has to do with the relationship between the local public sphere of culture and the high levels of professional competences characterising the local cultural system. The questions in this regard can be formulated as follows: how much of these (personal) competences are really available to be involved in the processes of collective reflexivity that shape the local public sphere of culture? How much do these competences participate in an enlargement of the cognitive resources available to the public discussion? It is a cultural translation of a more general issue of the public sphere, concerning the production and reproduction of a personal interest in applying one's own competence to the collective treatment and elaboration of social problems, a personal interest that is not a self-reproductive, natural and always given quality of social life (Borghi 2006a).

More generally, we can observe also in Modena the general shift described by Vestheim, in terms of a growing hegemony of what is here defined as a reductive, economically one-sided, interpretation of culture exercised also by the public actor. The historical part of the broader research project has offered many evidences of a gradual shift, through time, from a pedagogic (that does not mean paternalist) conception of public action in the cultural field – centred on imperatives of promoting access to cultural life and devices to a broader public, emphasizing the civic and democratic value of culture – to an idea of cultural activities as, mainly, subject (as commodities) to a market-like evaluation (through indexes of consumption, number of participants, capacity to attract tourists, and so on). That has been largely becoming a taken for granted perspective for the public actor as well. More generally, cultural projects and activities are mainly judged and evaluated (by many actors of the local cultural system) in terms of territorial marketing and looking at their strictly immediate economic feedbacks. There appears to prevail, at least among some of the main actors of the territorial socio-economic development, an idea of culture as something merely functional to the 'territorial brand', consisting of few, stereotypical static pictures linked to the city's self-representation (Ferrari's cars, Lambrusco wine, balsamic vinegar and so on).

At the same time, it has to be underlined that the research itself has been producing some interesting effects, revitalizing the local public debate about cultural issues, realizing some relevantly attended and participated seminars and debates. As we will see in the case of the disputed place, a disused foundry which is involved in a process of regeneration, local public opinion still seems to be highly interested in the cultural sphere. And this attention, together with a fully, non reductive interpretation of 'culture' and 'development', can be considered as one of the main resources to prevent a privatistic drift, that may be foreseen by international trends and by this very synthetic premise concerning the town of Modena.

Before presenting the case study, we will introduce the perspectives we used in order to define what we mean by 'public action', and the idea of 'culture' which is implied in the present research.

Searching for publicness in time of governance

As we previously observed, the presence of a relevant private actor such as the Fondazione, which is deeply involved in financing public activities in the cultural field, it is not a problem in itself: in other words, the dichotomy between the state (or the local public authority) and the market, and the identification of publicness with any direct and indirect emanation of the state is no longer possible. This was the classical liberal vision of the separation between public and private, that, at a deeper glance, appears already in itself rather unsatisfactory; as Paul Hirst (2000: 20) wrote, 'the liberal architecture looks less and less convincing as a descriptive account of modern advanced societies. In fact it would be better to see the state as a part of an "organizational society", with large hierarchically controlled institutions on both sides of the public-private divide that are either unanswerable to or only weakly accountable to citizens'. But without going mistakenly too far in this equalizing public and private organizations),[6] we have to take into consideration that current societies are structurally marked by the overlapping and combination of public and private agencies, and by an increasing process through which previously social informal relationships and social (volunteer) and civil activities are absorbed by big organizations and corporations (Perrow 1996). So, it is not difficult to agree with Paul Hirst (2000: 21–22), when he writes that we 'need to rethink the notion of democratic government to fit the reality of an organizational society'.

This need is also more evident in times in which public action is undergoing many and profound changes and it can be easily observed the ambiguous success of a term usually considered capable of summarizing them: *governance*. Without going into a detailed discussion of this term and its (ideological and cognitive) premises and meanings,[7] we use it here only for recalling three main levels of social and institutional change:

- the level of the actors participating the decision-making process: the number of actors increased either vertically (from EU Council to the local government of a small town) or horizontally (at each level of the vertical line, the public actor has to cooperate with other actors, public as well or private, profit and non-profit), according to the regulative principle of the subsidiarity;
- the level immediately consequent from what above recalled, that is the validation of a plurality of rationality models and normative criteria for the production and application of collectively binding decisions;

---

6 From its origins, public 'institutional program' (Dubet 2003) is intrinsically, programmatically, self-conceiving as responsible to citizens (through mechanisms of the public sphere and of the political system).

7 About that discussion, see Offe 2009; Pierre 2000; Borghi 2006b; for its meaning as far as urban policies are concerned, see Le Galès 2006; Sebastiani 2007.

- finally, the level of the coordination's forms (institutions, networks, associations, and so on), that such a twofold pluralization (of actors and rationality models) necessarily needs.[8]

In synthesis: neither the public actor, nor the techno-procedural rationality of public administration, nor the hierarchical-bureaucratic principle of coordination are exclusive of each other.

So, these changes make any substantive definition of publicness – such as the classical liberal identification of the public dimension with the state's organizational space – simply impossible. In the perspective we adopt, publicness depends much more on the properties characterizing the actions of a plurality of (public and private) agencies and on the qualities and the aims of their relationships than on the *a priori* supposed nature of the agencies in themselves (Bifulco and de Leonardis 2005). This perspective, in which publicness has to do with the process of treating a matter rather than with the nature of the actors involved, is rooted in a specific conception of the public sphere, of the public good and of public policies. According to this framework, the public sphere has, indeed, to be considered not only as a set of mechanisms linking society to the political system, based on specific institutions (connected with law enforcement, public opinion formation, public administration, and so on); but also as a general social horizon of experience through which matters relevant for all members of society take form and are integrated (Negt and Kluge 1993; Fraser 1990, Krause 2005). The public sphere has a structural power, being 'the site where the capacities of individuals to participate in public life are produced and where the production of the public's horizon of experience or the "limits of the possible" are produced' (Davis 2005: 137). In this perspective, there is a strong relationship between the public sphere and the identification of the public good. Far from being a specialists' or experts' matter, the public good cannot be described as the mere aggregation of the private interests of many individuals. Instead, it has to be conceived of as a 'social and cultural project of the public sphere', produced in and through a public process and not ascertainable independently of it (Calhoun 1998: 32).

So, the public sphere is not – as it is often conceived – only a space in which information plays a relevant role and in which decisions are taken. It is also 'an arena of reflexive modification of the people who enter it, of their ideas, and of its own modes of discourse', in which our debate on the public good – what is good for us – is always, as well, a discourse about our identity: who we want to be

---

8   The very schematic nature of this synthesis is evident. In the more complex reality we can easily see many signs of changes going exactly in the opposite direction: the subsidiarity principle that 'revealed to be a evident failure' (Ginsborg 2006: 45), the progressive power concentration, the systematic reduction of visibility of the spaces (in the global and in the local processes) in which that power is concretely exercised and a growing submission of the different rationality criteria to the economic and financial principles (Crouch 2004; Pizzorno 2001; Hertz 2001).

(Calhoun 1998: 33). So, public institutions (in our case, providers of cultural goods and activities) have a specific, pivotal role, as they should recognize[9] themselves as a 'formative context' (Unger 1987) and assume this nature of formative context as an explicit terrain of action: intervening in the social realm with the awareness that social services are relationships that reproduce relationships, identifies the specificity of public institutions with the space 'where questions of technical efficacy ("what works") can be integrated with value questions' and with the role – among others – of sometimes taking on 'impossible tasks' (Hoggett 2006: 13–14).

In this perspective, following Bifulco and de Leonardis (2005; de Leonardis 2006), publicness may arise when four properties are fulfilled. First of all, a boundary can be fixed between what is public and what is private, based on the quality of visibility: public processes are exposed to public visibility, whereas the secret is a quality of the private. A second property is about the claim of *universalistic validity* that publicness assumes as a constitutive element – whereas the private usually refers to particularistic interests and points of view – submitting practices and decisions to specific procedures aiming at generalizing them. Third, opposite to the exclusiveness that characterizes the private (for example, private property), publicness designs what is 'in-common': goods are recognized and treated as commons and they constitute that social property (education, social protection, health, and so on) in which the effective access to citizenship of all people is concretely rooted. Finally, publicness has to be conceived as a space through which society reflexively recognizes itself as a collective agency needing regulative (vertical) devices, that go beyond the self-regulation of (horizontal) one-to-one exchanges and agreements: so, the fourth property of becoming public has to do with practices of *institution building* (the law is the most formal version of it, but not the only one).

Culture and territory: Towards the 'capacity to aspire'?

Considering the issues of the instrumental nature of arguments in favour of public intervention in culture, our research project assumed a specific normative comparative point of view: the conception of culture as a necessary anthropological meta-capacity, the 'capacity to aspire' (Appadurai 2004). This conception is interested in overcoming any definition of culture as something only related to the past. As Appadurai (2004: 60) writes,

> in spite of many important technical moves in the understanding of culture, the future remains a stranger to most anthropological models of culture. By default, and also for independent reasons, economics has become the science of the future, and when human beings are seen as having a future, the keywords such as wants, needs, expectations, calculations, have become hardwired into the

---

9   The conditional mode here stresses that such a recognition is an eventual result of a social process, as I said, rather than an intrinsic attribute of the involved actors.

discourse of economics. In a word, the cultural actor is a person of and from the past, and the economic actor a person of the future.

A promising way for escaping such a vision is to define culture as the 'capacity to aspire': extending to the cultural dimension Sen's (1985) approach to capability[10] – the freedom of being and doing – that perspective permits to deepen the processes through which the possibility of conceiving (or aspiring to) a bettering of one's own life, the possibility of growing in one's own dignity and social rights, are strengthened or weakened. More generally, the concept of the 'capacity to aspire' emphasises the socio-cultural bases necessary for not considering an inescapable fate one's own current existential condition. Aspiring to 'something else and better' is not a natural given feeling; it needs to be fed and sustained: culture is the terrain on which the promotion (or the inhibition) of that feeling is concretely realized. It is a perspective that – at least indirectly – receives many inspirations and confirmations from different research paths concerning the relationship between the normative roots and the strategic or instrumental motives of social action: the studies about the relationship between economic rationality and normative dimensions (Borghi and Vitale 2006); the growing attention – as far as the relations between citizens and institutions, firms or organizations are concerned – not only to attitudes of total attachment (loyalty) or to the opposite ones (exit), but also to what is strictly linked to a capacity to aspire, that is *voice* (Hirschmann 1970); the research programme centred on a sociological analysis of the critical capacities of social actors (in place of the traditional perspective of realizing a critical sociology) (Boltanski and Thévenot 1991; Boltanski and Chiapello 2005). In this sense, we can also revise the way in which culture is invoked as a tool of development. Considering the 'capacity to aspire' as the main insight offered by culture, we can stress the difference between 'growth' and 'development'. The former is mainly related to economic parameters; the latter is a multidimensional concern – involving sustainability, social cohesion, territorial embeddedness, social justice, social recognition of the individual life project, with the consequent pluralization of meanings and rationalities – working at different levels (social, environmental, cognitive).

The case of the disused foundry and of the public debate about its destiny shows different possibilities for constructing the relationship between culture and urban spaces: on the one side, urban spaces have their own history, (evolving) identities, their material bonds and possibilities and their relationships with the surrounding urban environment; on the other side, citizens express and manifest (also) regarding urban spaces their 'capacity to aspire'. These interactions and relationships between urban spaces and culture (in terms of capacity to aspire) have

---

10   The concept of 'capacity to aspire' is an application of Sen's concept of *capability* – the human right to the freedom of being and doing – to the cultural field. 'In more general terms' – Appadurai writes (2004) – 'Sen's work is a major invitation to anthropology to widen its conceptions of how human beings engage their own futures'.

been the terrain of the public debate about the destiny of the disused foundry and, more generally, of a debate about territorial and urban development. According to the perspective of research we adopt, different regimes of justification should be taken into account, avoiding the frequent conflation between development and growth: contrary to what the economist and reductive torsion of common sense often states, growth 'is not the solution, but it is the problem. A problem, therefore, which admits solutions yet. But these solutions are external to the growth itself, they are in another paradigm, the development paradigm' (Donolo 2007: 17). Development is here defined in terms of commons and public goods growing, entitlements' enlargement, individual and collective capabilities' empowerment (Donolo 2007: 4). The conflict about legitimate representations, codes and the grammars – in other words *the regimes of justification* (Boltanski and Thévenot 1991) – concerning the territorial development becomes central here. In the case we will discuss later, for instance, there is evidently a conflict, among others, about the meaning of a specific urban space (a disused foundry), between a vocabulary and a grammar of justification belonging to the market mode of coordination, to the 'cité marchande', in Boltanski and Thévenot's (1991) words, on the one side; and a political-moral order of evaluation, according to which that space is defined and evaluated in relationship with relevant city's self-representations, based on its history, its (past and future) cultural and political identity.

Of course, it is a conflict concerning power, as always; but in this context power assumes a different meaning and, coinciding more and more with 'creating and perceiving the sense of what is communicated', is exercised through the control of the 'way in which the sense is produced and received' (Melucci 2000: 136). So, in that context, the local system is less conceivable as a space characterized by the production of any specific good, and more appropriately as 'the mode of producing and reproducing itself' (Ceruti 1987: 13; Dematteis 1994: 14). Local development is less conceivable as an issue of markets and competition on given costs and advantages, and more appropriately as an issue of sense making and of grammars, vocabularies, languages, conventions, modes of evaluation and regimes of justification through which situations are interpreted, actors coordinate, uncertainty reduced. In other words, culture and economy have to be conceived as strictly interwoven, but in a very different way orthodox economic thought used to take for granted (Amin and Thrift 2007).

So, according to this perspective, a crucial aspect to be focused on is the necessity of pointing out the potentials of development in a local system. The concept of 'potentials' (Donolo 2007) refers to the conditional nature of social reality, to the possibility of pointing out underground, latent and weakly visible possibilities of development. Social and institutional innovation more than homogeneity with the past, changes and transformations more than conformism towards (sometime invented) traditions and consolidated ways of doing, in this perspective, need to be recognized, estimated, promoted.

Spaces of publicness, culture as the capacity to aspire to something different, development as a collective production of meanings: despite general trends and concrete characteristics of the local cultural system, the case study will show the possibility of seeing in action some of the perspectives we briefly exposed above.

A Disputed Place

Trying to understand the ways in which a specific urban context is facing the growing relevance of culture in local development and what this change can tell us in terms of reinforcement of public action, we experienced that a good empirical starting point consists of choosing a specific 'object', useful to see in action some forces of the local sphere. In particular, from the end of 2006 to 2008, we had the opportunity to closely follow a decision-making process concerning a huge building in the industrial part of the town, a decommissioned foundry (known in Modena as 'Ex-Fonderie Riunite'). After more than twenty years of abandonment, the place became the stage of debates on different strategies and of innovative experiences of decision-making, mainly rooted, as we will see, in the symbolic relevance of the place.

The building is part of a large area involved in a relatively recent process of urban renewal, far from being concluded, that we can consider as an effect of a wide de-industrialization of urban landscape. The ex-foundry looks like a big island coming from the past. It is surrounded by large empty spaces, where it is possible to see the first signs of the future arrangement of the district, mainly dedicated to residence and services. As a whole, the area is 40,000 m², of which 11,740 m² are taken up by the big old warehouses and the impressive entrance.

In Modena, industrialization was the dominant pattern of physical, social and urban development since the 1930s, when several heavy industrial buildings were constructed in the northern part of the city, close to the city centre. Around them, large parts of the city developed as working-class districts. At the beginning of the 1980s, most of the industrial production and employment moved outside the town, shaping a landscape marked by huge empty spaces, boundaries, dangerous zones and only few new buildings, as a tangible result of a strong process of urban change. In re-shaping this part of the city, demolition has been the general trend exhibited by the local municipality in recent years, in order to build new residential areas and private and public services.

The decommissioned foundry is a remarkable exception: the announced privatization and the option of demolition generated widespread negative public opinion, which set up several discussions in the public arena. From the point of view of local decision-makers, this reaction could have been interpreted in several ways: as an obstacle to already established plans, which needs to be moved around; as a problem, in need of negotiated solutions; or as the signal of something un-attended,[11] and requiring specific considerations.

---

11   Compared to the considered 'natural' course of things: in the same urban area many other restructuring actions were realized without meeting any resistance or contestation.

The debate around this place is seen as an opportunity for the local public sphere to re-think the passage from an industrial development pattern to a new one – evidently, still in the way to be defined – in a perspective of publicness (as previously defined), re-inforcement of collective capacities to design alternatives, and taking into account which idea of urban development is implied.

The foundry and the city: Notes on history and the role of memory

The place we are focusing on started its activity during the 1930s, producing predominantly war products. Between 1940 and 1948, the foundry grew from employing 150 to over 550 workers, becoming one of the biggest in the town. As the number of workers increased, claims to obtain better working conditions became more frequent and vocal, according with a phase of strong conflicts across the whole country. Some examples of the Italian political climate, which was shifting in a conservative direction, were the attempt on the life of Togliatti, the leader of the Communist Party; the exclusion of the Communist Party, which contributed in a decisive way to Italian liberation during the war, in the parliamentary election, and the violent repression by the police of workers' strikes in the south of Italy, where several people were killed.

In Modena, this difficult passage was tragically marked by the deaths of six people killed by the police, during a strike following the lock-out of the foundry on 9 January 1950. This event has been and is still memorialized in the town, representing a first, tangible element of the urban memory connected to the foundry.

Workers' claims continued during the 1950s and 1960s, supported by a socialist-communist inspired trade union, the FIOM (Federazione Italiana Operai Metalmeccanici, Italian Federation of Mechanical Factory Workers). This period can be summarized as an opposition between two different points of view concerning the factory. Workers looked upon the factory as a social asset, and, immediately after World War II, they seemed to achieve significant results in this direction. The owner considered it as a totally private estate, and he did not recognize negotiation as a positive management tool (Osti Guerrazzi and Siligardi 2002).

At the end of the 1960s, the foundry was declining in productivity because of the lack of innovation and the general economic depression which hit traditional foundries hardest. When debts became unsustainable, the owner was forced to sell out. To avoid total decommission and discharge, workers occupied the foundry for 52 days; after an intense political phase, they took over the factory and established a cooperative society, actively supported by the local municipality in obtaining loans from the banks, a unique decision in Italian occupational history (Officina Emilia 2007: 44–48). The company is still active, but production was transferred to a more accessible site in 1983.

When the old building was decommissioned, it was bought by the local municipality, together with the surrounding land, expressing an attention towards the place. Furthermore, the front of the building was declared as historical heritage, preventing any relevant physical change.[12] Nevertheless, the building was totally abandoned for more than two decades, excluding some summer cultural initiatives in the late 1990s, confirming the difficulties in managing ex-industrial buildings, both from a financial and a physical point of view (Petrucci and Dansero 1995).

A first project was defined in 2001,[13] proposing to convert the building into a site for public health services: however, the idea was soon abandoned because the central hospital administration found a different solution. The story of the ex-foundry was again coming to a standstill, when at the end of 2005, the local press reported the Councillor for Town Planning's decision to sell the entire area to private investors. This event proved to be the turning-point in the story.

In press reviews at that time public opinion was strongly polarized against the decision, expressing deep disappointment. Heated debate began in the city. This was actually promoted by the local municipality, which met citizens and associations in several public meetings in order to discuss the future of Ex-Fonderie Riunite. In this phase, several proposals were put forward, most of them oriented towards the memory of industrial labour and the urban social history. All the same, the idea of a traditional museum clearly appeared unsuitable for obvious spatial and financial reasons, but also because citizens, associations and institutions seemed to express an unanimous wish for something more innovative for the city.

At this point, it seems necessary to resume some lines on which local memory is associated with this place, as emerged from interviews, local bibliography, and documentaries.

Firstly, factory work marked the passage from living and working in the countryside to an urban life-style: the possibility of a monthly salary opened the doors of mass-consumption society for people who decided to make the jump from rural to urban life. In workers' memories, the description of extreme work conditions is always accompanied by the satisfaction of supporting the frail home economies, typical of the post war period.[14] The work in the foundry was also the source of a new social identity as a part of a wide labour movement, with strong ideological and political connections to local administration. In this way, industrialization established a common values background between new citizens and the political standpoint (Osti Guerrazzi and Siligardi 2002; Bertucelli 2001). This socio-political cohesion grounds the success of the Emilia Romagna 'model', as recognized by David Harvey (1993: 359), which described the regional development as a peculiar mix of cooperative entrepreneurship, craft skills

---

12   For an accurate description of architectural values, see Officina Emilia (2007), available also in English.

13   References concerning planning in Modena is available on http://urbanistica.comune.modena.it/ (accessed October 2007).

14   Several evidences of this period are collected in a survey realised by the local municipality and by district council (Assessorato all''Istruzione e Circoscrizione 2 del Comune di Modena 1999).

and local communist government engaged for creating employment. Even so, the 1950s and 1960s were difficult years, with the dramatic junctures sketchily described above, such as the 9 January 1950 and the birth, in the late1960s, of the mutual company led by workers. In Modena, factory work is also associated to the 'myth of well-done work',[15] still considered as a part of local identity. In the foundry, workers could learn how to design models, an activity which required project skills, thereby improving their own professional status. Furthermore, the industrial age is probably seen by younger generations as an evocative and nostalgic background, as rural life was for their parents. It was an historical phase they don't live in, but in which they grew up culturally, as the foundation of local memories and pride.[16]

So, for many people in Modena, entering the community through factory work meant experiencing a different society based on mass consumption, to share values with the wider community and gave them the possibility of improving their own skills through working.

This first decision-building phase, and the reaction provoked by the option of privatization, are strictly connected to these memories and to a demand of visibility and open confrontation, and some first considerations are allowed.

First of all, the local civil society, in different forms and at different levels, seemed to be capable of mobilization, claiming visibility and to consider the place as an in-common value: in other words, they required publicness, both for the management of the building and for the process which would define the concrete destination. It is interesting to notice that the previous project, *id est* the possibility to host public health services, was not received in such a conflictual way, even if it was very far from emphasizing the place's identity. We can argue that, in this phase, the preservation of a common interest was considered much more acceptable than any clear affirmation of a privatistic logic.

Moreover, urban memory, as an expression of local culture which is often taken for granted, but also considered as a passive feature (something that does not have any concrete effect on the present), was actively engaged in the claims: the reasons to prevent the foundry demolition were not shaped on situated interests, but on collective social memories (Hayden 1995), considered as a starting-point in imagining possible futures. In this sense, urban memory manifested itself as a tool for change, far from any nostalgic desire for preservation. Much more than the yearly memorialization of 9 January, this decisional impasse and the necessity to fill the gap between local decision-makers and the public opinion, let urban memories emerge as a part of local active forces, and as a 'potential' of innovation.

---

15 As summed up by Giorgio Prampolini (president of 'Amici delle Fonderie' Association, and participant at the participative process) during the interview, and reported by many other people during public debates, or in documentaries.

16 Interview with Anna Maria Pedretti, historian, specialist in local and oral history.

From local potentialities to collective resources

This atmosphere of uncertainty and public debate laid the framework for the proposal of a participative process, launched in the first half of 2007. This was done in order to elaborate on a concrete project together with citizens. It was promoted and realized by a team constituted by members of local government together with an external group of counsellors,[17] also involving some citizens as volunteers.

The first step in the process occurred during the Memorial Day, 9 January 2007. The memorial celebration was followed by a public discussion concerning the history of the site, with some protagonists, documentaries and music, and the participative process was officially presented to the town. The goal was to establish a proposal for the local municipality catering for inclusivity and defining new assets for the site. The main steps included the collaboration of citizens, associations, schools and young people, with neighbourhood meetings, advertisements, distribution of informative materials, the creation of a website[18] and interviews with local stakeholders; a public discussion in a two-day public meeting,[19] the setting up of a round table for representatives of the proposals (formed by around 20 people, and named 'Tavolo di confronto creativo' ['Table of creative discussion']), and, finally, the submission of the project to the local council, after six months of intensive work.

The range of participants at the public discussion and at the round table was extremely heterogeneous, including members of associations, representatives from the University (including the rector, and the coordinator of a project concerning industrial territorial development), members of local institutions (such as the local historical archive and the council of cultural associations) and private citizens (some of them proposing a united project, some not). There was also a notable presence of young people.

The main guideline, formerly defined by the consultants' staff, was to establish an 'inclusive' proposal through consensus building.[20] The focus lay in bringing different positions together instead of negotiating around them to hopefully reach a totally new idea which could be agreed upon by all.

---

17   The external team was leaded by Marianella Sclavi, scholar of consensus building approach and participation, and professor of Urban Ethnology at Politecnico di Milano.

18   The website (www.comune.modena.it/exfonderie/) was created to present the history of the building and the participative process, and it was possible to upload ideas and proposals.

19   Using the Open Space Technology, a method devised by Harrison Owen in early Eighties (see the website http://ho-image.com).

20   The consensus building approach, developed in Anglo-Saxon contexts, has been translated in Italian governance culture mainly by Marianella Sclavi, the consultant who coordinated the participative process in Modena.

Looking through the minutes,[21] one notices that the participants joined the round table with different opinions and approaches. During the process, they established rules of discussion and some shared cornerstones, facing physical and economic matters, helped by members of the local municipality.[22]

A common vision for the future of the place was defined as based on: memory, intended in its capacity to suggest new directions and perspectives for the future; design, as a medium between the traditional local attitude towards technology and a modern contribution of knowledge and creativity; arts, considered both in a sense of production and consumption, also taking into account the deficit of cultural activities in the district; science and technology, associated, together with design, with the possibility of a new University department inside the building, and together with history, in combining new technologies with the past industrial history. The final project – DAST, Design, Art, Science and Technology – consists of four parts: a University Department of Industrial Design; 'Fonderia delle Arti', a space oriented towards the realization and supply of artistic activities; 'Fabbrica dei Saperi', dedicated to scientific educational programmes, especially focusing on industrial innovation, creativity and applied sciences; 'Polo della Memoria', where it will be possible to host the local historical archive (Istituto Storico della Resistenza) and all local documentary sources concerning industrial development, occupational history and social history of Modena. Several overlaps between the four parts were conceived, as well as a coordinated management of common spaces.

The basic idea is that a mixed and interdisciplinary approach can nourish creativity and innovation, a mixture seen by participants as one of the most interesting challenges for the DAST project.[23] The attempt was clearly oriented towards a solution able to comprehend industrialism as a 'structure of feelings', (Byrne 2002) and an innovative pattern based on culture as a part of the collective urban future. As an important added value, citizens who decided to be part of the process expressed personal wishes and desires, but at the same time they felt the responsibility to propose something reasonable and useful for the entire city, looking at themselves both as someone planning for the city and as potential users.[24]

---

21   Materials about the site (article history and architecture, pictures, documentaries), description of the participative methodology, minutes of the public debates are all available on: www.comune.modena.it/exfonderie.

22   For example: 'to do something the city would be proud of' or to 'conserve memories for the future'; free translation from the Table of creative discussion, 2007.

23   Interview with Federica Rocchi, member of a spontaneous group 'Fonderia delle Arti' and participant in the participative process.

24   Interview with Francesco Raphael Frieri, Assessore al Bilancio (councillor in charge of local budget and participation) in Modena Municipality.

The final project was presented and discussed by local council in June 2007, which essentially accepted the proposal, even if many details and, more relevant, the financial aspects, still needed to be clarified.[25]

Ex-Fonderie Riunite and the Local Public Sphere

The experience of Ex-Fonderie Riunite in Modena can be seen as a process of reinforcement of the local public sphere in several ways.

Firstly, the final project DAST required a public reflection concerning the relationship between culture and regeneration in the town: it clearly revealed a demand for a much more culture-oriented approach to physical regeneration, able to include memory, artistic performances and knowledge-based development, in step with many other urban renewal experiences all over Europe (URBACT 2007). In this sense, the silence of the Culture Department of the local municipality in the process was quite resonant. During the interview, the Councillor in charge of cultural activities described the gap between his own field of action and the spatial issues. Modena, he admitted, lacks coordination between public actions in the fields of urban planning and cultural activities; moreover, the historical centre is still considered the privileged setting for the main cultural initiatives,[26] in tune with an idea of culture as a 'brand', where the traditional historic city is considered as the perfect stage. As Beatriz Garcìa described: '... Despite the general use of cultural initiatives as catalysts for urban regeneration, the development of urban cultural policies as an element of city governance has been far slower and less consistent. This has often meant that the high level of investment required to produce hallmark cultural events and infrastructure is not framed by an assessment of long term cultural legacies or coherent strategies that seek to secure a balanced spatial and social distribution of benefits' (Garcìa 2004: 321).

Also, the traditional functional division of local government in Italy does not help to integrate cultural issues into planning, in a condition where managers of cultural activities and planning and regeneration managers '... (do) not naturally think of themselves as collaborators' (Evans 2005: 970). So, one contribution of the experience of Ex-Fonderie Riunite has been to put the issue of collaboration between participative initiatives, planning and cultural activities on the public agenda, highlighting that it is far from being natural and well-structured.

This result has to be seen not only as a step towards a more effective way to match cultural activities and physical regeneration, but above all as a part of the construction of 'publicness', intended as previously presented. The launch of a

---

25   During 2008, the local municipality announced a competition, to physically design the future of Ex-Fonderie Riunite; the winner was publicly presented on 9 January 2009 (for further information: http://www.comune.modena.it/fonderie).

26   Interview with Mario Lugli, councillor in charge of cultural activities in Modena Municipality.

participative process, which was an answer to a decisional impasse, due to the relevance that the site had in the local context, became an opportunity to open the decisional process to a public confrontation. The local municipality faced the emergence of much more ambitious needs, expressed by participants in the will to design something able 'to make the city proud of it', against the more strictly functional outcome previously planned. In light of the fact, participation can be considered as a tool, among others, to 'explore' local potentialities, allowing innovative ideas to take shape. And, since a feature of innovation is the un-expected, openess and exploration may challenge and stress the limitations of the local decisional level. The project let emerge, through an action oriented to visibility and involvement, that the participative and inclusive degree of the processes of policy building can be thought as a necessity: deliberative and participative practices of institutional innovation concretely appeared to be an effective road to empowering the possibilities of citizens' voice, where these experiments are carefully structured and methodologically looked at.

In spite of limits, the presence of public leadership has been helpful in generating the process, allowing private citizens, associations and, more generally, so-called civil society, to be part of the decision-making process, and to shift from a defensive and oppositional phase to a constructive one. On this occasion and taking into account the symbolic relevance of the place, the local municipality both recognized and steered the potential of the role of community in defining urban renewal. At the same time, some consideration of the participative process is required: the public actor entrusted what has been recognized as a collective good to a voluntary and heterogeneous group. On the one hand the different roles of people on the urban stage who took part in the process can be seen as an added value, because they allowed collaborations and unusual meetings, and in the end brought originality into the project. On the other hand, the risk of bypassing other possible discussion contexts and to reproduce in some ways power relationships which are present even outside the participative process, is tangible. The function of the public actor, in other words, should not be reduced to an 'accept or not accept' simplicity: it should be able to be culturally enhanced by participative processes (for example, as we said, reconsidering the use of cultural activities in urban regeneration), without abdicating their role as public interest preserver. In doing this, the political climate of Modena seems to be supported by a still lively capacity of *voice*, able to pass from opposition to active involvement. Considering that, another relevant question for the future of the local public sphere is how this openness of public discussion concerning visions of the city can be replicated in other urban contexts.

Some final conclusions can be drawn. Firstly, local cultures express a sense of persistence and continuity with the past, but also the need for renewal and of a new kind of development: they showed the capacity to collectively produce and re-produce sense-making, to have the strengths to induce the opening of spaces of opportunities in the local public sphere and to prevent the city to turn its planning and decision-making processes in a too privatistic direction. At least, they did on this occasion. On the other side, the Ex-Fonderie Riunite experience was also a confirmation of the absence of the main private actors in the local cultural public sphere, even when the relations between the production of urban affluence connected to industrial development and local values, memories and heritage is so evident.

Secondly, memory preservation has in fact been associated with cultural and knowledge-oriented proposals. Nevertheless, the growing relevance of cultural policies is not well-integrated with other policy fields, especially planning. In general, spatial matters and culture seem to be taken into account more in order to enhance the usage of the historical city than to support integrated development visions. The Ex-Fonderie Riunite experience showed that a collective production and re-production of sense-making, and the capacity to design alternatives for the future (as collective 'capacity to aspire') are still considered as a need for the city.

Thirdly, the most innovative ideas, fresh integrations (for example between arts and science, or labour history and university) and ambitious cultural visions came from an open space of confrontation, built in this case around a participative process. An 'empty' decisional space, that, if properly structured, linked to a decisional process and shaped in a perspective of publicness, may support the local communities' projectual potentialities in finding their own way to become a tangible collective resource.

Chapter 7

Transition, Memory and Narrations in the Urban Space: The Case of East German Cities

Barbara Grüning

Introduction

Twenty years after the fall of the wall one of the central issues regards urban transformation in East Germany. From a sociological perspective there are two interesting aspects of this question to consider.

First, it is to highlight how the processes of urban transformation, that include several urban and memory practices (and policies), construct specific 'urban imaginaries' (Huyssen 2008) by defining which layers of the history (and how many layers of the history) can be experienced in any singular city. On the other side it is also to pay attention to the 'urban imaginaries' (ibid.) created by the various narrations that circulate in the public space and that outline a conflictual arena where some narrations have more possibilities to influence the common sense about East German cities and East Germans.

Second, it is to understand whether it is possible to do an all-inclusive discourse for East German cities on the base of their shared social GDR past and thus to speak of a 'typical GDR city'. The GDR state tried indeed to remodel the town layout of East German cities in conformity with 'the sixteen principles of urban construction'.[1] However it is questionable to what degree this urban policy has been realized and whether the GDR urban policy remained unchanged during the forty years of the Regime. How is it to interpret, for example, the attempt of restoring the historic centre and the new attention on the (architectural) 'German cultural heritage'?

These critical points lead then to look at the material and symbolical traces of the different pasts 'survived' respectively in the urban spaces and in the 'spirit' (*Geist*) of East German cities after the Second World War and the German division. On the other hand, the symbolic traces are objectified in the urban space and give a meaning (or more meanings) to the material traces. In other words, the symbolic traces live through memory narrations and practices: if they are sometimes buried

---

1 Die 16 Grundsätze des Städtebaus, *Ministerialblatt der DDR* (25), 16 September 1950.

by the official tradition, the 'cultural memory' of a collectivity is always a virtual store, where shelved traces are always at disposal and can be re-acted in new cultural texts (for example, Assmann 1999). Here the 'rests' of the past not only crop up again in the surface but obtain a new meaning in relation to the new social context. To sum up, the issue is to understand how the dialectic between the traces that re-emerge in the public space and those that sink into oblivion shapes the identity of a East German city.

In this regard we can finally argue that speaking of East German cities allows us also to highlight the conflict about the meanings and relevance of the East German past for the present society, the difficulties of mutual acknowledgement between East and West Germans, such as the critical question for the German State of constructing a cultural and political shared identity based on a negative national history.[2]

In the first part of the chapter I will illustrate the dominant master narratives about East German cities in the public space, by focusing in particular on their temporal structure constructed on the separation between a 'before' and 'after' the fall of the wall.

In the second part I will pay attention to the tangle of symbolic and material traces of the city of Leipzig. The aim is to show how the city identity does not correspond just to one of its specific characters: neither to its modernist 'spirit' stressed by the urban transformation after the reunification, nor to its symbolic status as the most important city of the 'Peaceful Revolution',[3] nor to a 'typical East German city' in reason of its GDR past. It is rather built through the dialectic between the attempts to give it a stable definition and the polysemy of its cultural memory.

---

2   The main problematic is that in the current and scientific interpretations the German reunification is seen as regarding only East Germany. As a consequence the question of German reunification is formulated as: 'how to construct in the new *Bundesländer* a normality based on the parameters of the Federal Germany'. In this perspective the transition is interpreted as both a process of modernization and of normalization. This means that economically East Germany has to orientate towards the free market and its rhythms (modernization) and politically has to adapt to the federal institutions and to initiate a process of democratization (normalization). However the two processes also have a moral dimension. The widespread thesis of an influence of the German Democratic Republic (GDR) political culture on the mentality of East Germans leads to the conviction that they have to overcome, apart from antidemocratic opinions and attitudes, also 'traditional' customs and habits, considered antithetic to the postmodern orientation of the advanced modern societies (Berentzen 1990; Fritze 1997; Güsten 1990; Hanke 1991; Maaz 1992; Trommsdorf 1994; Winiarski 1991).

3   With 'pacific revolution' it is meant the protests of the GDR-citizens against the government in the last months of the regime.

Urban Imaginaries of East Germany After the Reunification

The urban transformation of East Germany concerns local, regional and federal institutions, private and economic actors, architects, urban planners and various associations that operate in the public sphere. On the whole, the face of East German cities through the construction of postmodern buildings, the renovation of historical centres (neglected by the GDR State), the modernization of infrastructures and environmental policies have improved. Then, the aim is not to criticize the single processes of urban transformation, but to analyze how different urban and memory practices such as 'media narrations' construct and 'crystallize in the space' (Wöhler 2008: 77) specific representations of East German society, by elaborating and giving a meaning to its material and symbolic traces.

The first aspect to highlight is how cities condense and thicken cultural developments (Huyssen 2008: 4). In this sense the urban transformations in different East Germans cities can be considered paradigmatic for reflecting more generally upon the German reunification and the different collective identities produced by (and emerged from) this transition phase. At the same time it is also important to pay attention to the specific identity of the cities. However the dominant master narratives neglect the 'peculiarities' of East German cities that are considered mostly only as 'ex-GDR cities' whose modernization or normalization indicates an integration and identification in the new state and in the new collective identity (and *vice versa*). This perspective stems also, as I underlined above, from an undifferentiated urban image of the GDR society.

The second aspect to pay attention to is the fact that the 'history' of East German cities is often based on the separation between 'before' and 'after' the fall of the wall, often understood as a moral distinction.

On the basis of those considerations I will illustrate five 'urban imaginaries' of East German cities, based on different ways of narrating the GDR past.

We can start by seeing how a postmodern architecture and the renovation of historical building represent a *post-national identity*, based on the acknowledgment of institutions and oriented to Europe and to the future.

Generally the postmodern architecture and the renovation of historical buildings are considered as opposite. However, a post-national identity does not exclude *a priori* what can be defined as 'traditional', for example the cultural 'canons' (Assmann 2007: 120–26). The canonized 'traditions' represent a neutralized past, a past that has been already normalized in the collective imaginary and integrated in the familiar reality. In this respect the question is to understand which collectivity we refer to when we speak of 'collective imagery' and 'familiar reality'. In East Germany the choice of renovating or reconstructing buildings of the 'remote' past has often given rise to polemics. It is the case, for example, of the 'Stadtschloss' and of the 'Garnisonkirche' in Potsdam, both destroyed in Second World War bombings and whose ruins were torn down by the GDR regime. In regard to the 'Stadtschloss' the project is to reconstruct the facade and to build, in its original site, a new building for the Regional Parliament. With regard to the 'Garnisonkirche', the final project of reconstruction, proposed by the evangelic church, supported and approved by the municipal and regional authorities, foresees the replacement of the original Prussian *Adler* (eagle) with the cross of Coventry, symbol of peace. The aim is to represent the church as a symbol of reconciliation, in order to 'close' the wounds of the past. At the same time it will also preserve the memory of antifascist partisans who fought against Nazism.[4]

The route that brought to this solution has been difficult and conflictual. The foundation 'Traditionsgemeinschaft Potsdamer Glockenspiel e.V', whose seat is in Iserlohn in West Germany,[5] initially refused to contribute with the money they had gathered through donations for this purpose, because they would have preferred to reconstruct the church truly and to give it no symbolic function. Moreover they claimed that the Prussian *Adler* had a neutral meaning and found it a defamation to define it as a symbol of war.

Two kinds of objections have arisen from a part of the citizens. The major worry[6] was that of a possible neutralization of the historical meaning of the church as place where Hindenburg handed power to Hitler, despite the symbolic intention of the final project. Second, the cost for the reconstruction of the two buildings could have been employed for renovating other historical and not historical parts of the town. This question is not of minor importance because it reveals a conflict-situation about who is entitled to define the identity of the city and which parts of the city are chosen to represent that identity.

It must be remarked that the institutional choice to reconstruct or to give a symbolic function to the buildings of the Second *Reich* does not aim to root a new German national identity in the Prussian past. As Beyme (1998) observes, the urban policies in this sense have been limited, despite the wide debates arising from single cases. In this respect an emblematic case is the project of the 'Humboldt-forum', an international forum of art, culture and science, that will replace the dismantled 'Palast der Republik' in Berlin. The medial and scientific interest (Varvantaskis 2009; Bianchetti and Berlanda 2009) is mostly turned to the question of eliminating a symbol of the past, the 'Palast der Republik', and of replacing it with a symbol of another past, the 'Berliner Schloss'. The latter residence of the Prussian King since 1701 stood upon the area where the forum will be built until the 1950s, when its ruins (the building has been heavily bombed during the Second World War) were removed by Ulbricht. However, only the facade of the 'Berliner Schloss' will be reconstructed: the Prussian architecture

---

4   Source: www.garnisonkirche-potsdam.org (accessed 10 May 2008).

5   The association was founded by the soldier of the 'Fallschirmjägerbataillon 271' in 1984. In 1991 the association managed to build a memorial 'Anstoss aus Iserlohn' in memory of the 'Garnisonkirche'. In the explanation-board there is no reference to the historical meeting between Hindenburg and Hitler.

6   This point regarded mostly political organizations of extreme left and student groups. The second objection was on the contrary not associable with a specific group.

has then a representative function, while the main building is conceptualized as modern and multi-functional.

Besides, the 'recycling' of a 'Prussian style'[7] depends on the architectonic materials that can be found in the place, even if the case of Berlin as new German capital is emblematic.

For the city of Dresden, for example, the project is to return to its *baroque* and *rococo* traits. Then, also Dresden has its symbol: the 'Frauenkirche'. After the bombing of 13 February 1945, its ruins were used as memorial during the GDR period. On 19 December 1989 Helmuth Kohl, the future 'Chancellor of the reunification', made a speech to the East German population in front of the ruins of the 'Frauenkirche' about a new era for a new Germany. Since 2005 the new reconstructed church is a symbol of reconciliation that allows a new beginning after two negative pasts.[8]

Thus, when it is possible, past and tradition are used as wrappers of a postmodern identity, in order to create an aesthetic compactness. This function cannot be played by the GDR past because it is still a 'living past', with emotional and experiential meanings and ties, which do not allow a politic of reconciliation. Moreover, it is to consider how the hegemonic discourses upon the processes of modernization and normalization define what is 'normal', in relation to the aesthetic canons and to the 'typical German', and what is 'modern',[9] taking as model the 'reconstructed' West German cities. It follows that 'overcoming' the GDR past is possible only through the elimination of its traces, so as to allow an *oubli de recommencement* defined by the inchoative form of the present (Augé 1998).

A further form of overcoming the past is represented by memorials. Through memorials East German cities receive a symbolic function as 'places of memory' of the GDR past.

The first observation concerns the difficulty of building a central memorial to commemorate the GDR past. The principal obstacle lies in finding an agreement among different 'entrepreneurs of memory' (Tota 2003) – institutions, historians, civic and political associations, and so on – about which content and which form the memorial should have. Besides, we find the same conflict field in the present panorama of the 'places of memory' situated in different East German cities. As a consequence we have also several ways of narrating the GRD-past. Dealing with

---

7   Beyme (1998) underlines also that the Prussian state did not have a 'defined' cultural identity. In constructing new buildings it recycled old architectonic styles, in particular neoclassicism.

8   A relevant symbol is the cross on the tower (8 metres high), made by the son of one of the English aviators who bombed the city. The cross was financed through the 'Dresden Trust', an English foundation. In this sense the new beginning received also an international recognition.

9   For example, privatizations processes, the building of new quarters, the renovation of the old ones, and the so called 'Westernization' define an imaginary of East Germany mostly as a 'far West' or a peacefully colonized land (Richter 2006; Carlini and Valle 1999; Boym 2001).

the institutional actors a distinction must be made between a supra-regional and a regional level.[10] In the first case the past of the GDR is concluded and constitutes the premise for a new national collective identity. In the second case there are no established normative identities to adhere to, but the principle of 'historical responsibility' as a result of an individual and collective reflection on the past and premise to construct a new citizenship, whose future form is open.

Furthermore, the role played by civic or victim associations is relevant. Some narrations are similar to those of the supra-regional institutions (for example, that of the memorial of 'Normannenstraße' in Berlin) or to those of the regional institutions (for example, that of the memorial 'Lindenstraße 54/55' in Potsdam). Another type of narration gives instead an absolute meaning to the 'stories of witness' (for example, the memorial of 'Hohenschönhausen' in Berlin) with the consequence that other interpretations of the past are refused, even if are sported by institutions or associations that recall the injustices and the suffering caused by the GDR regime.

If in the first two cases we can speak of an 'overcoming' of the past either through an institutional normalization or through the 'historical and reflexive elaboration', in the latter we have a 'persistence' of the past. In this case, the traces of the past, from the antifascist monuments to the toponymy of the cities,[11] do not only permeate the East German territory, but also its society. It follows that the past is considered totalizing and it must be then overcome in every aspect.

Finally, there are at least two further narrations where East German cities are defined by the GDR past.

The first narration is typical in media discourse. East German cities are here negatively portrayed as outdated and still fixed in their past, as demonstrated by the holes of the bullets of the Second World War in the buildings, by the 'apathy' of the province or by the people who continue to live in the phantasmagoric *Plattenbauten*.[12] In this sense the places are alienated from the temporal flow, and so excluded from the present and the future. Moreover, the overlap of the spatial and of the social dimensions brings to look at them as '*Gegenorte*', separated places, not much physically as culturally, that are considered as 'inadequate' and 'defective' (Hafner 2006).

---

10   For the supra-regional level we can consider the 'Haus der Geschichte' in Bonn, the 'Zeithistorisches Forum' in Leipzig, the 'Deutsches Historisches Museum' in Berlin, and the *Dokumentation und Informationszentren* (Documentation and information centres) instituted in different East German cities and which deal specifically with the theme 'Stasi' (shortened form of the Ministry for State Security); among the regional institutions we can quote the 'Stiftung Sächsische Gedenkstätte' and the 'Stiftung Brandenburgische Gedenkstätten'.

11   In an article published in the *Spiegel* on 3 October 2006, the director of the Memorial 'Hohenschönausen' included among the street-name that remember the 'GDR-communist past' those in memory of Rosa Luxemburg and Karl Liebknecht, the 'Straße der Freundschaft' (the street of friendship) and the 'Straße der Einigkeit' (the street of unity).

12   Prefabricated buildings.

The second narration is produced by marketing practices. East Germany is represented as an exotic place, by constructing of the 'typical *ost* (east)'. Also in this case we have a temporal subtraction as the 'typical east' is considered equivalent to the 'typical GDR'. Moreover, we have as well an experiential subtraction. By reducing the GDR past to a trade mark or a curiosity, *Ost-shops* or locals that aim to reproduce the 'typical East-GDR milieu'[13] offer experiences that are to consume at the moment and that are no constitutive for own identity.

In conclusion, even if the five narrations here presented produce different urban imaginaries of East German cities, they are based on the idea that it is possible to distinguish what belongs to the past, that means the GDR past, from what belongs to the present.

In the supra-regional institutional discourse the GDR past is considered concluded and it is not relevant for the construction of a postmodern landscape and identity in East Germany, that has to conform with the national standards.

In the discourses of some regional institutions or entrepreneurs of memory the GDR past is historically elaborated through stories of life which refer to experience of sufferance or injustice temporally concluded and spatially circumscribed to the commemoration place. It follows that the places of memory that cover a symbolic function for the present society are separated by the urban context, that represent only an abstract and symbolical referent for the construction of a new German historical consciousness.

The master narrative of 'a past that not passes' by defining an anomaly situation for the present creates also a spatial separation between the 'place of memory' and the 'external reality'. In this case, however, 'the urban context' assumes a negative characterization as still 'colonized' by the GDR ideology.

In media narrations, East German cities, in particular the provincial areas of East Germany, that are often considered as physically, culturally and morally imprinted by the 'GDR past', are seen as 'other' in respect of the Western society, that represents the 'norm'. This dichotomy between East and West implies also that the urban imaginary of East Germany is crystallized in common places.

In the last example, the 'typical East' or the 'typical GDR' characterizes some 'urban islands', from which it is possible to enter and go out, without the need of changing one's identity. The overlapping of past and present is here not the result of a persistence of the past in the present. It is instead the product of a sense of indifference in distinguishing them temporally.

To sum up, these urban imaginaries do not consider East German cities for their tangle of stories. The past is here objectified and de-individualized, which can be considered neutral or transformed in a symbol, an image that 'represents something else'. As a consequence we have a homogeneous representation of the GDR society such as of the East German society. Finally, with regard to the East

---

13 For example, the 'Café Gorki', the 'Ostel' or the 'Stasi-Kneipe' in Berlin. The latter two also trivialize some undemocratic aspects of the GDR-past.

German cities, this representation leads also to neglect of their peculiar identity, defined by the weave of different pasts.

Leipzig and its Memories

For the analysis of the city of Leipzig, of its stories and memories, I shall start by looking at the transition from the GDR regime to the FRG state not as a 'break' but as a narration of interrupted or continuous threads between past and present interlaced in the same plot. That allows one to consider the urban space as a 'narrative space' (Sennett 1992), a 'temporalized' space (Ricoeur 2008) formed by stories that overlap with each other. Then, the identity of a city is defined by the way these stories are woven in the time and with the places (Cellamare 2008). Besides, that makes it possible to focus on the social actors as *narrators*. That means to pay attention to their memories and everyday practices, to the different way of living, appropriating, using the spaces (Ricoeur 2008) and of relating oneself with the stories of the place. In this sense the city is not simply a store of stories or memories. Rather it is a 'palimpsest' for different memories and experiences (Huyssen 2003: 101) produced by the negotiation or the conflict among different ways to narrate, to practice and to give meaning to the places. Moreover these negotiations or conflicts are defined by a macro political, economical and socio-cultural frame (Amin and Thrift 2002). To sum up, from this perspective narrations are communication processes that depend on the context where they take place. This context eventually influences the rhythm and the temporality of the place and defines the possibility for a narration to mark materially and symbolically the urban landscape.

The analysis that I shall propose does not claim to be exhaustive. By illustrating some emblematic cases the aim is rather to highlight the complex relationship between the present and the different pasts, traditions and cultural heritages in the city of Leipzig, in order to consider it not only as an urban project, a place of memory or an 'East German city'.

I shall begin by showing the two main museums that tell the past of the GDR.

The 'Zeithistorisches Forum', which depends from the 'Haus der Geschichte', is an institutional museum. Here the history of the GDR is reconstructed by focusing on the protests against the regime in the course of the time, so to form a continuous process, which culminates in the peaceful revolution and ends with the reunification. This latter had negative consequences, as the high unemployment rate shows,[14] however the route adopted is presented as the only possibility. It is then a question of looking forward and adapting oneself to the new rhythms.

---

14 The museums underlines that also as during the GDR-regime the unemployment was hidden.

The 'Runde Ecke', which has its seat in the old building of the Ministry for State Security (*Stasi*), is directed by the *Bürgerkomitee*, a civic association founded during the peaceful revolution.

In the wide hall of this museum the peaceful revolution is reconstructed chronologically. The citizens are the main actors of the narration, which because of the absence of a closing event has a dynamic and open character. Neither the fall of the wall, nor the reunification are mentioned. The story continues instead with the occupation of the building (4 December 1989), the first special exhibition and its transformation in a permanent exhibition. If the exhibition rooms tell a 'story of the past' that is concluded,[15] in the passage the museum configures a still open and conflict- process of elaborating the GDR past. The conflict about how to interpret the GDR past does not involve the whole citizenship, but defined social groups (and media) of the society. On the contrary, as emerged in an interview with the director of the museum, the citizens of Leipzig would consider the 'Runde Ecke' as an element of their urban identity, not only for its historical and symbolical meaning, but also as background of their everyday experience. 'Procedural memory', which is constructed through habits and which defines the spatial and temporal orientation of individuals in everyday life (Welzer 2005) and symbolic memory, which has a founding and moral meaning for a collectivity, would so converge, legitimating at the same time the place. Instead the 'Zeithistorisches Forum' is not legitimated, because it is not an 'authentic place'. The lack of authenticity would depend on the fact that the exhibition is set in a place 'without past'. The aim of the director of the 'Runde Ecke' is then to underline how the 'Zeithistorisches Forum' cannot constitute an identification point for the city. It is not the 'product' of an urban story but of an exported narration that could take place in every other part of Germany.[16] The distance from the 'federal institutions' is visible also in the exposition. On a board the question mark about the 'Law on the Stasi documents' (StUG: *Stasi Unterlagen Gesetz*) stresses how the elaboration of the 'Stasi' issue cannot be considered concluded with the promulgation of the law. For the museum it is necessary for there to be a continuous dialogue in the society that, at the same time, legitimizes its function.

The activities of the *Bürgerkomitee* are not limited to the 'Runde Ecke', but actually extended to the city. First to be mentioned is the special exhibition on the occasion of the 15 year anniversary of the peaceful revolution. Yellow boards were positioned in front of the symbolic places of the revolution. Apart from a deictic function with the single building, they were interrelated with each other, so as to define both an everyday and a memory routes. In this way they made possible for the 'public' to create an emotional tie with the citizens who participated in the protests and with the city itself.

---

15   The ideological character of the GDR-society and how the *Stasi* was structured and operated.

16   The main seat of the 'Haus der Geschichte' is in Bonn.

A second remarkable activity of the *Bürgerkomitee* is the guided walk that takes place every Saturday afternoon that, starting in front of the 'Nikolaikirche',[17] touches the main places of the peaceful revolution. This is another example of how 'everyday life' and 'memory' can be tangled. Since the walk does not follow a chronological order, the narration has not only a historical character. It is more formed by stories and anecdotes that are interlaced with the physical traces of the places, as those left from the Soviet tanks during the workers protest on 17 June 1953. Then, the narration does not regard only the events of the peaceful revolution or protest acts during the GDR period. It explores and picks up the different stories that the place allows to tell. For example, crossing the historical centre the guide turns the attention to the statue of Goethe. Situated behind the old 'Stock Exchange building' it is oriented toward the 'Auerbachkeller' that, according to the guide, was not only a *topos* of the 'Faust', but also a restaurant regularly frequented by the writer.

Then, the memory of the citizens' protests during 1989 does not have only a symbolic meaning since the narration entangles it with other stories of the city. It follows also that the identity and the urban imagery of Leipzig cannot be reduced to a single event or to a concluded historical period.

In Leipzig we also find an historical monument that connects the city with the history of the Second *Reich* and with the failure of constructing a national memory and identity. The 'Völkerschlachtdenkmal' was built from 1894 to 1913 by the will of the 'Association of German patriots' in memory of the fight, which took place in Leipzig between the Napoleons troops on one side and the Prussian, Austrian, Russian and Swedish troops on the other side. It was the first monument in concrete, about 120,000 tonnes that, together to 2,000 m² of granite, form a 91-metre-high structure. Faded into oblivion in the period between the First and the Second World Wars, it found a new function during the GDR regime: the Russian participations in the struggle against the Napoleonic occupation was a sufficient reason to transform the monument in a symbol of the 'German-Soviet friendship' (Mosse 1975: 106). To sum up, the monumental character of the memorial, the mythological images of the reliefs and the ideal component of the 'liberation struggle' overshadow the differences between the cultural memory of the GDR state and that of the Second *Reich*, erasing in this way 30 years of history.

Behind the monument we find the South cemetery of Leipzig. The central part is occupied by the antifascist memorial, erected from 1980 to 1986. As a poster explains, following a communal ordinance the wall with the name of the 'communist tradition', the 'central monument' and the monument in memory of

---

17   The church is the symbol of the peaceful revolution. Since 1982 took place here the 'Monday Prayers' that in September 1989 paved the way to the 'Monday demonstrations' (*Montagsdemonstrationen*). The demonstrators transformed the streets of Leipzig in a forum of the public sphere more through their presence than through articulated political aims (Jessen 2009: 466).

the 'Kapp-Putsch'[18] have been moved between 1999 and 2000. The aim was to restore the old image of the cemetery in accordance with the project of 1901. Despite the attempt to erase the traces of the GDR period, the central path,[19] the graves of the communist fighters, and the statue of bronze dedicated to the victims of Fascism mark an ineffaceable transformation; the impossibility, also for a sacred place, of ignoring the flow of time. Even though the cemetery creates a bridge with an eternal dimension, it remains a terrain place.

Beside the antifascist memorial, there is also another memorial not marked on the map and difficult to find without the help of an expert employee of the cemetery. The central monument of this memorial is a simple irregular grey granite stone in memory of 'the victims of the dictatorship 1945–1989'. On another stone the victims are grouped in three categories: those who were executed, those who died in prison and those who died in the attempt to escape from East Germany. Two other stones commemorate the victims of the protest on 17 June 1953. Finally, we find also some individual graves of victims of the 'workers' protest', supposedly buried in this part of the cemetery.

Then, the aim of erasing the cultural memory (or part of it) of the GDR state is not to replace it with another memory, but to restore an apparently neutral image, by trying to ignore the irrevocable transformations lead by the time. Even if the cemetery has an antithetic function with respect to the 'Völkerschlachtdenkmal', used to celebrate a heroic memory, they share an a-temporal vocation and they are both sacred places that may house different political memories.

If monuments and public places, by becoming a symbol, can remove the human experiences from the space, the fictional narrations, mediating between the pole of the witness and the pole of the imagination (Jedlowski 2009), turn the attention to the details of the history and give the place back to the time.

In 1984 the East German writer Erich Loest[20] published the novel *Völkerschlachtdenkmal*. The novel is structured along two temporal lines to which correspond a symmetrical spatial division between above and under the ground. The opposition of two spaces and two times define eventually the official and non-official dimensions of history and reality.

If the succession of events and battles constructs an ensemble of interrupted lines, the flow of time is nullified by the repetition and accumulation of skulls, from the struggle of 1813 to the Second World War, that cannot be distinguished from each other. If on one side the State fails to root a 'national story and identity', on the other side there is no witness: what remains of the past are human traces that cannot tell any story and that, without a narration, become undifferentiated. The everyday life passes between the ruins and the bunkers, marked by the desire of forgetting: 'we wanted to erase the memory of the war with the bunkers' (my translation, 180). The search for a shelter (whether the bunker or the crypt of the

---

18 Coup d'etat (*putsch*) attempted by the extreme right during the Weimar Republic.
19 This was still present in the original project.
20 Erich Loest left the GDR in 1979.

monument or a house) as the main aim of the life, eventually prevent to narrate oneself, to emerge as subject and to build a memory different from the official one.

If the 'Völkerschlachtdenkmal' resists time and the political changes, other buildings fall a prey to the new GDR ideology. The old university and the 'Paulinenkirche'[21] are blown up, in order to redesign the city-centre in accordance with the real socialist architecture. The citizens observe their demolition passively. The difficulty of narrating themselves and of considering themselves as subjects translates in the inability to fight for *their* places. Thus they leave the city to its fate. As the narrator comments at the end of the story, in some cities only ruins are left, in some others only the name.

In a later novel of the same author, *Nikolaikirche* (1995) the events are concentrated in the last years of the GDR state. Unlike *Völkerschlachtdenkmal* where the time is reduced to an indistinct cycle of construction and demolition, expansion and misery, celebration and silence, here every paragraph is introduced by a date: the neutrality of the time indication makes possible 'to catch' the flow of time.

Besides, the quick rhythm of the present time is interrupted by flashbacks that refer to a period between the end of the Second World War and the end of the 1960s. The flashbacks correspond to a self-consciousness process: once the episodes of the past are recalled in the present time, they lose their aura of naturalness and the possibility of being confused again in the amalgam of history.

To sum up, near a 'neutral' and not ideological time we have the time of the individual memory: in both cases the subject can appropriate the time again. Moreover, a new relationship with the places and the city is possible. In this respect we can compare the passages in the two novels where the author refers to the 'Paulinerkirche'.

In *Völkerschlachtdenkmal* (238–240), to describe and to comment on the 'Paulinerkirche' episode, the writer uses the metaphor of the spiral that comes back always to the same point. The fact that the individuals are not able to change events, and therefore to act and to become responsible for their own actions, make it possible to history to repeat itself. This repetition has not, however, the same function and temporality of the circle, which can also define a time of habits or of traditions. It expresses a downwards centripetal force that prevents the individuals from emerging, to acknowledge themselves as subjects and to guide their singular and collective destiny. They are dragged down without leaving traces.

---

21   The 'Paulinerkirche' was also meeting place for intellectual alternative groups, which were critical toward the regime, in particular toward a dogmatic interpretation of the Marxism. The new 'Paulinerkirche' will be inaugurated in 2010 after a long and difficult discussion among associations, which promoted the reconstruction of the church as symbol of opposition against the GDR, local institutions, which favoured the reconstruction of the 'Paulinerkirche', and the rector and pro-rectors of the university who contested the rebuilding of the church (Poumet 2009).

Instead, in *Nikolaikirche*, the spirit of the 'Paulinerkirche' is regained and continued, after twenty years, by the young people that meet every Monday in the 'Nikolaikirche'. Even though the people were passive when the authorities blew up the 'Paulinerkirche', its memory was not erased. In this case memory is a communicative and social practice that can change the present reality. It is not fixed in the past, but it moves from it towards the future by recalling the unkept promises and failures of the past (Ricoeur 2004). It follows also that this form of memory allows one to construct a 'dynamical' collective identity which is the product of common experiences based on shared acts[22] and transformed in routines, thus rooted in time and in place.

Then, it is the place itself, described in the novel as non-monumental, marked by the time and included in an urban space, that makes it possible to practice a dynamic memory, allowing it at the same time to be used and understood in non conventional ways.[23]

In 2007 in the Augustusplatz (ex-Marxplatz) the work of demolition of the University built under the GDR period began, in order to construct a more modern university with better infrastructure. By decision of the rector and the students, the bas-relief of Marx has been removed and placed in the campus in Jahnallee. The decision to save the bas-relief from the demolition has been criticized in relevant national newspapers (for example *Der Spiegel* and *Die Bildzeitung*), by parliament members and 'SED-victims'.[24]

Not only Augustusplatz, but the whole city, is an open and contested building place. If on one hand the urban transformation of Leipzig is to connect to the modernization processes started after the reunification, on the other hand Leipzig as liberal and merchant city has always favoured those initiatives that allow it to grow and develop. In 1895 the trade fair was built, which immediately gained a leading position among the German trade fairs; in 1897 a new university was built; in 1895 a new tribunal of the *Reich*; in 1912 the trade fair was enlarged with 40 new buildings and in the same year a new town hall, the highest in Germany, was erected, and in 1915 the train-station that is still one of the largest in Europe was constructed.

The liberal tradition did not prevent the city from becoming a fortress of Social Democracy. From 1860s to the National Socialism era the labour movement built its bastions in Leipzig, such as the *Brauereigarten* Stötteritz, several pubs and the House of Folk (1906), situated between the city-centre and the south-western suburb (Plagwitz) where the workers lived. Moreover, it formed a network of

---

22   The term act is here to be understood in the sense of Arendt 1958.

23   The novel has an epic character but it is not heroic. The plot focuses on the doubts, memories and difficult relationships of the members of a family, divided by the last events in Leipzig during the pacific revolution. What emerges are also different ways to identify themselves with the city, the society and the GDR-state.

24   SED stays for 'Sozialistische Einheitspartei Deutschlands', in English: 'Socialist Unity Party'.

sports, musical, children's and cultural associations, which were recognized and frequented by different social groups. During the GDR regime until 1968, the social democratic workers (like the intellectual, liberal and bourgeoisie milieus[25]) preserved their space of autonomy despite a formal adhesion to the SED and to the brigade activities. For example, the worker of the 'Kirow-Werk', besides forming a counter-public sphere in the factory, gave a 'new' meaning to the collective cultural activities, considering them as 'local', that means belonging to the city, as it was also before the National Socialism period. The events of 1968 and Honecker's political culture oriented to consumer goods led to the abandonment of the public life in favour of closer relationships. The urban politics also contributes to this change. In the residential district no new building was built after the 1930s, and all the public premises were forced to close, while in the new residential districts no public premises were opened. The participation in the 'peaceful revolution' was limited: on 7 October the workers were divided into demonstrators and those that defended the Republic (the *Kampfgruppe*[26] of the factory). However, because of the idea to share the same destiny, the crisis of the factory, the workers who had demonstrated were not punished. With reunification more factories closed down. The workers shifted the focus of their activities from the place of work to the *Gartenverein*,[27] from the claim for work to the claim for better social infrastructures and life conditions (Hofmann 1995).

Today a lot of buildings in Plagwitz, that was the most important industrial area of Leipzig, are empty. The district gives a sensation of abandonment and melancholy together. Above the roof of a restaurant at the crossroads between Karl-Heine-Straße and Gieserstrasse an old aeroplane of the GDR has been placed. Most of the time the restaurant stays closed. In the large dining room we find round tables covered with long white tablecloths, waiter-mannequins, a piano and old vehicles which confer a ghostly atmosphere on the room. Their unwieldy presence

---

25 Until 1948, before the electoral reform, Leipzig had a liberal majority. Moreover the liberal and bourgeoisie groups, such as the evangelic church, preserved their traditional cultural and education institutions. In particular during the Honecker era it was possible for alternative cultural and intellectual groups to create in the city their meeting and identifications spaces. Even the extradition of Biermann, and the more relevant for Leipzig extradition of some components of the rock group 'Renft' did not silence the alternative milieus. On the contrary they intensified their public presence. In autumn 1989 the different civic and political associations and organizations created from the alternative groups found a common goal in the protest against the dictatorship. After the fall of the wall and the election of the *Volkskammer* on 18 March 1990 they took different ways. The alternative milieus, which have preserved a cultural nature, created new youth cultural scenes with pubs, independent cinemas and theatres in the south district of the city (see Rink 1995).

26 Paramilitary organization in the factories.

27 Literally club of gardens. From the beginning German industrialization has been accompanied by the culture of the 'small garden' in the peripheral areas of the cities. In particular in the GDR-period the *Schrebergarten* or *Datsche* functioned as place for developing informal and more spontaneous relationships (Rudolph 2001: 363–379).

makes them objects of a phantasmagoria: illusions produced by an altered fantasy or by a space that lost its temporality, remains of the past in a present without other contents. Besides, the death of the social life of the district does not correspond to the end of the GDR state, but started in the 1970s. The place is only a physical and emotional frame used to recall the end of something else.

Conclusions: Traces and Narrative Space

The comparison among the various 'urban imaginaries', the multiple ways of reading a city and of acting on it and in it through urban and memory practices, highlights how the question about who is legitimated to remember the GDR past goes together with the question about who is legitimated to redefine the context of urban life in the present and for the future.

In East Germany, and the case of Leipzig is in this sense emblematic, we find a fragmentary urban reality crossed by strained lines. To grasp them, it is however necessary to search for the traces of the past and the signs of the present, hidden among the more visible urban and memory markers, that indicate respectively residues of past experiences and the ability to recollect the past in the place (Crinson 2005). These must not be thought of as separated, but as interlaced and also in relation to (and often in opposition to) the dominant urban imaginaries.

Then, the plot of traces and signs constructs a 'narrative space', a space filled with time in the everyday life (Sennett 1992), and it allows a better understanding of the urban landscape because the focus is on its materiality often neutralized by framing the city in cultural, spatial and temporal schemes, that divide dichotomously east from west, inside from outside, a time before from a time after. This perspective stresses then the fictive and constructed character of every separation. That means moreover that boundaries can be always negotiated, crossed and made more complex in respect of their seeming linearity. Moreover, it pays attention to how people experience a place, give it a meaning, relate their identity to it and translate their experience in stories and physical signs that, together with stories and signs of other individuals, construct the plural meaningfulness of the urban place and of the 'urban time' (Tyrer and Crinson 2005: 67). For example, in his novels Loest makes this process visible by personifying monuments and Leipzig itself, in other words by interlacing events that are distant in time. Personification orientates eventually the glance to their temporal relations. To this temporal movement also corresponds a spatial one. The *narrative space* favours then a moving perspective that blocks the freezing of the urban reality in *topoi*. By suggesting 'doubt' and 'incompleteness' it indeed forms a 'tragic space' (Sennett 1992) that denies a teleological understanding of history and urges to tell stories continually.

To sum up, the narrative place takes form from the transgression of temporal, spatial and symbolic boundaries and from the acknowledgment that the urban experiences of the other is constitutive to give meaning to the place. Moreover, the spatial and temporal movements are possible through an act of imagination. This act of imagination does not remove the materiality of a place, it allows it instead to overcome its predefined images. The imagination creates a glow of indeterminacy around the place, a temporal filter made of interrelated stories that makes it possible to decode the cultural codifications of the places 'taken for granted'.

We can say in conclusion that the narrative space, created by exploration practices, does not aim to find a logical and final order to the stories that it picks up, to construct an integral representation of the city, but it remains spatially, temporally and culturally an open (and conflictual) space.

Chapter 8

Transforming Spaces:
Translation as a Practice that Reveals
Changing E-Motional Structures in Space

Daniela Allocca[1]

This chapter presents an attempt to identify which narrative mechanisms are involved in social practices and in the construction of spaces, and in which way they could be able to influence our perception of space and *vice versa*. It begins with the necessity to adopt and/or adapt the reflections born from the literary plane to the sociological and architectural planes and to observe if, and how, writing involves reality, how it carries and produces it.

We have chosen to analyze a quasi-invisible and rarely considered practice (Venuti 1995) and though seemingly un-manifested, one that has a fundamental value and presence in the construction of quotidian spaces, a narrative micro-gesture that you will see constituted as a topological event in the construction of space: translation.

Rushdie's definition: 'We are translated men' (Rushdie 1981: 17) aptly describes the condition of the contemporary man, *tout court*. The practices and spaces of the everyday are constantly composed of translative processes. Consider refugees who upon arrival need linguistic mediators in order to be understood, workers who leave to seek their fortune in a foreign land, the totality of information that circulates on the Internet – all these are only a few examples of cases in which translation acts in manifest modes. For example, the passage of information through the Internet can be understood as a process of translation because that information must be encoded in the language of the web. However, it is possible to identify translative processes even in practices where they are not readily evident. To translate does not simply mean to translate from one language to another or between different semiotic codes. Translation can act, for example, in the encounter between two different cultures, as demonstrated by Bachmann-

1 I heartily thank mathematician and musician Patrik Faurot-Pigeon and literary critic and pantomime Lidia Cangiano who were so kind as to translate this article. I asked them to 'turn' my thoughts, to fold or unfold the text. I'm really grateful for the 'emotion' they put in this work; Faurot-Pigeon also helped me with regard to the topological question. I thank translator and dancer Elisa Ricci too, who helped me with German-English 'twist'; we also discussed the text and she helped me to unleash some knots.

Medick (1997, 2006). Intercultural processes must be understood to comprise the practices of translation. Braidotti (2006), for example, talks of *trans-positions*, the relocation of subjects, knowledge and culture in which the process of *trans-lare* invests subjectivity with all of its nuances. The transfer from one place to another or from one language to another is a displacement between fields of meaning and planes of significance in a process that must be understood in its dynamism, in its evolution, and never as a point of arrival.

Topology, introduced by the French mathematician Jules-Henri Poincaré with the 1895 publication of his paper *Analysis Situs* (*Analysis of Position*), is a branch of mathematics that deals with the analysis of characteristics that remain unchanged by transformational processes of form, considering the objects as bodies able to transform continuously in their dynamic and process meanings. The investigation of topological facets in the study of the relationship between writing/representation of space and translation permits, therefore, the analysis of the dynamic process of the transformation of spaces operated by the translative process. Taking into consideration the importance and variety of everyday processes of translation, we ask ourselves if, and in which way, the practice of translation is inherent within the perception and production of space. In order to investigate the possible relation between space and translation we will take into consideration the transnational literature in German language.

Mutterzunge and Remote Motherlands

By German transnational literature we mean the works of authors who, though it is not their native language, choose German as an artistic language, translating themselves. We choose to speak of transnational literature rather than utilizing the obsolete terms *Migrationsliteratur* and *Ausländerliteratur* initially adopted by critics and contested by authors who do not want to be labelled as immigrants or foreigners. The idea of a transnational literature allows us to underline the dynamism of contemporary cultural and literary phenomena (Wierlach and Bogner 2003; Ottmar 2005).

Since 1985, the Robert Bosch Foundation has instituted a prize dedicated specifically to authors writing in the German language whose native language is not German, the *Adalbert von Chasmisso Preis*.[2] The prize has become an important arena to identify new talents of German literature, many of which are also recognized in competitions in which there is no pre-imposed limitation regarding the linguistic 'maternity' of the authors. In particular, we are obliged to point out Emine Sevgi Özdamar 1999 winner of the Chamisso Prize, a Turkish-German writer who lives and works in Berlin and the first author in German as a non-native language to receive the prestigious Ingeborg Bachman Prize in 1991.

---

2   Cfr. http://www.bosch-stiftung.de/content/language1/html/4595.asp (30 September 2009).

Thanks to these writings, it is possible to identify the ways in which translation influences the writing and reading of urban space. We have chosen to focus on the city of Berlin as a highly representative contemporary urban space.

To translate oneself demands a capacity to adapt, a readiness to renounce the possibility of expressing the same thing and an acceptance of the transformation that the displacement, transference and transposition of translation entail. For this reason, the space of translation is open to the other, ready to receive the foreign. In fact, Antoine Berman chose to call his study on translation *La Traduction et la Lettre, ou l'Auberge du lontain/The Inn of the Remote* (1999),[3] using the inn to symbolize translative space. The inn is a structure at once foreign and intimate; it hosts the other but must be ready to make us feel at home for a single night. In the note to the Italian translation of Berman, Gino Giometti (2003), translator and curator, asserts that the second part of the title is the translation of an expression concealed in the song *Lanquan li jorn son lonc en may* by troubadour Jaufré Rudel and in the original Occitan is sung: *L'alberc de lonh*. The song demonstrates the essence of being remote and proximate at the same time. Translation should sustain the threshold between familiar and foreign, interior and exterior, as the translated text must remain in this mode – between – to maintain a distance that is also familiar. The authors who *choose* to write in a foreign language (Saalfeld 1999) move themselves into the space of transition between their native language and a foreign one, thus remaining always in a journey:

> A Japanese proverb says: Only the journey is beautiful – not the arrival. Perhaps one loves a foreign language exactly as one loves a journey. One makes many errors on the voyage, but struggles with the language, rolls the words left and right, works with it, discovers oneself.[4] (Özdamar 2001: 131)

'Only the journey is beautiful – not the arrival' wrote Özdamar. To write in a foreign language is a journey, full of the taste of discovery. It forces one to work and struggle with the language; one can never arrive, but remains always in transit. The writers who choose to write in a foreign language demonstrate the obsolescence of the conception of the native language as the creative centre of literature. The native language can be seen, rather, as the bulb language, as pointed out by Deleuze and Guattari in their introduction to *Mille Plateaux/A Thousand Plateaus* (1980: 14), a language able to develop ramifications that are more productive and long-lasting

---

3   For the English translation of this title see also the article: Bereziartu, X.M., Tranlation, The Inn of The Remote, in Zehar [Online], 100–103, available at: http://www.arteleku.net/zehar/wp-content/uploads/2008/08/mendiguren_en.pdf (accessed 15 February 2010).

4   'Ein japanisches Sprichwort sagt: Nur die Reise ist schön – nicht das Ankommen. Vielleicht liebt man an einer fremden Sprache genau diese Reise. Man macht auf der Reise viele Fehler, aber man kämpft mit der Sprache, man dreht die Wörter nach links und rechts, man arbeitet mit ihr, man entdeckt sie', Özdamar 2001: 131 (my translation).

than the bulb itself. A language rhizome, in this case German, is the language of transnational writers that deterritorializes the national language.

The writer Tawada Yōko[5] asserts that she does not care for people who show off their knowledge by speaking rapidly in their native language, almost as though they were dominated by that language and ready to say only what the language offers them in the moment. To speak a foreign language engages the subject in research, reflection, choice. One has no choice of native language, while one chooses the foreign language (Tawada 2002: 111).

In principle, translation implies an interpretive transition. Henri Meschonnic underlines in his *Poétique du traduire* (1999) that 'to translate' comes from the Greek verb *hermeneuein/understand* and that the Romans developed auxiliary verbs such as *vertere, convertere, transvertere, imitari, reddere* and *traslatare*, evidently because they were the first to have the need to translate others and themselves in order to arrive in contact with other cultures (Meschonnic 1999: 37). The narrative spaces in transnational writing are affected by this form of interpretation implicit in translation, and are therefore *interpretive, reversing, converting, subversive, imitative, restorative* and *translative* spaces, or as Emine Svegi Özdamar describes, turning spaces, because they are described by the tongue twisted in its own mouth (that is, the spaces):

> In meiner Sprache heißt Zunge: Sprache.

> [In my language, "tongue" means "language".]

> *Zunge hat keine Knochen, wohin man sie dreht, dreht sie sich dorthin.*

> [A tongue has no bones: twist it in any direction and it will turn that way.]

> *Ich saß mit meiner gedrehten Zunge in dieser Stadt Berlin.*

> [I sat with my twisted tongue in this city.] (Özdamar 1990: 9)

The writer Emine Sevgi Özdamar first arrived in Berlin in 1965 where she worked as a *Gastarbeiterin* (guest worker) for two years before returning to Turkey. She studied theatre and cinema in Istanbul, and upon returning to Berlin in 1976 succeeded in making her way working with theatre director Benno Besson. Her career in writing, however, was inaugurated by her compilation of stories, *Mutterzunge*, in which she produced works nourished by her experiences of migration and in which translation acts as a creative and dynamic force that allows

---

5   The Japanese writer Tawada Yōko, born in 1960 in Tokyo where she studied Russian literature, living since 1982 in Hamburg, Germany, where she immersed herself in the study of German literature and musicology, and since 2006 in Berlin, http://www. tawada.de (accessed 30 January 2010).

the continuous traversal of the threshold between the lived and imagined. The title of her first novel following this compilation of stories, *Das Leben ist eine Karawanserei hat zwei Türen aus einer kam ich rein aus der anderen ging ich raus/ Life is a caravanserai* (1992), demonstrates through this traversal the example of the lived space, at least as it is conceived by the author. The clarification that her language is a tongue without bones is an attempt to indicate mobility, a readiness to move between spaces.

In this story, the narrator moves through the city of Berlin looking for the *Mutterzunge*. It is the language rhizome that has lost the traces of its root. 'Wenn ich nur wüßte, wann ich meine Mutterzunge verloren habe' (Özdamar 1990: 9).

The narrator does not know when she has lost her tongue. The same interrogative formula is found repeated many times throughout the text: 'Wenn ich nur wüsste, in welchem Moment ich meine Mutterzunge verloren habe' (Özdamar 1990: 11). Perhaps she had lost her tongue before arriving in Germany. In the search for the *Mutterzunge*, the author discovers a 'trauma' in the history of the Turkish language caused by the 1923 reforms of Kemal Mustafa (Atatürk) that imposed the passage from the Arabic alphabet to the Latin alphabet and the cleansing of Arabic and Persian traces from the Turkish language:

> I screamed out poems on the anniversaries of Atatürk's death and wept, but he should not have forbidden the Arabic writing. This ban, it's though half of my head had been cut off. All the names in my family are Arabic: Fatma, Mustafa, Ali, Samra. Thank God, I still belong to a generation those grew up with a good many Arabic words. I looked for Arabic words, that are still in the Turkish language. (Özdamar 1994: 33–34)[6]

In effect, the trauma of separation appears in the first page of the story when the writer remembers the words of her mother, who notes that after the journey in Germany it were as though she had left half of her hair behind. This fractured dimension moves itself into her speech, a fragmented mode of speaking in which the narrator jumps from one point to another, thinking to have spoken a sentence that makes sense while she actually presents in the construction of the sentence a discontinuous dimension created by the alteration of movement: 'My mother said to me, "You know what? You just keep on talking, you think you're saying everything, but suddenly you jump over unspoken words, and you just keep

---

6 'Ich habe zu Atatürk-Todestagen schreiend Gedichte gelesen und geweint, aber er hätte die arabische Schrift nicht verbieten müssen. Dieses Verbot ist so, wie wenn die Hälfte von meinem Kopf abgeschnitten ist. Alle Namen von meiner Familie sind arabisch: Fatma, Mustafa, Ali, Samra. Gottseidank ich gehöre noch zu einer Generation, die mit vielen arabischen Wörtern aufgewachsen ist. Ich suchte arabische Wörter, die es noch in türkischer Sprache gibt' (Özdamar 1990: 29 in German text).

talking. And I, I jump with you and breathe easily" Then she said: "You left half your hair back in Alamania'" (Özdamar 1994: 9).[7]
   Where did the narrator lose her mother tongue? In Germany upon immigrating or in Turkey before emigrating? Or perhaps in the transit itself, in this self-transposition from one space to another, from one language to another?

> Once I sat in the Intercity Train Resturant, at a table where a man was already seated, happily reading a book. I thought, what is he reading? It was only the menu. Perhaps I lost my mother tongue in the IC-Resturant. (Özdamar 1990: 13)[8]

The narrator's doubt suggests to us that the loss of her mother tongue is not simply attributable to migration. In Özdamar's final story in the Berlin trilogy (1990, 2002, 2003) *Seltsame Sterne starren zur Erde, Wedding-Pankow 1976/77* (2003), you find a more mature narrator who remembers with more clarity and who decidedly reconnects the loss of her language to the political regime and the impossibility of expressing herself freely (Seyhan 1996; Venkant 2007). The search for the *Mutterzunge* brings her to (re)discover in Turkish the influences borrowed from Arabic and Persian, therefore hybrid of the two, a shared rhizomic essence of the same mother language. The road to the *Mutterzunge* is therefore constellated by trauma and separation, and thus she asks if it is possible to lose her mother tongue in her own land. The German language becomes an instrument of self-expression, but at the same time it is a poetic choice. The space between two languages, the inn both familiar and foreign, becomes a space of creation rather than of rebirth. The encounter with a foreign language brings the narrator to discover the double-meaning of the Turkish word *dil*, which means both language and tongue, an organ in as much as it is a language, and to compare it to the German word *Zunge* in the composite word 'Mutter*zunge*', which describes the language strictly as an organ. In the translation of the Turkish word *anadili*, the author decides to transform the German word in order to communicate the double sense of the Turkish word. In this transition between the two languages, in the moment in which she chooses to translate *anadili* as 'Mutter*zunge*' and not as 'Mutter*sprache*', she opens a space between the two languages that will be seen to be the exact space that offers the subject the possibility of recreating herself.
   The process of overcoming trauma is in fact a process of translating trauma (Ingram 2001). In the translation of Turkish to German, the lack of language reveals

---

7 'Meine Mutter sagte mir: "Weißt du, du sprichst so, du denkst, dass du alles erzählst, aber plötzlich springst du über nichtgesagte Wörter, dann erzählst du wieder ruhig, ich springe dir mit, dann atme ich ruhig". Sie sagte dann: "Du hast die Hälfte deiner Haare in Alamania gelassen"' (Özdamar 1990: 9).

8 'Ich saß mal im IC-Zugrestaurant an einem Tisch, an einem anderem saß einen Mann, liest sehr gerne in einem Buch, ich dachte, was liest er? Es war die Speisekarte. Vielleicht habe ich meine Mutterzunge im IC-Restaurant verloren' (Özdamar 1990: 12).

the repression (Freud 1900) and remorse (De Martino 1961). In her self-translation, the narrator discovers that language, the tongue of her mother, is an organ that has no bones, that 'turns/translates itself' and that can go in every direction. In fact: 'The German verb *drehen* is the translation of the Turkish verb *çevirmek* that means *translate* and *turn* to' (Konuk 2001: 137). Therefore, the writer finds in translation the possibility of 'recovering' *her* mother tongue by recreating it as her *Mutterzunge*. It is in this language, which is neither Turkish nor German but a language which remains on the threshold between the two, a language which does not create the *medium* but is the *medium*, the *trans-*, *l'Auberge du lontain*, that she writes her award-winning work, and it is this language-threshold that represents urban spaces.

When the narrator of Özdamar's novels looks and describes the city, she *translates* parts of the city. In the novel *Die Brücke von goldenen Horn/The Bridge of the Golden Horn* (2002), one finds a narrator that arrives in Berlin and works as a *Gastarbeitern* at Telefunken. The *Gastarbeiterinnen* live in the *Woynam* (the German word *Wohnheim/residential accomodation, hostel* transcribed by the author using the Turkish orthography) and their life revolves principally between the factory and the *Woynam*. Each day on their way to work they pass the *Anhalter Bahnhof*, a train station destroyed during the 1945 bombardment of Berlin, and today one of the few spaces still not completely recuperated or restored. Through a Turkish translation this station becomes in the eyes of Özdamar the *beleidigte Bahnhof*, or the *offended station*:

> From the right bus window I saw the newspaper, from the left bus window I saw the station Anhalter Bahnhof, standing as the Hebbel Theatre in front of our Woynam. We called it the broken station. The Turkish word for "broken" means also offended. So the name of the station was also "the offended station". (Özdamar 2002: 25)[9]

The city is written and translated; through a kind of *translating eye* which watches and describes the urban space. A quasi-surreal game with this urban space can be in Tawada Yōko's works too (Brandt 2006a). Tawada often transfers the visual relation of reading Japanese ideograms to the Latin alphabet, this placing herself in the category of 'translators with eyes' (Tawada 1988: 31; Sgambati 2007). Tawada plays at deconstructing and reconstructing the city. In this way you see here the perceptive modality of spaces, but above all that the alphabet allows the creation of other spaces (Foucault 1980).

---

9 'Aus dem rechten Busfenster sah ich die Zeitung, aus dem linken Busfenster sah ich den Anhalter Bahnhof, der wie das Hebbeltheater gegenüber unserem Woynam stand. Wir nannten ihn den zerbrochenen Bahnhof. Das türkische Wort für "zerbrochen" bedeutete gleichzeitig auch beleidigt. So hieß er auch "der beleidigte Bahnhof"' (Özdamar 2002: 25).

By Warszawa Express I arrived in Berlin Zoological Garden and discovered in "Berlin" a B, in "Zoological" a C and in the "Garden" an A. The Alphabet always reminded me of the Middle East. Vilém Flusser wrote: "The A still shows the horns of the syriac Taurus, the B still shows the domes of the Semitic house, the C (G) still shows the camel's hump in the Near Eastern desert." You write the alphabet in order to evoke the desert in the language. The desert is the reason, the mind of a mathematician. He rejects any moist corruption and puts countless but countable grains of sand into clear light. In Berlin, I looked at the dome of the Semitic house, in the zoo I saw the hump of a camel, and in the garden the horns of *his* syriac Taurus. (Tawada 2007: 12)[10]

Thanks to this alphabetic game the author renders Berlin as a zoo. She asserts: 'One writes the alphabet in order to re-evoke the desert in language'. The desert indicates the space of transformation, the space of translation, the *atopy* in language that permits the birth of other spaces. The desert is also the space evoked in *El Aleph* by Borges (1949), topological space par excellence (Borsò 2007), in which one renders possible the coexistence of space and time, space in which enters in action creative possibilities of construction and deconstruction.[11]

In the example given by Tawada's writing, one observes clearly the operative topological structure. Topology deals with the study of space, and in particular the similarities between spaces, and the identification of 'maps' that show two spaces to be congruous. In this case the author traces a map, a code, from which she is able to recognize in the city of Berlin alphabetic elements observed by Flusser and recalled by Tawada in her own words:

> In Berlin, I looked at the dome of the Semitic house, in the zoo I saw the hump of
> a camel, and in the garden the horns of *his* syriac Taurus. (Tawada 2007: 12)

From a mathematical perspective we have two topological spaces – the one representing Berlin, call it T, and the one representing Flusser's text, call it V. We can reconstruct Tawada's map, a literary one, in topological terms by defining a map F between the two spaces which relates each element in T with and element

---

10   'Mit dem Warszawa-Express kam ich in Berlin Zoologhischer Garten an und entdeckte in "Berlin" ein B, im "Zoologischen" ein C und im "Garten" ein A. Das Alphabet erinnerte mich immer an der Nahen Osten. Vilém Flusser schrieb: "Das A zeigt noch immer die Hörner der syriakischen Stiers, das B noch immer die Kuppeln des semitischen Hauses, das C (G) noch immer den Buckel des Kamels in der vorderasiatischen Wüste". Man schreibt das Alphabet, um die Wüste in der Sprache wachzurufen. Die Wüste ist die Vernunft, der Geist eines Mathematikers. Er lehnt jede feuchte Korruption ab und setzt unzählige dennoch zählbare Sandkörner ins klare Licht. Im Berlin blickte ich auf die Kuppel des semitischen Hauses, im Zoo sah ich den Buckel eines Kamels und in dem Garten die Hörner seiner syriakischen Stiers' (Tawada 2008: 12).

11   See also Manning 2007.

in V, thereby mapping the one onto the other despite their being geometrically unequal. Thus we have:

T = {'Berlin' : 'Zoologhischen' : 'Garden'}
V = {'the domes of the Semitic house' : 'the camel's hump'
    : 'the Syriac Taurus'}

and F: T→V where F maps:

'Berlin'	→	'the domesof the Semitic house'
'Zoologhischern'	→	'the camel's hump'
'Garten'	→	'the Syriac Taurus'.

This topological mechanism can be assimilated to the literary mechanism of Tawada's writing which narrates space through translation. Through the use of the alphabet as a multidimensional visual piano, the spaces produced in these writings are modified in their topological structure. *Translation* brings to creation *distorted* spaces, surfaces of intersection between figure and space otherwise foreign to each other in which opposing logics cross each other and gives life to the new and animate spaces.

Both writers have the ability to narrate space through translation, a characteristic that can be assimilated to the topological mechanism that gives a map from space T to space V so that same points of T can be found in V despite their being geometrically unequal:

> In Berlin, I looked at the dome of the Semitic house, in the zoo I saw the hump of a camel, and in the garden the horns of *his* syriac Taurus. (Tawada 2007: 12)

The author, in other words, transforms the spaces of the city into an alphabet, and thanks to this alphabet-code-map, she transforms the city into a zoo. This mode of representation of spaces is made possible exactly by a 'translation with eyes' a translation that unties itself as much from audible links of significance as from semantic links of significance. The translating eye undoes reality, tripping up significance and opening up the possibility of the creation of new conceptions of space. We are confronted with a process that acts on the topological structure of spatial perception, and as Barthes points out, this is what always occurs in the encounter with a foreign language:

> Le rêve: connaître une langue étrangère (étrange) [...]; défaire notre 'réel' sous l'effet d'autre découpage, d'autre syntaxes; découvrir des positions inouïes du sujet dans l'énonciation, déplacer sa topologie. (Barthes 2005 [1970]: 15)[12]

---

12 'The dream : to know a foreign language to unpack our 'truth' under the effect of other zoning, other syntax; to discover unheard positions of the subject in the statement, to move its topology' (my translation).

This possibility of the sudden alteration of space, typical of literature but empowered by foreign linguistics, reveals the potential of translation in the process of production of spaces. The space made of the distance between two languages facilitates topological action, the 'betrayal' of space that generates transposition, the transformation of space. Obviously, we do not mean to assert here that the transformation of spaces is a mechanism implemented solely by translation, but that on the basis of the process of translation there is a potential for the topological modification of spaces and the perception thereof. Consider that to translate is a trans-portation and therefore implemented by modifications in space, and therefore the necessity to translate is a viaticum for these authors towards the transformation of spaces.

Translation opens a space in which to create new meanings and transform spaces, but such a possibility is also utilized in the relationship with other semiotic codes, as is the case in the experiment with music of Tawada Yōko in collaboration with pianist Aki Takase, in which, the writer notes, the conversion into musical code permits the discovery of new meanings of words. 'When I look at their faces, I can see that they listen differently. A new passage has opened up, one that is too often closed when people listen to poetry' (Brandt 2006a). The conversion to another code – the movement, the transfer, the translation – allows a topological transformation, an expansion of the significance of words. Consequently, the same occurs with spaces.

Then our spaces, the spaces where we are living, are formed and perceived through topological ways, one of which is the translation. The topology performs an emerging mental attitude through which people begin perceiving their own spaces and begin building these spaces throughout topological ways.

The presence of topological processes of transformation in narration can be applied to the field of architecture where one recognizes an increase in the use of topology in design (Di Cristina 2004). An example of topological action in architecture is given by the work of Peter Eiseman,[13] who bases his work on the correspondence between language and architecture, and considers architecture as a narrative structure, taking as a point of reference the theories of Noam Chomsky.

Here Günzel (2008) speaks of topological urban space, leaving as a question the effect of the use of topology in architecture in real space. Perhaps the work of Bertrand Westphal (2007) can help us to understand that the separation between conceived spaces and real spaces is fictitious, imposed by an old pattern.

The space of translation is like a topological piano, for example, the desert that Tawada refers to is a surface, or more precisely, a *hypersurface*, to utilize the notion introduced by René Thom in the explanation of catastrophe theory and borrowed from Stephan Perrella (1998). A hypersurface in architecture is elicited by incommensurate relations between form and image:

---

13   See the website: http://www.tschumi.com (accessed 13 February 2010).

The effects of hypersurface are also other than that of either form or image. Information culture is spilling out into the built environment, creating a need for surfaces through which data may traverse (hypersurfaces). Topology in architecture comes about due to the shift from the interest in language theories (Derrida) to matter and substance (Deleuze) in its theoretical discourses.

The hypersurface is the space that renders possible topological action. In architecture it is utilized to create transformations, modifications of form and structure.[14]

The physical movement between spaces creates a *torsion* of space that transfers into the linguistic plane. Meschonnic, in his poetics of translation, speaks about a translation that translates what words do and not the words themselves:

> Ce n'est pas l'hétérogenéité des langues entre elles qui fait problème. C'est l'enseignement de la transparence et de l'effacement. L'idée régnante continue, malgré tout ce qui est dit et affiché, de faire comme si la diversité des langues était un mal, à effacer. Ce n'est donc pas l'hétérogeneité des langues qui fait la différence entre les traductions, mais la poétique ou l'absence de poétique. Où cette hétérogeneité est un des moyens du texte. (Meschonnic 1999: 127)[15]

In that case translation must be active, must act and translate the action of words: 'faire que la traduction aussi soit porteuse et non portée' (Meschonnic 1999: 131). By looking at translation as an active and supporting force in the writings of Özdamar and Tawada, one can affirm the existence of poetry in the translating gaze. The *translating eye* acts by means of torsion and asserts itself as the interpreter of reality. Translation is therefore transformation, transposition of spaces, transposition in space. According to the percepts of geocriticism narrated space drifts into reality. These narrated spaces are also twisted spaces exemplifying where the urban space undergoes a twist.

The translated space is a space transformed, or if we like, 'distorted'. The space of translation creates a sort of *atopia* that renders possible a topological transformation of the space.

The action of translation, of the rhizome language, renders possible superposition where it would seem impossible, thereby revealing the creative value of the translative act. In this way, these writings create spaces in continuous

---

14 Hypersurface can be assimilated with the desert that one finds in writing, and the presence of the desert as a topological space can be found in films such as *Zabriskie Point* by Michelangelo Antonioni (1970), or a rereading of 'the Zone' in *Stalker* by Andreij Tarkowskij (1979).

15 'It is not the heterogeneity between tongues to make a problem. It is teaching transparency of the blotting out. The main idea continues, after all that is said and posted, to act as the diversity of tongues is evil, to erase. Than it is no the heterogenity of tongues which makes difference between translations, but the poetical or the absence of any poetic where this heterogeneity is one of the means of the text'.

transformation because they are always subjected to the performative element of *translation*; they move the spaces, turning them. Thanks to observations stemming from the use of topology in architecture one can understand the use of translation as a transformative agent which contributes concretely to the animation of spaces and their transformation, creating relations and eliciting emotional states that otherwise would remain unexpressed.

Dis*torsions*

In an essay on the topology of torsion Berressem (1996) identifies the chiasmus as the figure of speech lent by poetics to architecture. Chiasmus renders visible the interior of the exterior and the exterior of the interior.

Interior of the exterior

χ

Exterior of the interior

The mechanism through which one links the exterior with the interior is the same utilized by Cornelius M. Escher in his numerous lithographs such as *Relativity* (1953) and *Waterfall* (1961) and that Eiseman realizes in his project for the *Max Reinhardt Haus* in Berlin (1990). The chiasmus realizes the continuity of the Möbius strip and that Escher would realize in a series of lithographs, the first of which is *Möbius Strip* 1963.

The mechanism of the chiasmus is the same that acts at the psychological level in the traversal from real space to imaginary space, as is shown by Lacan's scheme in his work *La topique de l'imaginaire/The topic of imaginary* (Lacan 1991: 83–103). In the work, Lacan shows through the experiment *Experience du bouquet renversé/The experience of turned bouquet* how imaginary space, in this case represented by the heterotopic surface of the mirror, presents an unreal image; according to the action of reflection, the bouquet in the mirror is an imaginary bouquet, an illusion created through torsion as it occurs in the optical illusions of Escher. The mirror creates an illusive image, conferring unity to that which is disjoined and creating continuity between external and internal. Hypersurfaces are the parents of the heterotopic space of the Lacanian mirror.

The mirror is the space par *excellence* of the *elsewhere/otherness* because it finds itself in an inaccessible space, where we can never find ourselves with our real bodies, as Foucault outlines in his work on heterotopia (1980). Exactly for these characteristics, the mirror becomes a central element in some of the writings on migration (Weber 2009).

Özdamar, for example, utilizes in her writing the mirror as a mediated and median surface between Turkey and Germany but also between the world of the living and the world of the dead as shown by the story *Der Hof im Spiegel/The courtyard in the mirror* contained in the homonymous collection (Özdamar 2001). In this story the narrator describes what, across three mirrors positioned inside her house, she sees take place in the courtyard and buildings opposite, and in so doing the courtyard enters the mirrors, creating proximity with the other inhabitants that reflects an oriental urban character. There is an analogy that runs between the mirror and translation, the same that exists between the *bouquet renversé* of Lacan and the *gedrehte Zunge* of Özdamar (1990: 9). The language of Özdamar is a reflected language that exists only in a mirror in which we can never exist with our body. Thanks to the use of the mirror, Özdamar's translation transfers itself to the visual plane. The mirror therefore creates here a hypersurface on which to realize topological transformations. This type of mechanism of translation is visible, for example, in the title of the story *Karagöz in Alamania, Schwarzauge in Deutschland. Karagöz in Alamania, Blackeye in Germany* in the compilation *Der Hof im Spiegel/The courtyard in the mirror* where Karagöz means in Turkish exactly *Schwarzauge/Blackeye* and *Alamania* is the Turkish name for Germany.

Karagöz in Alamania → Mirror → Schwarzauge in Deutschland

The author translates by turning the words, and she turns them by putting the language in the mirror, realizing through this process the coexistence of the two languages. Thus in the moment in which the process of production of spaces utilizes translation, it twists the space, folds the space. Özdamar uses torsion and folding to create a transformation in the space. Topology is, in fact, 'a "geometry of refolded sheets" [...] that allows the switch from two dimensions to three dimensions; through folding the two-dimensional surface is transformed into a three-dimensional surface, catching the space between its folds'. (Di Cristina 2004: 17).

The essay by Gilles Deleuze *Le pli. Leibniz et le Baroque/The Fold: Leibniz and the Baroque* (1988) shows how the Baroque, with its conception of total art, has been useful in founding a primary mode of connection between various arts that trespass on each other. The extension of the baroque fold that passes from painting into sculpture and continues further to realize itself in architecture creates extensive unity between the arts that becomes a response to the illusions of reality:

> Already the world has been seen as a theatre, a dream, an illusion, as Leibniz says, a vestment of Harlequin; the baroque answer consists in not falling into illusions, nor escaping them, but in realizing something in the illusions themselves, in communicating to them a spiritual presence that returns to their folds and their fragments a collective unity. (Deleuze 1980)

The action of these writers who turn spaces is exactly the process of realizing something in illusions themselves, creating spaces of withstand, of creation and rebirth, of openness to the senses, acting on the interior of illusionary spaces. The considerations of Benjamin on baroque characteristics of modernity are found echoed in reflections on postmodernity. The fundamental concept of Benjamin's text *Ursprung des deutschen Trauerspiels/The Origin of German Tragic Drama* (1967), and translated in Italian with the title: *Il drama barocco Tedesco/The German Baroque Drama* (1971), is the correlation between modernity and the baroque hinging on the awareness of transience and ruin at the base of cultural and artistic production of the baroque and modernity. The relation to postmodernity is given not only by considerations on the state of ruin and transience, but also in the perception and production of spaces in which we observe a return of the baroque fold. In postmodernity one observes the disappearance of some opposing binaries such as that between copy and original, true and false, reality and simulation, exterior and interior.[16]

The fold, the torsion, topology, the translation of space, all work exactly on the boundary between the exterior and interior, wherein the Möbius strip, for example, nullifies this distinction. In the movement between exterior and interior, or better in an exterior that becomes internal and *vice versa*, in a latency that is made evident, or in a transparency that is made opaque, the translator's gesture reveals itself.

The space of transition between external and internal is also able to delineate Leibniz's monad, and therefore Deleuze identifies in movement an element that recreates the monad, but no longer in its static form but rather in its dynamic form. *Monadology* transforms itself into *nomadology*. Deleuze takes as an example the story of artist Tony Smith, published in 1966, in which the artists narrates his journey along a highway under construction on the periphery of New York (Careri 2006), to demonstrate that the experience of the journey recreates a sort of monadic space. The dark backdrop of the highway represents the dark backgrounds of baroque art from which the forms of bodies emerge. The fold realizes the continuity of the Möbius strip, creating continuity between the interior and exterior, and such continuity finds itself also in cellular nomads. The voyage creates a form of monadic space; to be travelling is the space of these writers, the space-threshold where internal and external are inverted, the space of nomadology and of topological torsion, the space of the translation of a *language/Sprache* that transforms itself into a *Zunge*/organ without bones, *Mutterzunge* both mobile and nomadic.

In the case of Özdamar her familiarity with 'the state of travel' is not only the result of her personal experience of immigration, but also a reference to the choice of perspective tied to a perception of the world and of herself as a subject in transit; so it is in a train that the first novel, *Das Leben ist ein Karawanserei*, begins and it is the journey that carries all of the creation of a nomadic language (Ghaussy 1999). Tawada Yōko also arrives in Europe by train, to be precise, by the Tran Siberian Railroad, and by being in transit finds a form of stability of identity (Kraenzle 2006). Through the voyage the subject in transit creates a form of monadic-

---

16   Online available at: http://design.iuav.it/~comunicarti/postmoderno.htm.

nomadic space; this space is no longer the topographic space but a topological space in which it is possible to act on the structures of the space themselves, and it is here that the space is turned, undergoes a torsion, is translated, and creates the illusionary structures that are but the answer to the illusions of the world, representing a self-imposed fold that encounters the fluidity of contemporary spaces (Bauman 2002).

Giordana Bruno, in her *Atlas of Emotion*,[17] shows how the images of cinema create a sort of emotional atlas in which they can move and carry from place to place images which in their own turn are linked to memories of life. What we mean here by emotion is the capacity to move space, to turn spaces by translating them. 'I studied' – says Gehry – 'many folds and have started to see them as substitutes for decoration, as a way to express emotion in a building ...' (Di Cristina 2004: 99).

Thus the translating eye reveals its transformative capacity using urban spaces as hypersurfaces and allowing the experience of transit to act on spaces by emotionalizing them. For this reason it is more correct to talk not of emotional topography but rather of emotional topology, choreographies of space.

The desert in language invoked by Tawada is the hypersurface on which translation acts. The practice of translation, which in this way has to do with the passage from striated space to smooth space as described by Deleuze and Guattari in *Mille plateaux* (1980), is the space created by the nomadic subject. The space of these literatures, then, cannot be considered as the space 'between' but as the movement between spaces; it is the dynamic process that they put in action, the torsion that realizes itself in space, the translation of space, that implies their subversion (*transvertere*) and animation.

Bressem puts these spatial modifications in the city in relation to the bellicose events that have created a perception of urban space as a hypersurface on which a totalized fantasy sometimes acts. In this he rediscovers the baroque foundation of what he calls *Architexturen*. We believe that in this it is possible to find a link with those transnational writings that often are the result not only of migration but also of exile; therefore writing creates a means of narration and translation for the trauma of war, and further, that of separation and displacement. Marica Bodrožić, born in 1973 in Zadvarije, former Yugoslavia, (today Croatian territory), and who moved to Germany in 1983 where her parents worked as *Gastarbeiter*, declares

---

17 'It is not surprising to conclude, then, that, the museum of emotion pictures, as it repictures fragments of an intimate geography, ferries across a reversible "transport". Emotion, as we have show, reveals itself to be a matter of voyage: a moving form of epistemological passion and historic force. Its Latin root suggests the route this motion will take: a moving out, a migration, a transference from place to place. The physical effect of the pull of emotion is inscribed in the very experience of spatial transfer and dislocation and, in such a way, underwrites the fabrication of cultural travel. It is here, in this very *emotion*, that the moving image was fashioned, with its own psychogeographic version of the transition of movere' (Bruno 2002: 262).

that, thanks to the German language, she began to perceive space in a different way. German showed her the border between the speakable and unspeakable.

> In the German language I began to understand borders and to believe in life. [...] Even if the memory can never be thought as a line in space, it is something similar to that, with a transcendental continuity. Akin with the breath, she is, and with the presence of images. (Bodrožić 2007: 18)[18]

To be always in movement is, for Bodrožić, to discover her own country that, as for many exiles, is based on language more than territory (Bodrožić 2007: 94). The practice of translation shows practically her relation to a psychoanalysis whose method is founded on the possibility of translating blocks, fears, and traumas into words. For Özdamar, as for other writers, the choice of a foreign language as the language for their writing is a poetic choice, linked, however, also to the impossibility of expressing themselves in their own mother tongue. In the story *Mutterzunge*, the first of the collection, the narrator finds herself in Berlin and in this city begins the reemergence, as in a dream, of sentences from 'the tongue of her mother' or *Muttersätze*,[19] that she perceives, however, as sentences from a foreign language.[20] The ghostly modality of the *Muttersätze* recalls the unconscious process of the reemergence of repressed matter identified by Sigmund Freud. The *Mutterzunge* itself can be considered as an image of this 'repressed matter', inasmuch as the writer asserts to mean with this noun the 'tongue in the mouth of her mother', therefore the language of her corporeal matter.

Translation can be considered as a practice that helps to unfold the folded and refold the unfolded, a dynamic practice that helps to move space, and to transfer, as the fold in architecture, emotions in space. Translation is a transformative action that does not modify the meaning that generates it, inasmuch as translation is a practice that transforms by transporting texts, regenerating them. The dynamism situated in the practice of translation renders (fr)agile existence and in that way

---

18 'In der deutsche Sprache habe ich begonnen, diese Grenzen zu verstehen und an das Leben zu glauben. [...] Selbst wenn diese Erinnerung nie als eine Linie im Raum gedacht werden kann, ist sie doch etwas ähnliches und einer überirdischen Kontinuität zuzuschreiben. Verwandt mit dem Atem ist sie, und mit der Anwesenheit der Bilder' (Bodrožić 2007).

19 'Ich erinnere mich an ein anderes Wort in meiner Mutterzunge, es war im Traum. [...] Noch ein Wort in meiner Mutterzunge kam mal im Traum vorbei', Özdamar 1990: 12. 'I remember another word in my mother tongue. It was in a dream. [...] Another word in my tongue one came to me in a dream', Özdamar 1994 (English translation), 12–13.

20 'Ich erinnere mich jetzt an Muttersätze, die sie in ihrer Mutterzunge gesagt hat, nur dann, wenn ich ihre Stimme mir vorstelle, die Sätze selbst kamen in meine Ohren wie eine von mir gut gelernte Fremdsprache', Özdamar 1990: 9. 'I can remember sentences now, sentences she said me in her mother tongue, except that when I imagine her voice, the sentences themselves sound in my ears like a foreign language', Özdamar 1994 (English translation), 9.

leads it through the folds of the postmodern baroque; the translation configures itself in that sense as a practice not only useful, but also necessary. In this way translation reenters as one of those processes able to fold space and thus allowing the emotional structures to move the space, generating '"topological events" that are points where change can happen' (De Cristina 2004: 98). Berlin, in this case as an example of the traumatic events of the twentieth century, whether at the architectural level (Eiseman, Libeskind, Kolhaas) or in its narration, presents a baroque configuration of space that, besides delineating itself in an alternation between full and empty, also configures itself in the performative degree of its spaces, allowing itself to translate, transport, recycle; and in so doing also a space of reception of identities ready to transform themselves. To conclude you can assert that there is a kind of translating skills that is the skill to translate the identity crossing the space you're living. The transnational literature shows how the dislocation and living between different languages increase these skills and help the nomadic subject to deterritorialize the space. I consider these skills very important in the 'art of city making' (Landry 2006), because the translation skills are the capacity to change, to trans-form, that is to give our space a different form, and therefore to release the performative capability of our space.

Bibliography

AA.VV. 2007. *D.A.S.T. alle Fonderie Riunite*. Available online at: http://www. comune.modena.it/exfonderie/documenti/presentazioneDAST.pdf (accessed 2009).

Adelson, A.L. 2005. *The Turkish Turn in Contemporary German Literature: Toward a New Critical Grammar of Migration*. Basingstoke: Palgrave Macmillan.

Adey, P. 2008. Airports, mobility and the calculative architecture of affective control. *Geoforum*, 39: 438–451.

Akrich, M. 1992. The de-scription of technical objects, in *Shaping Technology/ Building Society. Studies in Sociotechnical Change* edited by W.E. Bijker and J. Law. Cambridge, MA: The MIT Press, 205–224.

Akrich, M. and Latour, B. 1992. A summary of a convenient vocabulary for the semiotics of human and nonhuman assemblies, in *Shaping Technology, Building Society: Studies in Sociotechnical Change* edited by W.E. Bijker and J. Law. Cambridge, MA: The MIT Press, 259–264.

Allen, J., Cars, G. and Madanipour, A. 2000. *Social Exclusion in European Neighbourhoods. Processes, Experiences and Responses*. Final Report. Bruxelles: European Union.

Alsayyad, N. and Roy, A. 2006. Medieval modernity: On citizenship and urbanism in a global era. *Space and Polity*, 10(1): 1–20.

Amin, A. and Thrift, N. 2002. *Cities: Reimagining the Urban*. Oxford: Polity Press.

Amin, A. and Thrift, N. 2007. Cultural economy and cities. *Progress in Human Geography*, 31(2): 143–161.

Appadurai, A. 1996. *Modernity at Large*. Minneapolis: University of Minnesota Press.

Appadurai, A. 2004. The capacity to aspire: Culture and the terms of recognition, in *Culture and Public Action* edited by R. Vijayendra and M. Walton. Stanford: Stanford University Press.

Arendt, H. 1958. *The Human Condition*. Chicago: Chicago University Press.

Assessorato all'Istruzione, Circoscrizione 2 and Comune di Modena. 1999. *Sacca-Crocetta: quartiere industriale della città tra il 1930 e il 1970*. Modena: Comune di Modena.

Assmann, A. 1999. *Erinnerungsräume: Formen und Wandlungendes kulturellen Gedächtnisses*. München: Beck.

Assmann, A. 2007. *Geschichte im Gedächtnis. Von der individuellen Erfahrung zur öffentlichen Inszenierung*. München: Beck.

Atkinson, R., Buck, N. and Kintrea, K. 2005. Neighbourhoods and poverty: Linking place and social exclusion, in *Changing Cities, Rethinking Competitiveness,*

Cohesion an Governance edited by N. Buck, I. Gordon, A. Harding and I. Turok. Houndsmills and New York: Palgrave.

Augé, M. 1995. *Non-Places: Introduction to an Anthropology of Supermodernity*. London: Verso.

Augé, M. 1998. *Les Formes de l'oubli*. Paris: Pagot.

Bachmann-Medick, D. 1997. *Übersetzung als Repräsentation fremder Kulturen*. Berlin: Schmidt.

Bachmann-Medick, D. 2006. *Cultural Turns. Neuorientierungen in den Kulturwissenschaften*. Reinbek bei Hamburg: Rowohlt.

Bagnasco, A. 2003. *Società fuori squadra. Come cambia l'organizzazione sociale*. Bologna: Il Mulino.

Balducci, A. 2001. Senza quartiere. *Territorio*, 19: 7–95.

Ballard, R., Habib, A. and Valodia, I. (eds) 2006. *Voices of Protest. Social Movements in Post-Apartheid S. Africa*. Scottsville: University of KwaZulu-Natal Press.

Barrientos, A. and Santibañez, C. 2009. Social policy for poverty reduction in lower-income. *Latin America: Lessons and Challenges. Social Policy and Administration*, 43(4): 409–424.

Barry, A. 2001. *Political Machines. Governing a Technological Society*. New York: The Athlone Press.

Barthes, R. [1970] 2005. *L'Empire des Signes*. Paris: Édition du Seuil.

Bauman, Z. 2002. *Liquid Modernity*. Oxford: Polity Press.

Beiguelman, G., Bambozzi, L., Bastos, M. and Minelli, R. (eds) 2008. *Appropriations of the (Un)Common: Public and Private Spaces in Times of Mobility*. Instituto Sergio Motta: São Paulo.

Benassi, P., Dima, S.G., Lisotti, A. and Vigarani, M. 2006. *Modena in cifre – Edizione 2006*. Modena: Comune di Modena.

Benjamin, W. 1967. *Ursprung des deutschen Trauerspiels*. Frankfurt am Main: Suhrkamp.

Benjamin, W. 1971. *Il dramma barocco tedesco*. Torino: Einaudi.

Benjamin, W. 1985. Naples, in *One Way Street and Other Writings* edited by W. Benjamin. London: Verso, 167–176.

Berentzen, D. 1990. Der autoritäre Charakter – Made in DDR. *Psychologie heute*, 4: 32–35.

Beressem, H. 1996. Architexturen. Überlegungen zu einer Topologie der Torsion, in *DisPositionen. Beiträge zur Dekonstrution von Raum und Zeit. Philosophischer Schriften 33* edited by M. Scholl and C.G. Tholen. Kassel: Universität Gesamthochschule, 51–79.

Bereziartu, X.M. 2008. Translation, The Inn of The Remote. *Zehar*, 63: 100–103.

Bergquist, C., Peñaranda, R. and Sánchez, G. 2001. *Violence in Colombia, 1990–2000: Waging War and Negotiating Peace*. New York: Rowman & Littlefield.

Berman, A. 1984. *L'Épreuve de l'Étranger*. Paris: Gallimard.

Berman, A. 1999. *La Traduction et la Lettre ou l'Auberge du Lontain*. Paris: Édition du Seuil.

Bertucelli, L. 2001. 'Costruire la democrazia'. La Camera del lavoro di Modena (1945–1962), in *Un secolo di sindacato. La Camera del lavoro a Modena nel Novecento* edited by L. Ganapini. Roma: Ediesse.

Bessy, C. and Chateauraynaud, F. 1995. *Experts et faussaires: pour une sociologie de la perception.* Paris: Métailié.

Beyme, K. von 1998. *Kulturpolitik und nationale Identität.* Wiesbaden: Westdeutscher Verlag.

Bhabha, H.K. 1985. Signs taken for wonders: Questions of ambivalence and authority under a tree outside Delhi, May 1817. *Europe and its Others: Proceedings of the Essex Conference on the Sociology of Literature, July 1984.* Vol. 1. Edited by F. Barker, P. Hulme, M. Iversen, and D. Loxley. Colchester: University of Essex, 89–106.

Bianchetti, C. and Berlanda, T. 2009. I paradossi del castello di Berlino, in *Oltre il muro. Berlino e i linguaggi della riunificazione* edited by A. Chiarloni. Milano: FrancoAngeli.

Bifulco, L. and De Leonardis, O. 2003. Partnership o partecipazione. Una conversazione sul tema, in *Lo spazio europeo fra pianificazione e governance* edited by F. Karrer and S. Arnofi. Firenze: Alinea, 87–105.

Bifulco, L. and De Leonardis, O. 2005. Sulle tracce dell'azione pubblica, in *Le politiche sociali. Temi e prospettive emergenti* edited by L. Bifulco. Roma: Carocci.

Bifulco, L., Bricocoli, M. and Monteleone, R. 2008. Activation and local welfare in Italy. Trends, issues and a case study. *Social Policy & Administration*, 2: 143–159.

Blomley, N. 2004. *Unsettling the City. Urban Land and the Politics of Property.* New York/London: Routledge.

Bodrožić, M. 2007. *Sterne erben, Sterne färben. Meine Ankunft in Wörtern.* Frankfurt am Main: Suhrkamp.

Boje, D.M. 2001. *Narrative Methods for Organization & Communication Research.* London: Sage.

Boltanski, L. and Chiapello, E. 2005. *The New Spirit of Capitalism.* London/New York: Verso.

Boltanski, L. and Thévenot, L. 1991. *De la justification.* Paris: Gallimard.

Borges, J.L. 1998. L'Aleph, in *Tutte le opere* (ed.) Milano: Mondadori, 886–901.

Borghi, V. 2006a. Tra cittadini e istituzioni. Riflessioni sull'introduzione di dispositivi partecipativi nelle pratiche istituzionali locali. *Rivista delle politiche sociali*, 2: 147–181.

Borghi, V. 2006b. Metamorfosi della sfera pubblica? Questioni organizzative e governance pubblico-privato nelle policies. *Studi Organizzativi*, 2: 111–126.

Borghi, V. and Chicchi, F. (eds) 2008. *Le istituzioni dello sviluppo.* Milano: FrancoAngeli.

Borghi, V. and Rizza, R. 2006. *L'organizzazione sociale del lavoro.* Milano: BrunoMondadori.

Borghi, V. and Vitale, T. (eds) 2006. *Le convenzioni del lavoro, il lavoro delle convenzioni*. Milano: FrancoAngeli.

Borsò, V. 2007. Topologie als literaturwissenschaftliche Methode: die Schrift des Raums und der Raum der Schrift, in *Topologie* edited by S. Günzel. Bielefeld: Transcript Verlag, 279–296.

Botero Gómez, F. 1994. *Cien Años de la Vida de Medellín*. Medellín: Editorial Universidad de Antioquia.

Botero Herrera, F. 1996. *Medellín 1890–1950. Historia Urbana y Juego de Intereses*. Medellín: Editorial Universidad de Antioquia.

Bourdieu, P. 1987. *Distinction: A Social Critique of the Judgement of Taste*. Cambridge, MA: Harvard University Press.

Boym, S. 2001. *The Future of Nostalgia*. New York: Basic Books.

Braidotti, R. 2006. *Transpositions: On Nomadic Ethics*. Cambridge: Polity Press.

Brand, P. 1995. Ecologism and urban space: Nature, urbanization and city planning in Medellín, Colombia. *Planning Practice and Research*, 10(1).

Brand, P. and Prada, F. 2003. *La Invención de Futuros Urbanos: Estrategias de Competitividad Económica y Sostenibilidad Ambiental en las Cuatro Ciudades Principales de Colombia*. Medellín: Colciencias and Universidad Nacional de Colombia.

Brandt, B. 2006a. Schnitt durchs Auge: Das surrealistische Bild bei Yoko Tawada, Emine Sevgi Özdamar und Herta Müller in *Text + Kritik. IX Special issue on Literatur und Migration* edited by H.L. Arnold. München: Edition Text + Kritik, 74–84.

Brandt, B. 2006b. A post-Communist eye: An interview with Yoko Tawada. *WLT World Literature Today*, 80(1): 43–46.

Bressem, H. 1996. Architexturen. Überlegungen zu einer Topologie der Torsion, in *DisPositionen. Beiträge zur Dekonstrution von Raum und Zeit* edited by M. Scholl and C. Tholen. Kassel: Universität Gesamthochschule, 51–79.

Breton, V., Garcia, F. and Roca, A. 1999. Los limites del desarrollo. Modelos 'rotos' y modelos 'por construir', in *América Latina y África*. Barcelona: Icari. Institut Catala d'Antropología.

Briata, P., Bricocoli, M. and Tedesco, C. 2009. *Città in periferia. Politiche urbane e progetti locali in Francia*. Gran Bretagna e Italia. Roma: Carocci.

Bricocoli, M. 2002. Uno sporco lavoro di quartiere. Il Contratto di Quartiere a Cinisello Balsamo (MI). *Animazione Sociale*, 3: 54–63.

Bricocoli, M. 2007. Territorio, contrattualizzazione e politiche urbane, in *La contrattualizzazione delle politiche sociali* edited by R. Monteleone. Roma: Officina, 140–164.

Bricocoli, M., De Leonardis, O. and Tosi, A. 2008. L'Italie. Inflexion néolibérale et politiques locales, in *Villes, violence et dépendance sociale. Les politiques de cohésion en Europe* edited by J. Donzelot. Paris: La Documentation Française.

Bricocoli, M. and Savoldi, P. 2008. *Villes en Observation*. Paris: Éditions du Puca.

Brighenti, A. 2006. On territory as relationship and law as territory. *Canadian Journal of Law and Society/Revue Canadienne Droit et Société*, 21(2): 65–86.

Brighenti, A. 2007. Visibility: A category for the social sciences. *Current Sociology*, 55(3): 323–342.

Brighenti, A. 2010. Democracy and its visibilities, in *Surveillance and Democracy* edited by K.D. Haggerty and M. Samatas. London: Routledge.

Bruno, G. 2002. *Atlas of Emotions*. London: Verso.

Brundtland Commission. 1987. *Our Common Future*. Oxford: Oxford University Press.

Byrne, D. 2002. Industrial culture in a post-industrial world. The case of the North East of England. *City*, 6(3): 279–289.

Caldeira, T.P.R. 2001. *City of Walls: Crime, Segregation, and Citizenship in São Paulo*. Berkeley: University of California Press.

Calhoun, C. 1998. The public good as a social and cultural project, in *Private Action and the Public Good* edited by E.S. Clemens and W.W. Powell. New Haven/London: Yale University Press.

Calimani, R. 2001. *Storia del ghetto di Venezia*. Milano: Mondadori.

Callon, M. 1999. Actor-network theory: The market test, in *Actor Network and After* edited by J. Law and J. Hassard. Oxford: Blackwell.

Callon, M. and Latour, B. 1981. Unscrewing the big Leviathan: How actors macrostructure reality and how sociologists help them to do so, in *Advances in Social Theory and Methodology: Toward an Integration of Micro- and Macro-Sociologies* edited by K.D. Knorr-Cetina and A.V. Cicourel. Boston: Routledge.

Cardoso, F. and Faletto, E. 1979. *Dependencia y Desarrollo en América Latina*. México: Alianza Editorial.

Careri, F. 2006. *Walkscapes. Camminare Come Pratica Estetica*. Torino: Einaudi.

Carlini, E. and Valle, P. 1999. Le città in movimento. Geografia dell'est urbano negli anni Novanta, in *La Cortina Invisibile* edited by E. Banchelli. Bergamo: Bergamo University Press, 143–160.

Carreira, A.M. 2007. El desarrollo o las múltiples formas de decir siempre lo mismo. *Revista Universidad EAFIT*, 43(147): 48–55.

Castel, R. 2007. *La discrimination négative. Citoyens où indigenes?* Paris: Editions du Seuil.

Castells, M., Fernandez-Ardevol, M., Linchuan Qiu, J. and Sey, A. 2004. The Mobile Communication Society. A cross-cultural analysis of available evidence on the social uses of wireless communication technology. Paper to the Conference: *International Workshop on Wireless Communication Policies and Prospects: A Global Perspective*, Los Angeles, 8–9 October.

Cellamare, C. 2008. *Fare città. Pratiche urbane e storie di luoghi*. Milano: Eleuthera.

Ceruti, M. 1987. L'impresa di fronte alla sfida della complessità, in *Il divenire dell'impresa* edited by AA.VV. Milano: Anabasi.

Chmielewska, E. 2005. Logos or the resonance of branding. *Space and Culture*, 8(4): 349–380.

Choay, F. 2006. *Pour une Antropologie de l'Espace*. Paris: Editions du Seuil.

Cochoy, F. 2004. Is the modern consumer a Buridan's donkey? Product packaging and consumer choice, in *Elusive Consumption* edited by K. Ekström and H. Brembeck. Oxford/New York: Berg, 205–227.

Cochoy, F. and Grandclément, C. 2005. Publicizing Goldilocks' choice at the supermarket: The political work of product packaging, shopping carts, and shopping talk, in *Making Things Public: Atmospheres of Democracy* edited by B. Latour and P. Weibel. Cambridge, MA: The MIT Press, 646–659.

Cooren, F. 2004. Textual agency: How texts do things in organizational settings. *Organization*, 11(3): 373–393.

Corboz, A. 2008. *Ordine sparso: saggi sull'arte, il metodo, la città, il territorio*. Milano: Angeli.

Cortés, F. 2009. *La economía informal en Colombia*. Available online at: http://redassei.blogspot.com/2009/10/economia-informal-en-colombia.html (accessed 6 January 2010).

Cremaschi, M. 2001. Quartiere e territorio nei programmi integrati. *Territorio*, 19: 38–44.

Cremaschi, M. 2009. New neighbourhoods in Europe. Paper to the Conference: *Future City – Future Bauhaus*, International Conference, Weimar, 4–6 November.

Crinson, M. 2005. Urban memory – an introduction, in *Urban Memory. History and Amnesia in the Modern City* edited by M. Crinson. London/New York: Routledge.

Cronin, A.M. 2008. Urban space and entrepreneurial property relations: Resistance and the vernacular of outdoor advertising and graffiti, in *Consuming the Entrepreneurial City: Image, Memory and Spectacle* edited by A.M. Cronin and H. Kevin. New York: Routledge.

Crosta, P. 2003. Reti translocali. Le pratiche d'uso del territorio come 'politiche' e come 'politica'. *Foedus*, 7: 5–18.

Crosta, P. 2007. Interrogare i processi di costruzione di 'pubblico', come 'prove' di democrazia, in *Democrazia locale. Apprendere dall'esperienza* edited by L. Pellizzoni. Gorizia: ISIG/Gorizia DSU/Trieste.

Crosta, P. (ed.) 2009. *Casi di politiche urbane. La pratica delle pratiche d'uso del territorio*. Milano: FrancoAngeli.

Crouch, C. 2004. *Post Democracy (Themes for the 21st Century)*. Cambridge: Polity Press.

Czarniawska, B. 2002. *A Tale of Three Cities, or the Glocalization of City Management*. Oxford: Oxford University Press.

Czarniawska, B. 2004a. *Narratives in Social Science Research*. London: Sage.

Czarniawska, B. 2004b. On time, space, and action nets. *Organization*, 11(6): 773–791.

Czarniawska, B. 2010. Women, the city, (dis)organizing. *Culture and Organization* 16(3): 3, 283–300.

Czarniawska, B. and Solli, R. 2001. Big city as a societal laboratory, in *Organizing Metropolitan Space and Discourse* edited by B. Czarniawska and R. Solli. Malmö: Liber.

Davis, M. 2005. The public spheres of unprotected workers. *Global Society*, 19(2): 131–154.

De Certeau, M. 1984. *The Practice of Everyday Life*. Berkeley: University of California Press.

De Giorgi, A. 2000. *Zero tolleranza. Strategie e pratiche della società di controllo*. Roma: DeriveApprodi.

De Leonardis, O. 1997. Declino della sfera pubblica e privatismo. *Rassegna italiana di sociologia*, 38(2): 169–193.

De Leonardis, O. 2006. L'onda lunga della soggettivazione: una sfida per il welfare pubblico. *Rivista delle politiche sociali*, 2: 13–38.

De Leonardis, O. 2008. Una nuova questione sociale? Qualche interrogativo preliminare a proposito di territorializzazione delle politiche. *Territorio*, 46: 10–16.

De Leonardis, O. and Monteleone, R. 2007. Dai luoghi della cura alla cura dei luoghi. A Trieste e dintorni, in *La contrattualizzazione delle politiche sociali* edited by R. Monteleone. Roma: Officina, 135–161.

De Martino, E. [1961] 2002. *La terra del rimorso*. Milano: Il Saggiatore.

Delaney, D. 2004 Tracing displacements: Or evictions in the nomosphere. *Environment and Planning D*, 22(6): 847–860.

Deleuze, G. 1988. *Le Pli. Leibniz et le Baroque*. Paris: Les Éditions de Minuit.

Deleuze, G. and Guattari, F. 1980. *Mille Plateaux. Capitalisme et Schizofrénie*. Paris: Les Éditions de Minuit.

Dematteis, G. 1994. Possibilità e limiti dello sviluppo locale. *Sviluppo locale*, 1(10–30).

Dematteis, G. and Governa, F. 2005. *Territorialità, sviluppo locale, sostenibilità*. Milano: FrancoAngeli.

Denis, J. and Pontille, D. [forthcoming]. Placing subway signs. Practical properties of signs at work. *Visual Communication*, 9(4).

Departamento Administrativo Nacional de Estadistica. 2005. *Dirección de Censos y Demografía. Censo General 2005*. Available online at: http://www.ddhh-colombia.org/html/CENSOGENERALDEL2005.pdf (accessed 10 May 2009).

Di Cristina, G. 2004. *Architettura e Topologia. Per una teoria spaziale dell'Architettura*. Roma: Editrice Librerie Dedalo.

Die 16 Grundsätze des Städtebaus, *Ministerialblatt der DDR* (25), 16 September 1950.

Dikec, M. 2009. Space, politics and (in)justice. *Spatial Justice*, 1(September 2009).

Donald, J. 1999. *Imagining the Modern City*. London: Athlone Press.

Donolo, C. 1997. *L'intelligenza delle istituzioni*. Milano: Feltrinelli.

Donolo, C. 2005. Dalle politiche pubbliche alle pratiche sociali nella produzione di beni pubblici? *Stato e Mercato*, 1(33–65).

Donolo, C. 2007. *Sostenere lo sviluppo*. Milano: Bruno Mondadori.

Donzelot, J. 2006. *Quand la ville se défait: Quelle politique face à la crise des banlieues?* Paris: Éditions du Seuil.

Donzelot, J., Mével, C. and Wyvekens, A. 2003. *Faire Societé. La Politique de la Ville aux Etats-Unis et en France*. Paris: Éditions du Seuil.

Dubet, F. 2003. *Le déclin de l'institution*. Paris: Édition du Seuil.

Eckardt, F., Geelhaar, J., Colini, L., Willis, K.S., Chorianopoulos, K. and Hennig, R. (eds) 2008. *Mediacity. Situations, Practices, and Encounters*. Berlin: Frank & Timme.

Escobar, A. 1995. *Encountering Development*. Princeton: Princeton University Press.

Ette, O. 2005. *ZwischenWeltenSchreiben, Literatur ohne festen Wohnsitz* (Überlebenswissen II). Berlin: Kulturverlag Kadmos.

Evans, G. 2005. Measure for measure: Evaluating the evidence of culture's contribution to regeneration. *Urban Studies*, 42(5/6): 959–983.

Farías, I. and Bender, T. (eds) 2009. *Urban Assemblages. How Actor-Network Theory Changes Urban Studies*. London: Routledge.

Fenton, N. 2008. Mediating hope: New media, politics and resistance. *International Journal of Cultural Studies*, 11(2): 230–248.

Fludernik, M. 1998. *Hybridity and Postcolonialism: Twentieth Century Indian Literature*. Tübingen: Stauffenburg.

Förster, W. 2006. *Wohnen. Housing in the 20th and 21st Centuries*. New York: Prestel Publishing.

Foucault, M. 1977. *Discipline and Punish*. New York: Pantheon Books.

Foucault, M. 1980. Des espaces autres, in *Dit et écrits (1954–1988)* edited by M. Foucault. Paris: Gallimard, 4, 752–762.

Foucault, M. 1982. The subject and the power, in *Michel Foucault: Beyond Structuralism and Hermeneutics* edited by H.F. Dreyfus and P. Rabinow. Brighton: Harvester Press, 202–226.

Foucault, M. 1991. Governmentality, in *The Foucault Effect. Studies in Governmentality* edited by G. Burchell, C. Gordon and P. Miller. London: Harvester Wheatsheaf.

Fraenkel, B. 2006. Actes écrits, actes oraux: la performativité à l'épreuve de l'écriture. *Études de Communication*, 29: 69–93.

Fraser, N. 1990. Talking about needs: Interpretive contexts as political conflicts in welfare-states societies, in *Feminism and Political Theory* edited by C. Sustein. Chicago: Chicago University Press.

Fraser, V. 2004. Art and Architecture in Latin America, in *Cambridge Companion to Modern Latin American Culture* edited by J. King. Cambridge: Cambridge University Press, 202–235.

Freud, S. 1900. *Die Traumdeutung*. Leipzig: Deuticke.

Fritze, L. 1997. *Die Gegenwart des Vergangenen. Über das Weiterleben der DDR nach ihrem Ende.* Weimar: Böhlau.

Fuller, G. 2002. The arrow-directional semiotics: Way-finding in transit. *Social Semiotics*, 12(3): 131–178.

Gagliardi, P. 1990a. Artifacts as pathways and remains of organizational life, in *Symbols and Artifacts: Views of the Corporate Landscape* edited by P. Gagliardi. New York: Aldine de Gruyter, 3–38.

Gagliardi, P. 1990b. *Symbols and Artifacts: Views of the Corporate Landscape.* New York: Aldine de Gruyter.

Galster, G. 2001. On the nature of neighbourhood. *Urban Studies*, 38(12): 2111–2124.

Garay, L.J. 2002. *Colombia entre la exclusión y el desarrollo.* Bogotá: Contraloría de la República.

Garcìa, B. 2004. Cultural policy and urban regeneration in Western European cities: Lessons from experience, prospects for the future. *Local Economy*, 19(4): 312–326.

García-Canclini, N. 1995. *Hybrid Cultures: Strategies for Entering and Leaving Modernity.* Minneapolis: University of Minnesota Press.

García-Canclini, N. 2004. *Diferentes, Desiguales y Desconectados. Mapas de la Interculturalidad.* Barcelona: Gedisa.

Garfinkel, H. 1996. Ethnomethodology's program. *Social Psychology Quarterly*, 59(1): 5–21.

Geddes, M. and Benington, J. (eds) 2001. *Local Partnership and Social Exclusion in the European Union. New Forms of Local Social Governance?* London: Routledge.

Ghaussy, S. 1999. Das vaterland verlassen: Nomadic language and 'feminine writing' in Emine Sevgi Özdamar's 'Das Leben ist eine Karawanserei'. *The German Quarterly*, 72(1): 1–16.

Ginsborg, P. 1998. *L'Italia del tempo presente. Famiglia, società civile, Stato 1980-1996.* Torino: Einaudi.

Ginsborg, P. 2006. *La democrazia che non c'è.* Torino: Einaudi.

Ginzburg, C. 1979. Spie. Radici di un paradigma indiziario, in *Miti, Emblemi, Spie* edited by C. Ginzburg. Torino: Einaudi.

Giometti, G. 2003. Introduzione, in *La traduzione e la lettera o l'albergo nella lontananza* edited by A. Berman. Macerata: Quodlibet.

Goffman, E. 1959. *The Presentation of Self in Everyday Life.* Garden City, NY: Doubleday Anchor.

González, N. 2006. *Colombia en la Pintura de Fernando Botero: El Realismo Mágico en el Imaginario de Botero.* Available online at: http://www.tesisenx arxa.net/TESIS_UPC/AVAILABLE/TDX-0109107-123829//01Ngr01de01.pdf (accessed 9 April 2007).

Göttische, D. 2006. Emine Sevgi Özdamars Erzählung Der Hof im Spiegel: Spielräume einer postkolonialen Lektüre deutsch-türkischer Literatur. *German Life and Letters*, 59(4): 515–525.

Governa, F. and Saccomani, S. 2004. From urban renewal to local development. New conceptions and governance practices in the Italian peripheries. *Planning Theory and Practice*, 5(3): 327–348.

Graham, S. and Marvin, S. 2001. *Splintering Urbanism: Networked Infrastructures, Technological Mobilities and the Urban Condition*. London/New York: Routledge & Kegan Paul.

Gray, C. 2007. Commodification and instrumentality in cultural policy. *International Journal of Cultural Policy*, 13(2): 203–215.

Greimas, A. 1976 (1989). *The Social Sciences. A Semiotic View*. Minneapolis, MN: University of Minnesota Press.

Guattari, F. 1992. Le Capitalisme Mondial Intégré et la révolution moléculaire. *Le lien social*, 181: 1–9.

Guizeli, V. 1984. *Social Transformations and the Origins of Social Housing in Greece 1900–1930*. Athens: Epikerotita (in Greek).

Günzel, S. 2008. Topologie und Städtischer Raum. *der architekt*, 3: 8–10.

Güsten, S. 1990. Kulturschock lähmt die ex-DDR. Wie die Menschen ihre neue soziale Realität verarbeiten. *Frankfurter Rundschau*, 31 December 1990, 29.

Hafner, S. 2006. Wie auch Großsiedlungen Ghettos werden. Beiträge zur Entschlüsselung der Produktionsmechanismen von 'Gegenorten', in *Themenorte* edited by M. Flitner and J. Lousseau. Berlin: LIT Verlag, 75–90.

Haggerty, K. and Ericson, R. 2000. The surveillant assemblage. *British Journal of Sociology*, 51(4): 605–622.

Hanke, I. 1991. Die Ungleiche Nation, in *Deutsche Vereinigung. Probleme der Integration und der Identifikation* edited by B. Muszynski. Opladen: Westdeutscher Verlag, 45–60.

Hanstein, M. 2003. *Fernando Botero*. Cologne: Taschen.

Harding, D. 2003. *Writing the City: Urban Visions and Literary Modernism*. London: Routledge.

Harvey, D. 1993. *La crisi della modernità*. Milano: Il Saggiatore.

Harvey, D. 2006. The Political Economy of Public Space, in *The Politics of Public Space* edited by S. Low and N. Smith. New York: Routledge, 17–34.

Hayden, D. 1995. *The Power of Place*. Cambridge, MA: MIT Press.

Hénaff, M. and Strong, T. 2001. The Condition of Public Space: Vision, Speech and Theatricality, in *Public Space and Democracy* edited by M. Hénaff and T. Strong. Minneapolis: University of Minnesota Press, 1–31.

Henao, H. 1990. Territorios, espacios e instituciones de la socialización en la Antioquia actual. *Realidad Social*, 1: 115–157.

Hertz, N. 2001. *The Silent Takeover: Global Capitalism and the Death of Democracy*. London: The Free Press.

Hirschmann, A.O. 1970. *Exit, Voice and Loyalty. Responses to Decline in Firms, Organization and States*. Cambridge, MA: Harvard University Press.

Hirschon, R. 1989. *Heirs of the Greek Catastrophe. The Social Life of Asia Minor Refugees in Piraeus*. Oxford: Clarendon Press.

Hirst, P. 2000. Democracy and governance, in *Debating Governance* edited by J. Pierre. Oxford: Oxford University Press, 13–35.

Hofmann, M. 1995. Die Leipziger Metallarbeiter Etappen sozialer Erfahrungs-geschichte. Milieubiographie eins Arbeitermilieus in Leipzig, in *Soziale Milieus in Ostdeutschland* edited by M. Vester, M. Hofmann and I. Zierke. Köln: Bund Verlag, 36–192.

Hoggett, P. 2006. Conflict, ambivalence, and the contested purpose of public organizations. *Human Relations*, 59(2): 175–194.

Hubbard, P. 2006. *Key Ideas in Geography: City*. London: Routledge.

Hutchins, E. 1995a. *Cognition in the Wild*. Cambridge, MA: The MIT Press.

Hutchins, E. 1995b. How a cockpit remembers its speeds. *Cognitive Science*, 19: 265–288.

Huxley, T.H. 2008 (1880). *On the Method of Zadig. Essay #1 from 'Science and Hebrew Tradition'*. (Online). Available at: http://www.gutenberg.org/files/2627/2627-h/2627-h.htm (accessed 9 July 2009).

Huyssen, A. 2003. *Present Pasts: Urban Palimpsests and the Politics of Memory*. Stanford: Stanford University Press.

Huyssen, A. 2008. Introduction: World cultures, world cities, in *Other Cities, Other Worlds. Urban Imaginaries in a Globalizing Age* edited by A. Huyssen. Durham and London: Duke University Press, 1–23.

Ingold, T. 2000. *The Perception of the Environment*. New York: Routledge.

Ingram, S. 2001. Translation studies and psychoanalytic transference. *TTR: Traduction, Terminologie, Rédaction*, 14(1): 95–115. Available online at: http://id.erudit.org/iderudit/00530ar (accessed 28 November 2009).

Islam, Y.M. and Doyle K.O. 2008. Distance education via SMS technology in rural Bangladesh. *American Behavioral Scientist*, 52(1): 87–96.

Iveson, K. 2007. *Publics and the City*. Oxford: Blackwell.

Iveson, K. 2009. The city versus the media? Mapping the mobile geographies of public address. *International Journal of Urban and Regional Research*, 33(1): 241–245.

Jedlowski, P. 2009. *Il racconto come dimora. Heimat e le memorie d'Europa*. Torino: Bollati Boringhieri.

Jessen, R. 2009. Die Montagsdemonstrationen, in *Erinnerungsorte der DDR* edited by M. Sabrow. München: Beck, 466–480.

Kanizsa, G. 1955. Margini quasi-percettivi in campi con stimolazione omogenea. *Rivista di Psicologia*, 49(1): 7–30.

Kanizsa, G. 1979. *Organization in vision: essays on gestalt perception*. New York: Praeger.

Kärrholm, M. 2007. The materiality of territorial production. *Space and Culture*, 10(4): 437–453.

Kaufmann, V. and Montulet, B. 2009. Between social and spatial mobilities: The issue of social fluidity, in *Tracing Mobilities: Towards a Cosmopolitan Perspective* edited by W. Canzler, V. Kaufmann and S. Kesselring. Farnham: Ashgate.

Kellerman, A. 2006. *Personal Mobilities*. New York: Routledge.

Konuk, K. 2001. *Identität im Prozeß: Literatur von Autorinnen aus und in der Türkei in deutscher, englischer und türkischer Sprache*. Essen: Die Blaue Eule.

Kraenzle, C. 2006. Travelling without moving: Physical and linguistic mobility in Yoko Tawada's Übersetzungen. *Transit*, 2(1).

Krause, M. 2005. The production of counter-publics and counter-publics of production. An interview with Oskar Negt. *European Journal of Social Theory*, 9(1): 119–128.

Kwan, M.-P. 2007. Mobile communications, social networks, and urban travel. *The Professional Geographer*, 59(4): 434–446.

La Vendedora de Rosas (dir. V. Gaviria, 1998)

La virgen de los sicarios (dir. B. Schroeder, 2000).

Lacan, J. 1973. La topique de l'imaginaire, in *Les écrits techniques de Freud* edited by J. Lacan. Paris: Édition du Seuil, 83–103.

Lacan, J. 1991. *The Seminar of Jacques Lacan: Freud's Papers on Technique* (Vol. Book I). New York: Norton & Company.

Lacoste, M. 1997. L'information à visage humain: la place des agents dans un système d'information-voyageurs, in *Les traversées de la gare. Une méthode des trajets pour analyser l'information-voyageurs* edited by D. Bayart, M. Borzeix, M. Lacoste and J. Threureau. Paris: RATP, Département du développement, unité prospective, 25–81.

Laino, G. and Padovani, L. 2000. Le partenariat pour rénover l'action publique. L'expérience italienne. *Pôle Sud*, 12: 27–46.

Landry, C. 2006. *The Art of City Making*. London: Earthscan.

Lash, S. and Urry, J. 1994. *Economies of Signs and Space*. London: Sage.

Latour, B. 1993. *We Have Never Been Modern*. Cambridge: Harvard University Press.

Latour, B. 2005a. From Realpolitik to Dingpolitik or how to make things public, in *Making Things Public. Atmospheres of Democracy* edited by B. Latour and P. Weibel. Cambridge, MA: The MIT Press, 14–41.

Latour, B. 2005b. *Reassembling the Social: An Introduction to Actor-Network Theory*. Oxford: Oxford University Press.

Latour, B. and Hermant, É. 1998. *Paris ville invisible*. Paris: Les empêcheurs de penser en rond/La Découverte.

Latour, B. and Weibel, P. (eds) 2005. *Making Things Public: Atmospheres of Democracy*. Cambridge, MA: The MIT Press.

Law, J. and Hassard, J. 1999. *Actor Network and After*. Oxford: Blackwell.

Lawless, P. 2004. Locating and explaining area-based urban initiatives: New deal for communities in England. *Environment and Planning C*, 22: 383–399.

Le Galès, P. 2006. *Le città euroepee*. Bologna: Il Mulino.

Lefebvre, H. 1996. *Writings on Cities* edited by E. Kofman and E. Lebas. Oxford: Blackwell.

Lianos, M. 2001. *Le nouveau contrôle social: toile institutionnelle, normative et lien social*. Paris: L'Harmattan.

Loest, E. 2003. *Völkerschlachtdenkmal*. München: Deutscher Taschenbuch Verlag.

Loest, E. 2004. *Nikolaikirche*. München: Deutscher Taschenbuch Verlag.

Londoño-Vega, P. 2002. *Religion, Culture and Society in Colombia: Medellín and Antioquia, 1850–1930*. Oxford: Oxford University Press.

López, H. 1996. *Ensayos sobre Economía Laboral Colombiana*. Bogotá: FONADE and Carlos Valencia Editores.

Lucie-Smith, E. 1993. *Latin American Art of the Twentieth Century*. London: Thames and Hudson.

Lukes, S. 2005. *Power: A Radical View*. Basingstoke: Palgrave Macmillan.

Lynch, K. 1960. *The Image of the City*. Cambridge, MA: The MIT Press.

Lyon, D. 2001. *Surveillance Society. Monitoring Everyday Life*. Buckingham: Open University Press.

Maaz, H.J. 1992. *Der Gefühlsstau. Ein Psychogramm der DDR*. München: Vollständige Taschenbuchausgabe.

Magatti, M. 2007. *La città abbandonata. Dove sono e come cambiano le periferie italiane*. Bologna: Il Mulino.

Maglaveras, N. Koutkiasa, V., Chouvardaa, I., Goulisb, D.G., Avramidesb, A., Adamidisc, D., Louridasc, G. and Balasd, E.A. 2002. Home care delivery through the mobile telecommunications platform. *International Journal of Medical Informatics*, 68(3): 99–111.

Magnaghi, A. 2006. *Il progetto locale*. Torino: Bollati Boringhieri.

Manning, E. 2007. Wandering the law. Nomadic desertscapes and topological dreamings, in *Literary Landscapes, Landscapes in Literature* edited by M. Bottalico, M.T. Chialant and E. Rao. Roma: Carocci, 257–276.

March, J.G. and Olsen, J.P. 1989. *Rediscovering Institutions: The Organizational Basis of Politics*. New York: The Free Press.

Marcuse, P. 1995. Not chaos, but walls: Postmodernism and the partitioned city, in *Postmodern Cities and Spaces* edited by S. Watson and K. Gibson. Oxford: Blackwell.

Marcuse, P. and Van Kempten, R. (eds) 2000. *Globalizing Cities: A New Spatial Order?* Oxford: Blackwell.

Marcuse, P. and Van Kempten, R. (eds) 2002. *Of States and Cities. The Partitioning of Urban Space*. Oxford: Oxford University Press.

Martín-Barbero, J. 1987. *De los Medios a las Mediaciones*. México: Gustavo Gili.

Massey, D. 2005. *For Space*. London: Sage.

Massiotta, S. 2006. *La sperimentazione micro-win a Trieste: cornici, dispositivi, pratiche di integrazione delle politiche pubbliche*. Tesi di Master in Sviluppo Locale e Qualità Sociale. Milano, Università degli Studi di Milano Bicocca.

Mastropaolo, A. 2001. Democrazia, neodemocrazia, postdemocrazia: tre paradigmi a confronto. *Diritto pubblico comparato ed europeo*, 4: 1612–1635.

Max-Neef, M. 1991. *Human Scale Development. Conception, Application and Further Reflections*. London: Apex Press.

McIlwaine, C. and Moser, C. 2003. Poverty, violence and livelihood security in urban Colombia and Guatemala. *Progress in Development Studies*, 3(2): 113–130.

McQuire, S. 2008. *The Media City: Media, Architecture and Urban Space*. London: Sage.

Melucci, A. 2000. *Culture in gioco: differenze per convivere*. Milano: Il Saggiatore.

Merton, R. and Barber, E. 2006. *The Travels and Adventures of Serendipity*. Princeton, NJ: Princeton University Press.

Meschonnic, H. 1999. *Poétique du Traduire*. Lagrasse: Éditions Verdier.

Michalopoulos, E. 1960. Chasing the Refugees Again. *Avgi (Newspaper)*. 8 May 1960.

Miller, V. 2006. The unmappable. Vagueness and spatial experience. *Space and Culture*, 9(4): 453–467.

Mingione, E., Nuvolati, G., Grana, M., Morlicchio, E. and Tuorto, D. 2001. *Nation and City Contexts, Urban Development Programmes and Neighbourhood Selection*. Italian National report. Ugis project. Milano: Fondazione Bignaschi.

Mitchell, W.J.T. 2003. *Me++: The Cyborg Self and the Networked City*. Cambridge, MA: The MIT Press.

Monteleone, R. (ed.) 2007. *La contrattualizzazione nelle politiche sociali. Forme ed effetti*. Roma: Officina.

Mosse, J. 1975. *La nazionalizzazione delle masse*. Bologna: Il Mulino.

Mumford, L. 1996 (1938). *The Culture of Cities*. New York: Harcourt Brace.

Negt, O. and Kluge, A. 1993. *Public Sphere and Experience. Analysis of the Bourgeois and Proletarian Public Sphere*. Minneapolis: University of Minnesota Press.

Netz, R. 2004. *Barbed Wire: An Ecology of Modernity*. Middletown, CT: Wesleyan University Press.

Norman, D. 1991. Cognitive artifacts, in *Designing Interaction: Psychology at the Human-Computer Interface* edited by J.M. Carroll. Cambridge: Cambridge University Press, 17–38.

Ocampo, G.I. and Dover, R.V.H. 2006. Del estado privado al neo-estatismo: el caso de las Empresas Públicas de Medellín como aproximación a las relaciones entre estado, empresa y política, in *Globalización, Cultura y Poder en Colombia: Una mirada Interdisciplinar* edited by F. González and G.I. Ocampo. Medellín: Colciencias, Universidad de Antioquia and Editorial La Carreta.

Offe, C. 2009. Governance: An empty signifier? *Constellations*, 16(4): 550–562.

Officina Emilia 2007. *La fabbrica col cortile. Le Ex Fonderie Riunite di Modena, Storia e Architettura*. Modena: Edizioni ArteStampa.

Osti Guerrazzi, A. and Siligardi, C. 2002. *Storia del sindacato a Modena, 1880–1980*. Roma: Ediesse.

Ottmar, E. 2005. *ZwischenWeltenSchreiben. Literatur ohne festen Wohnsitz* (Überlebenswissen II). Berlin: Kulturverlag Kadmos.

Özdamar, E.S. 1990. *Mutterzunge*. Berlin: Rotbuch Verlag.

Özdamar, E.S. 1994. *Mother Tongue*. Toronto: Coach House Press.

Özdamar, E.S. 2001. *Der Hof im Spiegel*. Köln: Kiepenheuer & Witsch.

Özdamar, E.S. 2002. *Die Brücke von goldenen Horn*. Köln: Kipenheuer & Witsch.

Özdamar, E.S. 2003. *Seltsame Sterne starren zur Erde. Weddig-Pankow 1976/77*. Köln: Kipenheuer & Witsch.

Pain, R. Grundy, S., Gill, S., Towner, E., Sparks, G. and Hughes, K. 2005. 'So long as I take my mobile': Mobile phones, urban life and geographies of young people's safety. *International Journal of Urban and Regional Research*, 29(4): 814–830.

Palermo, P.C. 2002. *Il programma Urban e I 'innovazione delle politiche urbane*. Milano: FrancoAngeli.

Papavasileiou, E. 2003. A Personal Account and an Appeal. *Kiriakatiki Avgi (Newspaper)*, 11 February 2003.

Park, R. 1940. News as a form of knowledge. *American Journal of Sociology*, 45: 669–686.

Park, R. and Burgess, E. 1925. *The City. Suggestions for Investigation of Human Behavior in the Human Environment*. Chicago: The University of Chicago Press.

Park, R., Burgess, E. and McKenzie, R.D. 1925. *The City*. Chicago: University of Chicago Press.

Parra Vera, O. 2006. De la ciudadanía autoritaria a una ciudadanía social diferenciada y participativa. Apuntes sobre el debate vendedores ambulantes-espacio público. *Estudios Políticos*, 28: 31–59.

Pasqui, G. 2005. *Territori: progettare lo sviluppo*. Roma: Carocci.

Perrella, S. 1998. *Hypersurface Theory: Architecture><Culture*. (Online). Available at: http://architettura.supereva.com/extended/19981201/index_en. htm (accessed 30 September 2009).

Perrow, C. 1996. The bounded career and the demise of civil society, in *The Boundaryless Career* edited by M.B. Arthur and D.M. Rousseau. Oxford: Oxford University Press.

Petrucci, A. 1993. *Public Lettering. Script, Power, and Culture*. Chicago: The University of Chicago Press.

Petrucci, M.A. and Dansero, E. 1995. Aree dimesse, tra degrado e riqualificazione ambientale. *Geotema*, 3: 69–78.

Pickvance, C.G. 1995. Where have urban movements gone? in *Europe at the Margins: New Mosaics of Inequality* edited by C. Hadjimichalis and D. Sadler. London: John Wiley and Sons.

Pierre, J. (ed.) 2000. *Debating Governance*. Oxford: Oxford University Press.

Pizzorno, A. 2001. Natura della disuguaglianza, potere politico e potere privato nella società in via di globalizzazione. *Stato e mercato*, 62: 201–236.

Poumet, J. 2009. Die Universitätskirche Leipzig, in *Erinnerungsorte der DDR* edited by M. Sabrow. München: Beck, 536–544.

Power, A. 1993. *From Hovels to High Rise. State Housing in Europe since 1850.* London: Routledge.

Power, A. 1997. *Estates on the Edge.* London: Macmillan.

Putnam, R.D. 2000. *Bowling Alone: The Collapse and Revival of American Community.* New York: Simon & Schuster.

Raab, J. and Butler, M. (eds) 2008. *Hybrid Americas. Contacts, Contrasts, and Confluences, in New World Literatures and Cultures.* Berlin: LIT Verlag.

Ramírez Guerrero, J. 2002. *Capacitación Laboral para el Sector Informal en Colombia.* Paper to the Conference: 90th Conferencia Internacional del Trabajo, Geneva (Switzerland), 3–20 June.

RATP 1993. *Politique de l'information des voyageurs.* Point sur la mise en œuvre, Annexe au Conseil d'Administration du 29 Octobre 1993.

RATP 1997, *Signalétique multimodale. La RATP fait signe aux voyageurs,* Document de présentation interne, Département des projets, Conception de l'information.

RATP 2002, *La signalétique multimodale. Code des espaces voyageurs,* Document de présentation interne.

Richter, S. 2006. Bauschildmalerei und Objektsmarketing in der Berliner Mitte in *Themenorte* edited by M. Flitner and J. Lousseau. Berlin: LIT Verlag, 75–90.

Ricoeur, P. 2000. *La mémoire, l'histoire, l'oubli.* Paris: Éditions du Seuil.

Ricoeur, P. 2004. *Ricordare, dimenticare, perdonare.* Bologna: Il Mulino.

Ricoeur, P. 2008. Architettura e narratività in *Leggere la città. Quattro testi di Paul Ricoeur* edited by F. Riva. Troina: Città Aperta Edizioni.

Rink, D. 1995. Leipzig: Gewinnerin unter den Verlieren? Zwischen alten und neuen Eliten, in *Soziale Milieus in Ostdeutschland* edited by M. Vester, M. Hofmann and I. Zierke. Köln: Bund Verlag, 51–90.

Robson, B. 1988. *Those Inner Cities: Reconciling the Social and Economic Aims of Urban Policy.* Oxford: Clarendon Press.

Rodriguez, R. 2001. Colombia's Fernando Botero. *Revista Hispánica,* July/August 2001: 95–99.

Roldán, M. 2003. Wounded Medellín: Narcotics traffic against a background of industrial decline, in *Wounded Cities: Destruction and Reconstruction in a Globalized World* edited by J. Schneider and I. Susser. Basingtoke: Berg Publishers.

Roncayolo, M. 1990. *La Ville et ses territoires.* Paris: Gallimard.

Rudolph, H. 2001. Der Schrebergarten, in *Deutsche Erinnerungsorte* edited by E. François and H. Schulze. München: Beck Verlag, 363–379.

Rushdie, S. 1981. *Imaginary Homelands.* London: Granta Books.

Saalfeld, L. (ed.) 1999. *Ich Habe eine Fremde Sprache Gewählt. Ausländische Schriftsteller Schreiben Deutsch.* Gerlingen: Bleicher Verlag.

Schütz, A. 1970. *On Phenomenology and Social Relations.* Chicago: University of Chicago Press.

Sebastiani, C. 2007. *La politica delle città*. Bologna: Il Mulino.

Secretaría de Transportes y Tránsito de la Ciudad de Medellín, 2007, *Código de Tránsito* Art. 76, Proyecto Ley 087/2007.

Sen, A. 1982. *Choice, Welfare and Measurement*. Oxford: Basil Blackwell.

Sen, A. 1985. Well-being, agency and freedom. The Dewey Lectures 1984. *The Journal of Philosophy*, LXXXII(4): 169–221.

Sen, A. 1999. *Development as Freedom*. Oxford: Oxford University Press.

Sennett, R. 1970. *The Uses of Disorder*. New York: Knopf.

Sennett, R. 1992. *The Conscience of the Eye: The Design and Social Life of the City*. New York: Norton & Company.

Sennett, R. 2003. *Respect. In a World of Inequality*. New York: Norton.

Seyhan, A. 1996. Lost in translation: Re-membering the mother tongue in Emine Sevgi Özdamar's Das Leben ist eine Karawanserei. *The German Quarterly*, 69(4): 414–426.

Sgambati, G. 2007. *Celan liest Japanisch. Traduzione come manifestazione di significati nascosti*. L'opera e la vita. Paul Celan e gli Studi Comparatistici, Napoli, Università degli Studi di Napoli l'Orientale.

Shenhav, Y. 2002. *Manufacturing Rationality: The Engineering Foundations of the Managerial Revolution*. Oxford: Oxford University Press.

Simmel, G. 1989. La ville, in *Philosophie de la modernité* edited by P. Editeur. Paris: Payot, 169–199.

Simmel, G. 1994 (1909). Bridge and door. *Theory, Culture & Society*, 11(1): 5–10.

Simmel, G. 1997 (1909). Bridge and door, in *Rethinking Architecture* edited by N. Leach. London: Routledge, 66–69.

Simon, H. and Kaplan, C. 1989. *Foundations of Cognitive Science*. Cambridge, MA: The MIT Press.

Sloterdijk, P. 2005 *Im Weltinnenraum des Kapitals*. Frankfurt am Main: Suhrkamp.

Smith, N. 2002. New globalism, new urbanism: Gentrification as global urban strategy. *Antipode*, 34(3): 427–450.

Soja, E. 2000. *Postmetropolis*. Oxford: Blackwell.

Stavrides, S. 2002. Inhabitation and otherness: Refugees and immigrant, in the city, in *Athens 2002 Absolute Realism (8th International Exhibition of Architecture, Venice Biennale)* edited by T. Koubis, T. Moutsopoulos and R. Scoffier. *Athens.* Hellenic Ministry of Culture – Association of Greek Architects, 133–145.

Stavrides, S. 2005. Prosfygica facades, in *Athens in Transition* edited by C. Calari and K. Daflos. Athens: Futura, 109–114.

Stavrides, S. 2006. Heterotopias and the experience of porous urban space, in *Loose Space: Possibility and Diversity in Urban Life* edited by K.A. Franck and Q. Stevens. London: Routledge.

Stierle, K. 2001. *La Capitale des signes. Paris et son discours*. Paris: Éditions de la Maison des Sciences de l'homme.

Suchar, C. S. 2007. Grounding visual sociology research in shooting scripts. *Qualitative Sociology*, 20(1): 33–55.

Suchman, L. 2007. *Human-Machine Reconfigurations. Plans and Situated Actions*. 2nd Edition. Cambridge: Cambridge University Press.

Svoronos, N. 1972. *Histoire de la Grece Moderne*. Paris: PUF.

Székely, M. 2003. The 1990s in Latin America: Another decade of persistent inequality, but with somewhat lower poverty. *Journal of Applied Economics*, 6(2): 317–339.

Tarde, G. 1969 (1901). The opinion and the crowd in *Gabriel Tarde: On Communication and Social Influence* edited by T. Clark. Chicago: University of Chicago Press.

Tawada, Y. 1996. *Talisman*. Tübingen: Konkursverlag.

Tawada, Y. 1998. *Talisman*. Tübingen: Konkursbuch Claudia Gehrke Verlag.

Tawada, Y. 2002. *Überseezungen*. Tübingen: Konkursbuch.

Tawada, Y. 2007. *Sprachpolizei und Spielpolyglotte*. Tübingen: Konkursbuch Claudia Gehrke Verlag.

Thrift, N. 2005. *Knowing Capitalism*. Los Angeles: Sage.

Tobón, N. 1985. *La Arquitectura de la Colonización Antioqueña*. Bogotá: Fondo de Cultura Cafetera and Benjamin Villegas Editores.

Todorov, T. 1977. *The Poetics of Prose*. Oxford: Blackwell.

Tosi, A. 1994. *Abitanti. Le nuove strategie dell'azione abitativa*. Bologna: Il Mulino.

Tosi, A. 2001. Quartiere. *Territorio*, 19: 10–14.

Tota, A. 2003. *La città ferita*. Bologna: Il Mulino.

Tripodi, L. 2008. Space of exposure. *Lo squaderno*, 8: 9–13. Available online at http://www.losquaderno.professionaldreamers.net.

Trommsdorf, G. 1994. Psychologische Probleme bei den Transformationsprozessen in Ostdeutschland, in *Psychologische Aspekte des sozio-politischen Wandels in Ostdeutschland* edited by G. Trommsdorf. Berlin: Aldine De Gruyter, 19–42.

Turner, V. 1977. *The Ritual Process*. Ithaka: Cornell University Press.

Tyrer, P. and Crinson, M. 2005. Totemic Park: Symbolic representation in post-industrial place, in *Urban Memory. History and Amnesia in the Modern City* edited by M. Crinson. London: Routledge, 99–117.

Unger, R.M. 1987. *False Necessity*. Cambridge: Cambridge University Press.

URBACT 2007. *Cultural and Urban Regeneration. Case Studies's Summaries, France*. URBACT Culture Network.

Urry, J. 2004. The 'system' of automobility. *Theory, Culture & Society*, 21(4/5): 25–39.

Urry, J. 2007. *Mobilities*. Cambridge: Polity.

Urry, J. 2009. Moving on the mobility turn, in *Tracing Mobilities: Towards a Cosmopolitan Perspective* edited by W. Canzler, V. Kaufmann and S. Kesselring. Farnham: Ashgate.

Van Gennepp, A. 1960. *The Rites of Passage*. London: Routledge & Kegan Paul.

Varvantaskis, C. 2009. A memory to dismantlement. *Memory Studies*, 2: 27–38.

Vayssière, B. 1988. *Reconstruction – deconstruction: le hard-french ou l'architecture française des trente glorieuses*. Paris: Picard.

Velázquez, M. 2006. Medellín and its violence, in *The Armed Conflict in Medellín-Colombia Understanding and Responses* edited by A.E. Hincapie. Medellín: Universidad Pontificia Bolivariana.

Venkant, B. Mani, 2007. Slouching Histories, Lurking Memories: Emine Sevgi Özdamar's Seltsame Sterne Starren zur Erde, in *Cosmopolitical Claims. Turkish-German Literatures from Nadolny to Pamuk*. Iowa: University of Iowa Press, Iowa, 87–117.

Venuti, L. 1995. *The Translator's Invisibility. A History of Translation*. London: Routledge.

Vestheim, G. 2007. Cultural policy and democracy: Theoretical reflections. *International Journal of cultural policy*, 13(2): 217–236.

Vlachos, G., Yannitsaris, G. and Hadjicostas, E. 1978. Housing the Asia minor refugees in Athens and Piraeus between 1920 and 1940. *Architecture in Greece*, 12: 117–124.

Wacquant, L. 2008. *Urban Outcasts*. Cambridge: Polity Press.

Wagner, J. 2006. Visible materials, visualised theory and images of social research. *Visual Studies*, 21(1): 55–69.

Weber, A. 2009. *Im Spiegel der Migration. Transkulturelles Erzählen und Sprachpolitik bei Emine Sevgi Özdamar.* Bielefeld: Transcript.

Weick, K. 1976. Educational organizations as loosely coupled systems. *Administrative Science Quarterly*, 21(1): 1–19.

Weick, K. 1979. *The Social Psychology of Organizing*. Reading: Addison-Wesley.

Weick, K. 1995. *Sensemaking in Organizations*. Thousand Oaks, CA: Sage.

Weizman, E. 2007. *Hollow Land*. London: Verso.

Welzer, H. 2005. *Das kommunikative Gedächtnis*. München: Beck Verlag.

Westphal, B. 2007. *La Géocritque. Rèel, ficition, espace*. Paris: Les Édition du Minuit

Wiart, A., Le Roux, A. and Lomazzi, M. 1998. Signalétique, le nouveau fil d'Ariane. Vie du rail et des transports. *Edition professionnelle*, 57: 30–35.

Wierlacher, A. and Bogner, A. (eds) 2003. *Handbuch interkulturelle Germanistik*. Stuttgart/Weimar: Verlag J. B. Metzler.

Winiarski, R. 1991. Vom Buckel zum Ellenbogen. *Report Psychologie*, 45(5–6): 12–13.

Winkler, A. 2008. *Torino City Report, CASE Report*. London School of Economics: Centre for Analysis of Social Exclusion.

Wirth, L. 1964. *On Cities and Social Life*. Chicago: The University of Chicago Press.

Wöhler, K. 2008. Raumkonsum als Produktion von Orten, in *Räume des Konsums. Über den Funktionswandel von Räumlichkeit im Zeitalter des Konsums* edited by K. U. Hellmann and G. Zurstiege. Wiesbaden: Verlag für Sozialwissenschaften, 69–86.

Woolcock, M. 2001. The place of social capital in understanding social and economic outcomes. *ISUMA: Canadian Journal of Policy Research*, 2(1): 1–10.

Woolgar, S. 1991. Configuring the user: The case of usability trials, in *Sociology of Monsters: Essays on Power, Technology and Domination* edited by J. Law. London: Routledge, 58–97.

Zabriskie Point (dir. M. Antonioni, 1970)

Zajczyk, F., Cavalca, G. and Palvarini, P. 2007. Modelli di insediamento e nuovi bisogni abitativi, in *Personal Manager. Casa: acquisto e locazione* edited by AA.VV. Milano: Università Bocconi Editori.

Zapf, H. 1999. The theoretical discourse of hybridity and the post-colonial time-space of the Americas. *ZAA (Zeitschrift Fur Anglistik Und Amerikanistik)*, 47(4): 302–310.

Zimm, M. 2005. *Losing the Plot. Architecture and Narrativity in Fin-de-Siecle Media Cultures*. Stockholm: Axl Books.

Zukin, S. 1995. *The Cultures of Cities*. Cambridge, MA: Blackwell.

Index